The European Heritage in Economics and the Social Sciences

Series Editor:
Jürgen Georg Backhaus

For further volumes:
http://www.springer.com/series/5902

Jürgen Georg Backhaus
Editor

Physiocracy, Antiphysiocracy and Pfeiffer

To Leland with
fond wishes.

26 July 2011

Springer

Editor
Prof. Dr. Jürgen Georg Backhaus
Krupp Chair in Public Finance and
Fiscal Sociology, University of Erfurt
Nordhäuser Str. 63
99089 Erfurt Thüringen
Germany
juergen.backhaus@uni-erfurt.de

ISBN 978-1-4419-7496-9 e-ISBN 978-1-4419-7497-6
DOI 10.1007/978-1-4419-7497-6
Springer New York Dordrecht Heidelberg London

Library of Congress Control Number: 2011929225

Printed on acid-free paper

Springer is part of Springer Science+Business Media (www.springer.com)

TABLEAU ÉCONOMIQUE

Objets a considerer. 1º trois sortes de Depenses. 2º leur Source. 3º leurs avances, 4º leur Distribution, 5º leurs Effets, 6º leur Reproduction, 7º leurs Rapports entr'elles, 8º leurs Rapports avec la population, 9º avec l'Agriculture, 10º avec l'Industrie, 11º avec le Commerce, 12º avec la masse des richesses d'une Nation.

DÉPENSES Productives *Relatives a l'Agriculture &c.*	DÉPENSES DU REVENU *l'Impôt compris se partagent a la Classe productive et a la Classe stérile*	DÉPENSES Stériles *Relatives a l'Industrie &c.*
Avances annuelles *pour produire un Revenu de 2000# sont 2000#*	Revenu *Annuel de*	Avances annuelles *pour les Ouvrages des Dépenses stériles sont*
2000# produisent net	*2000#*	*1000#*
Productions	*moitié passe icy*	Ouvrages &c.
1000# .. .. reproduisent net	*1000# .. ..*	*1000# .. ..*
500 .. .. reproduisent net	*500 .. ..*	*500 .. ..*
250 .. .. reproduisent net	*250 .. ..*	*250 .. ..*
125 .. .. reproduisent net	*125 .. ..*	*125 .. ..*
62 10 .. reproduisent net	*62 10*	*62 10 ..*
31 5 .. reproduisent net	*31 5*	*31 5 ..*
15 12 6 reproduisent net	*15 12 6*	*15 12 6*
7 16 3 reproduisent net	*7 16 3*	*7 16 3*
3 18 2 reproduisent net	*3 18 2*	*3 18 2*
1 19 1 reproduisent net	*1 19 1*	*1 19 1*
0 19 6 reproduisent net	*0 19 6*	*0 19 6*
0 9 9 reproduisent net	*0 9 9*	*0 9 9*
0 5 .. reproduisent net	*0 5 ..*	*0 5 ..*
0 2 6 reproduisent net	*0 2 6*	*0 2 6*
0 1 3 reproduisent net	*0 1 3*	*0 1 3*
0 0 8 reproduisent net	*0 0 8*	*0 0 8*
Total *2000# .. ..*	Total *2000# .. ..*	Total *2000# .. ..*

Il n'est pas nécessaire de s'attacher a l'intelligence de ce Tableau avant la lecture des 7 premiers Chapitres, il suffit a chaque chapitre de faire attention a la partie du Tableau qui y a rapport.

Prachtausgabe des Tableau économique, enthalten in den „Elemens de la Philosophie rurale" (1767) des Marquis von Mirabeau

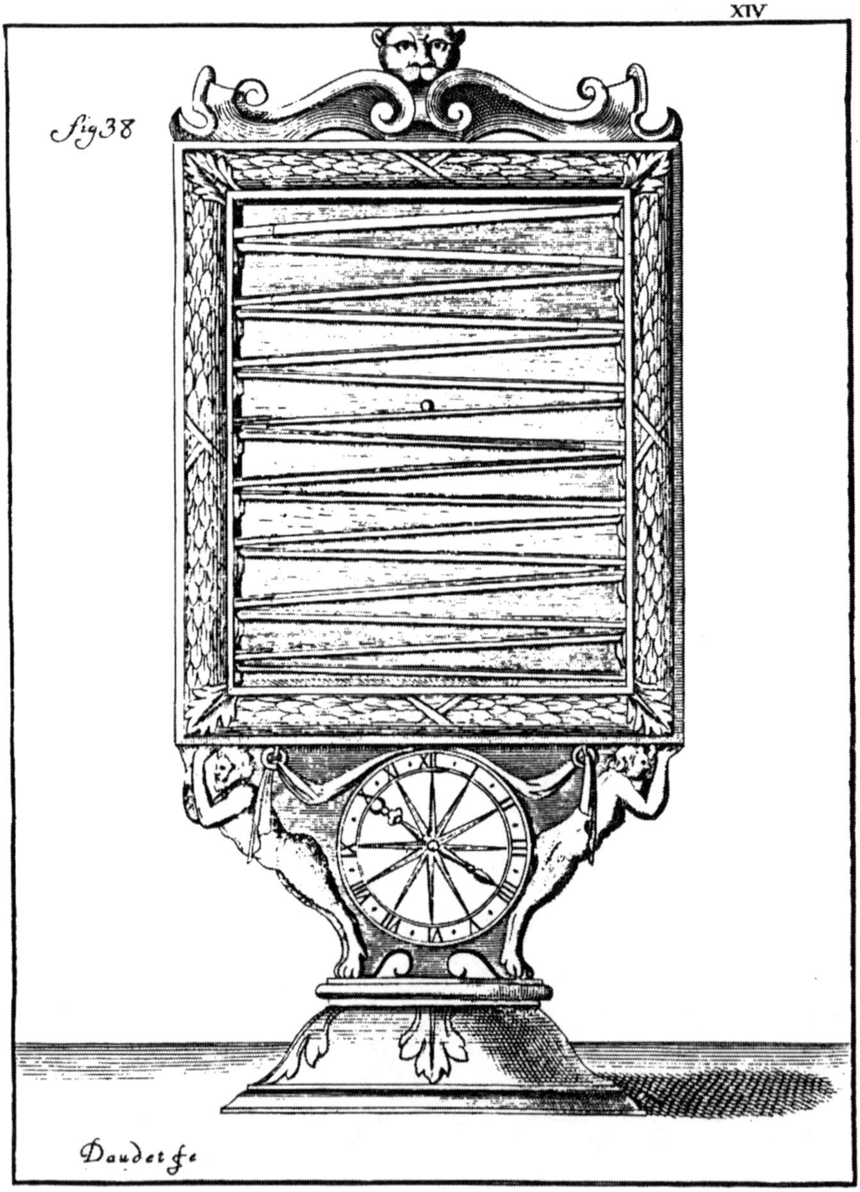
fig 38
Daudet fe

Contents

Chapter 1
The Physiocrats, The Antiphysiocrats, and Pfeiffer in Particular

Jürgen G. Backhaus

Physiocracy was probably the shortest lived school in the history of economic thought. While of obvious advantage in France to point out the pitfalls and costs of Colbertism, across the Rhine Physiocracy was not a step ahead, as it replaced Cameralism with its wise and comprehensive policy doctrines. For this reason, Physiocracy in the German literature has its greatest impact in provoking Antiphysiocracy. In this volume, Physiocracy is immediately paired with Antiphysiocracy, and with the unique figure of Johann Friederich (von) Pfeiffer (1718–1787).

Pfeiffer was a self-taught economist. He was born in 1718 in Berlin and died in 1787 in Mainz. For the last 5 years of his life, it was in Mainz where he was a professor of cameral sciences. The reputation of the school of Mainz as a fortress of Cameralism owes much to his contributions. Until 1780, his eight previous works are largely reproductions of his vast reading. Pfeiffer first entered the military service in Prussia, was later state agricultural councilor there, carried through a land reform in the Mark Brandenburg between 1747 and 1750, honored by the title of a privy councilor, was used in the Prussian diplomatic service at various courts in Germany, and was named a professor at the Mainz academy in 1782. In 1780, after his more mainstream outline (Lehrbegriff) of all economic and cameral sciences in four volumes (1764–1778) he came out with his revolutionary "Anti-Physiocrat." This was topped a year later by his blueprint of the science of forestry, which is also the blueprint of the science of mining in its eighth chapter.[1]

[1] The nineteen most important publications by Pfeiffer are listed in the dissertation by Damianoff MD (1908) Die volkswirtschaftlichen Anschauungen Johannes Friedrich von Pfeiffers. Noske, Borna-Leipzig, a 1908 Erlangen dissertation:

1. *Der Teutsche Seidenbau*, Berlin 1748.
2. *Lehrbegriff sämtlicher ökonomischer und Cameralwissenschaften*, 4 vol, 1764–1778. Mannheim and Stuttgart.

J.G. Backhaus (✉)
Krupp Chair in Public Finance and Fiscal Sociology, University of Erfurt,
Nordhäuser Str. 63, 99089 Erfurt, Germany
e-mail: juergen.backhaus@uni-erfurt.de

J.G. Backhaus (ed.), *Physiocracy, Antiphysiocracy and Pfeiffer*, The European Heritage in Economics and the Social Sciences 10, DOI 10.1007/978-1-4419-7497-6_1,

The essays presented in this volume span the entire landscape of Physiocracy, Antiphysiocracy, and Pfeiffer in particular. Of him, Schumpeter writes: "[his] voluminous systematic works of the Justi-type, no doubt marked by strong practical sense, have earned for him high praise from several historians."[2] Kenneth Carpenter, formerly of Harvard University's Kress Library, finds that it was not the Bible that was the most widely spread book, as one might expect, but the Justi- and Pfeiffer-type literature that shaped the knowledge economy of the eighteenth century. In his essay "Manufactures in European Economic Literature of the Enlightenment: The Description des Arts et Métiers and the Schauplatz der Künste und Handwerke," Carpenter distinguishes two kinds of readers of those publications, persons who would be interested in science and scientific development, and practitioners. He concludes that science was no longer just for the elite, no longer only for the possessor of secrets, but was also to be shared with the uninitiated, the practitioner. In discussing translations, Carpenter emphasizes the issue that translations could not be trusted, but in the process, this furthered the discourse with the community,

---

3. *Geschichte der Steinkohlen und des Torfes*, Mannheim 1777.
4. *Entdecktes Geheimnis des Verbesserungsmittels der Steinkohlen und des Torfes und der Benutzungsart aller daraus zu ziehenden Produkte*, Mannheim 1777.
5. *Vermischte Verbesserungsvorschläge und freie Gedanken über verschiedene den Nahrungszustand, die Bevölkerung und Staatswirtschaft der Teutschen betreffende Gegenstände*, 2 vol, Frankfurt a. M. 1777/78.
6. *Allgemeine Polizeiwissenschaft*, 2 vol, Frankfurt a. M. 1779/80.
7. *Grundriß der wahren und falschen Staatskunst*, 2 vol, Berlin 1778/79.
8. *Die Manufakturen und Fabriken Deutschlands, nach ihrer heutigen Lage betrachtet und mit Vorschlägen zu ihrer Verbesserung begleitet*, 2 vol, Frankfurt a. M. 1780/81.
9. *Der Antiphysiokrat*, Frankfurt a. M. 1780.
10. *Grundriß der Finanzwissenschaft nebst einem Anhang über die Unausführbarkeit des physiokratischen Systems*, Frankfurt a. M. 1781.
11. *Grundriß der Forstwirtschaft*, Mannheim 1781.
12. *Universalcameralwissenschaft oder die vier wichtigsten Säulen, nämlich der Staatsregierungskunst, der Policeywissenschaft, der allgemeinen Staatsökonomie und der Finanzwissenschaft, zu akademischen Vorlesungen und zum Unterricht angehender Staatsbedienter*, 2 vols, Frankfurt a. M. 1782/83.
13. *Berichtigungen berühmter Staats-, Finanz-, Policey-, Cameral- und öknomischer Schriften dieses Jahrhunderts*, 6 vols, Frankfurt a. M. 1781–84.
14. *Grundriß der Staatswirtschaft zur Belehrung und Wahrung angehender Staatswirte*, Frankfurt a. M. 1782.
15. *Programm von der Notwendigkeit und dem Nutzen der in den Curmaynzischen Landen aufbelebenden Bergwerks- und Schmelzwissenschaften*, 1784.
16. *Nachricht an das Publikum von der Natur, den Bestandteilen, Eigenschaften, Zubereitung und Anwendung des Ducksteins oder des daraus bereiteten Druses*, Mainz 1784.
17. *Critische Briefe*, 4 brochures, Offenbach 1784/85.
18. *Prüfung der beträchtlichen Verbesserungsvorschläge der Glückseligkeit und Macht Deutschlands*, Frankfurt a. M. 1786.
19. *Grundsätze und Regeln der Staatswirtschaft*, edited by Nicolaus Moser, Mainz 1791.

---

[2] Joseph Alois Schumpeter, *History of Economic Analysis*. New York: Oxford University Press, 1954, p. 228.

and the development of new knowledge also created the tools for discourse. New knowledge is also at the core of Erik S. Reinert's (University of Tallinn) contribution "The Technological Dynamics of Capitalism: A Note on Antiphysiocracy, Colbertism, and 1848 Moments." He finds that neither the Physiocrats, nor the Antiphysiocrats were pure profit maximizers, they all had the well-being of the Commonweal in mind. Development of new techniques and practical knowledge is also the topic of the next essay. Sophus A. Reinert (Cambridge University) describes "Another Grand Tour: Cameralism and Antiphysiocracy in Baden, Tuscany, and Denmark-Norway."

The essay by Helge Peukert (University of Erfurt) is devoted to Johann August Schlettwein (1731–1802) who was probably the most productive of the German Physiocrats in a physiocratic sense. In the newly formed medium-sized Southern German States, lots of practical policy problems had to be resolved and presented many a challenge for a productive mind, inspired by Physiocracy or not.[3] Hans Frambach (University of Wuppertal) focuses on the political economic contributions of Johann Friedrich von Pfeiffer. He shows that Pfeiffer did not take an isolated stance, but wanted to make his knowledge available to several nations. Frambach asks, why Pfeiffer did not become a Physiocrat. The lasting point of Physiocracy is, of course, the Single Tax, and its Antithesis, formulated by Pfeiffer in the *Anti-Physiocrat,* has left us with a manifold and complex tax system. In addition, other more subtle differences are also analyzed by Frambach. One of the main practical emphases of physiocratic policy was the repopulation of the newly acquired lands. The price for these acquisitions was paid in human terms; the large contributions from Westphalia and the German Southern States to Napoleon's Russian Campaign. Gerhard Scheuerer (University of Erfurt) therefore discusses the Physiocrats' Laws of Population. Günther Chaloupek (Chamber of Labour, Vienna) suggests "On the Reception of Quesnay's Economic Thought in German History of Economics" that issues of shortage of food as raised by Cannais will remain important in the future. Sometimes, it is as important to overcome a novel but faulty doctrine as it is important to create new theoretical concepts and models. In this vein, the role of the State is highlighted by Marcel van Meerhaeghe (University of Ghent) in "Mature Cameralism according to Pfeiffer." For example, as is pointed out by van Meerhaeghe, the later or mature Cameralists recognized that trade between nations can be mutually beneficial and are thus in favor of free trade policies.

Pfeiffer's *Anti-Physiocrat* (1780) did much to reduce the impact of Physiocracy in Germany and put an enlightened science of state in its place. Yet, there was still a longer term effect, which consisted in the development of the science of forestry (Pfeiffer 1781). This was to be the first of the applied environmental sciences. Pfeiffer is the prime protagonist. His insights are far-sighted at the time. First, Pfeiffer describes his endeavor as a very broad research program, and second, he also is giving an interesting take of what a Cameralist would expect the use of his

[3] A counter example is the stale Friedrich Karl von Fulda (1774–1847) who deserves a footnote in the German history of economic thought for his obstinate opposition to Friedrich List.

scholarly endeavor to be, because the book is not only directed towards those in charge of public policy, but also to private owners (Gutsbesitzer) who have holdings of forestry land. As elaborated in the essay by Jürgen Backhaus, "Pfeiffer and the Foundation of the Science of Forestry," Werner Sombart in his *Modern Capitalism* foresees failure of capitalism. Why? Because of the price of wood. This is exactly the topic of Pfeiffer, who sees forestry as a precondition of modern capitalism. The issue of sustainable resources is also the topic of the next essay. A vast literature on sustainability has recently become available, but the history of economic thought perspective is typically omitted. A thorough look into the roots of this line of thought has been provided by Peter Deegen (University of Tharandt): "Establishing sustainability theory within classical forest science – the role of cameralism and classical political economy."

The essays presented in this book were originally discussed at the 19th annual Heilbronn Symposion in Economics and the Social Sciences, 15–17 June 2006. The effort by Erik, Fernanda, and Sophus Reinert is also acknowledged, who brought their collection of rare books on Pfeiffer to Heilbronn and presented them to the conference participants. We are grateful to the Lord Mayor of the City of Heilbronn and the City Council for their generous hospitality and support.

Chapter 2
Manufactures in European Economic Literature of the Enlightenment: The *Description des Arts et Métiers* and the *Schauplatz der Künste und Handwerke*

Kenneth Carpenter

The year 1750 marks the start of a great outpouring of economic literature. Besides documenting that in various ways, both statistical and otherwise, I will show that the fastest growing part of that literature, far from being generally descriptive of the economy or prescriptive in advancing arguments relating to economic policies, was practical. It was intended to be useful. It recounted best practices in agriculture, and it described how best to ply certain crafts and manufacture a variety of goods. The works mentioned in the title of this essay are above all exemplars of the new emphasis on producing goods. Finally, I will argue that these works had a significance that transcended their texts as embodiments of technological information. Implicitly, though rarely explicitly, they contributed to contemporary debates about economic freedom and the values attached to work, especially work with ones hands. They represented a break with old ways, and in their raising of aspirations, their use of the intellect to advance knowledge, they should be viewed as important elements in what we term the Enlightenment.

Documenting the Output of Economic Literature

The vastly increased output can be documented by counting the entries recorded in the catalog of the Goldsmiths' Library at the University of London and the Kress Collection at the Harvard Business School. In the year 1748 these two libraries,

K. Carpenter (✉)
Retired Editor, Harvard Library Bulletin, Harvard University,
16 Stafford Road, Newton Center, MA 02459, USA
e-mail: kencarpenter@comcast.net

J.G. Backhaus (ed.), *Physiocracy, Antiphysiocracy and Pfeiffer*, The European Heritage in Economics and the Social Sciences 10, DOI 10.1007/978-1-4419-7497-6_2,

both with international collections, had 103 titles. In 1749, there were 121. Then in 1750, the combined catalog recorded 176; and although the numbers for a given year could decline (there were 148 in 1751), the trajectory was upward.

A study of French output provides a detailed look at the total body of economic literature in the dominant language of the Continent.[1] Christine Théré has provided precise figures: 1740–1749, 96 titles; 1750–1759, 391 titles; 1760–1769, 612 titles; 1770–1779, 668 titles; 1780–1788, 756 titles.[2] Antoin Murphy, taking another approach, has described contemporary French awareness of the greatly increased output, which was reportedly even being read by the king and courtiers. As Murphy notes, "there was the feeling that the new subject matter would revolutionize attitudes on trade and the role of the government in this area."[3]

The consciousness of increased output resulted not only from growth in the absolute number of publications. Economic literature became a higher proportion of total book production. In the second half of the eighteenth century in France, general production tripled, while economics increased sevenfold.[4] The book-buying public in France necessarily came face to face with economic questions.

The French were not alone. The catalog of Italian economic literature in the Kress Collection at the Harvard Business School, a strong and representative collection though not a comprehensive one, records 37 titles during the 2 decades from 1730 to 1749, but 120 for the period from 1750 to 1769, more than three times as many.[5] Economic literature in English had long flourished and was the largest body, but trying to create statistics would be problematic for a variety of reasons. An increased demand around mid-century is, however, indicated by the numerous reprints. Some examples are as follows: Joshua Gee's *Trade and Navigation of Great Britain*, reprinted in Glasgow (1750) and London (1755); Josiah Child's *New Discourse of Trade* was reprinted in Glasgow in 1751; Sir Matthew Decker, *An essay on the causes of the decline of the foreign trade* (London, 1750; Dublin, 1751; Edinburgh, 1756); James Puckle, *England's path to wealth and honour* (1750); and Thomas Mun's *England's Treasure by Foreign Trade*, first published in 1664, was reprinted in Glasgow in 1755.

Most of these and other English works served as well as the source texts for translations, often heavily reworked, in Dutch, French, German, Italian, Spanish,

---

[1] Christine Théré, "Economic Publishing and Authors, 1566-1789," in Gilbert Faccarello, ed., *Studies in the History of French Political Economy, from Bodin to Walras* (London and New York: Routledge, 1998), 1–56. To identify the works of French economics over two and a half centuries was an extraordinary task, and similar research has not been carried out for other European cultural areas. If it were, the results would differ in various significant ways, but it does seem that economic literature generally increased markedly after mid-century.

[2] Théré, "Economic Publishing," 11. As Théré points out, these figures are for texts, so a multivolume work is counted as one. Furthermore, the figures are for texts and do not include revised editions and reprints, which means that the number of actual publications is much higher.

[3] Antoin Murphy, *Richard Cantillon: Entrepreneur and Economist* (Oxford: Oxford University Press, 1989), 308–09.

[4] Théré, "Economic Publishing," 21.

[5] *Italian Economic Literature in the Kress Library, 1475–1850*, comp. P. Barucci and K. Carpenter, in collaboration with A. Calcagni Abrami and R. Reinstein Rogers (Rome: Banco di Roma, 1985).

and Swedish. In France, the translations were often produced by members of the circle around Vincent de Gournay. They do not represent market demand, but the crucial figure behind a translation was often the publisher, who, stimulated by consciousness of the public interest in economics, paid someone to translate. Some books had a truly vast popularity. Thus, Girolamo Belloni's *Del commercio*, which first appeared in a Latin and Italian edition in 1750, was followed within the decade by four Italian editions, seven in French, plus English and German translations. The very diversity of Europe had become an advantage; it provided a body of texts to be translated into other vernaculars and adapted to local needs. The passion for economics was general, by no means confined to France.[6]

Bibliographical publishing as a sign of increased output. A indication of the upsurge in economic literature is the bibliographical publishing of that era. There was even in London a call for formation of a "*publick* mercantile library," which would be available for consultation by all citizens.[7] The author believed such a library would be the first in all Europe, but in fact, the Commerz-Bibliothek had been founded in Hamburg in 1735. It first published a catalog in 1750.[8] That catalog can be considered the second bibliographical work on economics, the first having been published in 1716 and revised in 1726 – J. B. von Rohr's *Compendieuse-Hausshaltungs Bibliotheck*. Then, after a 25 year hiatus, several others followed the Kommerz-Bibliothek catalog: G. H. Zincke, *Cameralisten Bibliothek* (1751); a third edition of Rohr's *Haushaltungs-Bibliothek* (1755); J. J. Moser's *Bibliothec von Oeconomischen- Cameral- Policey- Handlungs- Manufactur- Mechanischen und Bergwercks Gesetzen, Schrifften und kleinen Abhandlungen* (1758); and J. H. L. Bergius's *Kameralisten-Bibliothek* (1762). Some of these German works were surveys of the subject matter, from, of course, the vantage point of Cameralism, with added and annotated listings of books; others were more in the form of annotated indexes to periodicals, with minute subject headings in alphabetical order. Some covered literature in languages other than German. They are extraordinary monuments to diligence and, one might add, to a bibliographical world that, on the one hand, consisted of a large body of literature but was, on the other hand, still bounded. The first bibliography that looks to the modern eye like a digestible listing of books appeared in France in 1769, André Morellet's "Catalogue d'une bibliotheque d'économie politique," which was appended to his *Prospectus d'un nouveau dictionnaire de commerce* (1769). Morellet's 34p work was a classified list of titles in

[6] My *Economic Bestsellers before 1850* (1975) provides other instances. That work is available on the website of the Other Canon Foundation (http://www.othercanon.org). It is in process of being revised, and a more general bibliographical study of translations is well underway.

[7] *An essay on the many advantages accruing to the community, from the superior neatness, conveniences, decorations and embellishments of great and capital cities* (1754), 19–21. The author also details what should be included in the library.

[8] *Catalogus Librorum Bibliothecae Commercii Hamburgensis*, which recorded 1,158 volumes. On this library, see the description by Berta Backe-Dietrich in Bernhard Fabian, ed., *Handbuch der historischen Buchbestände in Deutschland* (2003): http://www.vifabbi.de/fabian? Commerzbibliothek_Der_Handelskammer.

English, French, Italian, and Latin. It has had great renown and is still useful, not for its comprehensiveness, but because it, the work of one engaged in the production of economic literature, lays out the contours of the field of economics at that time.

Categories of the Post-1750 Economic Literature

"Economic literature" is inherently a broad designation, which can mean many things. Théré, basing her categories on those of Morellet, has the following, with the number in parentheses being the total number of titles in the category published between 1550 and 1789: Politics (499), Political economy (387), Agricultural and manufacturing production (324), Population and aid (856), Trade and navigation (508), History and state of trade and the colonies (394), Money and credit (240), and Finances and taxation (450). These are the broad categories used in Morellet's Catalogue, but Théré has rearranged some of the subdivisions, and in her search for relevant titles has markedly altered the relative numerical importance of categories and subdivisions. This is not the place to analyze Morellet's categories and Théré's reworking, but a closer look at the category of Agricultural and manufacturing production is relevant. Théré has five subdivisions, one less than Morellet, since she moved out from Agriculture the 47 books on the grain trade and placed them under Trade and navigation. Her subdivisions are Agriculture in general (239); Wines, wood, and livestock (36); Mines and minerals (13); Fishing, fish, salt, etc. (7); and Manufacturing production (29). To simplify, she basically created a category of Agriculture in general and added 233 works to the ones that Morellet recorded under Farms and closures (Fermes, clotures). The same increase did not take place in Manufacturing production, and, indeed, Théré notes (p. 49) that around 70 titles describing craft and manufacturing techniques or means of communication were rejected.[9] Even with those rejections, the category of Agricultural and manufacturing production constituted 12.5% of the output of economic literature during the period from 1750 to 1769. From 1730 to 1749, it constituted only 5%. From 1750 to 1769, Agricultural and manufacturing production was the fastest-growing category of economic literature, since it more than doubled whereas no other category doubled. Political economy grew from 6 to 10%. The conclusion to be drawn is that the 2 decades after mid-century represent above all a turn to the practical and useful.

No one has done for other languages what Théré did for French, but there is a statistical account of German book production that treats Agriculture and

[9] She states that of the technical pamphlets found largely in "Anglo-Saxon sources" "only those which carried reflections on practical applications [of a supposed innovation] were taken into account" and that in the case of descriptive works, only those that dealt "with a sector of production or ... with the problem of quality of fraud" were included. I know that during the years from 1967 to 1980, when I was curator of the Kress Collection, I tended to view technological literature as belonging to another field, more so than I did agricultural. Hence, I find intriguing Dr. Théré's explanation, not of what to exclude, but rather of what to include. She kindly informs me that that no list of the works is in her thesis or otherwise available.

manufacturing (Landwirtschaft, Gewerbe, usw.) as a category. Ilsedore Rarisch records that the number of books in that category grew from 8 in 1740 to 60 in 1770, an increase of 650%, the largest of all the categories. She does not record where economics lies, but a reasonable guess is that it is included in Political science (Staatswissenschaften), which in that same period grew from 10 to 32 titles, for a change of 220%, making it the fourth largest. Her statistics show this practical literature was the fastest growing portion of German book production, rising from 1.1% in 1740 to 5.2% in 1770.[10]

Not all works related to agriculture are practical. Quite apart from the Physiocratic works, which were placed under Political economy, are works on various aspects of agrarian policy, for example, land tenure, closures, or taxation of agricultural products. Very different are those scientific works on how to farm. That is the literature that especially flourished after mid-century, indeed, starting in 1750. An historian has written that the results of "the great agricultural revolution … begun in England … were suddenly revealed [in France] in 1750."[11] The literary signpost of that was Duhamel du Monceau's *Traité de la culture des terres suivant les principes de M. Tull*, whose first volume was published in 1750, followed by five additional volumes between 1753 and 1761.

Duhamel du Monceau was also the principal figure behind the Academy of Sciences *Description des arts et métiers*. It, along with its German translation and Swiss re-edition, stands almost alone as works on manufactures, except, that is, for journals. Although I have drawn a distinction between agriculture and manufacturing, the journals, often published by newly formed societies, saw them as just different sides of the practical. One might say that Duhamel du Monceau exemplified this. The *Journal oeconomique*, for example, had the subtitle *Mémoires, notes et avis sur l'agriculture, les arts, le commerce, & tout ce qui peut y avoir rapport, ainsi qu'à la conservation & à l'augmentation des biens des familles, & c.* Its first issue, January 1751, naturally included a statement of purpose, which stated that a wise and simple "Œconomie," by means of agriculture, the arts and commerce, provides a full abundance of riches and all the commodities of life. ("Tel est le caractere de la simple & sage Œconomie, qui par le moyen de l'Agriculture, des Arts & du Commerce nous procure une plein abondance de richesses & toutes les commodités de la vie.")[12]

[10] Ilsedore Rarisch, *Industrialisierung und Literatur: Buchproduktion, Verlagswesen und Buchhandel in Deutschland im 19. Jahrhundert in ihrem statistischen Zusammenhang* (Berlin: Colloquium-Verlag, 1976), 12–14.

[11] André J. Bourde, *The Influence of England on the French Agronomes, 1750–1789* (Cambridge: At the University Press, 1953), 13. The distinction between agricultural and farming literature comes from pp. 3–5 of this work.

[12] Writings on commerce, if that term is not used as a term to mean political economy, could also be considered practical. In that category are above all merchants' manuals, which describe the trade of various parts of the world, provide information on commercial practices and laws, and perhaps give sample letters for the young businessman. The most famous such work, Jacques Savary's *Le parfait negociant* was first published in 1675, was almost immediately translated into German and Dutch; it went through many new editions, with the frequency picking up at mid-century. This category is, of course, not included in Théré's Agricultural and manufacturing production, and it is not considered in this essay.

A similar journal, with a focus on making available useful, practical information, was the journal of the Royal Swedish Academy of Sciences (Kungliga Svenska Vetenskaps Akademien). It so satisfied the goal that in 1749 there began publication of a German translation of the entire periodical, going back to its very first volume of 1741. The German title points up the emphasis on the practical: *Der Königl. Schwedischen Akademie der Wissenschaften Abhandlungen aus der Naturlehre, Haushaltungskunst und Mechanik*. The fact of a German translation of the entire work is also testimony to the demand for practical, useful information. "Useful" was the watchword, as shown by the title of another German periodical, *Nützliche Samlungen vom Jahre 1755*, which ran through 1758.

These periodicals, though they demonstrate the perceived need for a literature devoted to the mechanical arts, were not systematic. They did not satisfy the need for actionable information. Just as periodical articles could not do that, neither could an individual do so. Back in the sixteenth century Tomaso Garzoni had written an account of the various trades, translated into German in 1619 as *Piazza universale, das ist, Allgemeiner Schauwplatz, oder Marckt vnd Zusammenkunst aller Professionen, Künsten, Geschäfften, Händeln vnd Handwercken so in der gantzen Welt geübt werden*, but it could not contain the information that would enable someone with the book in hand to make something. Neither, a century and a half later, could Johann Heinrich Gottlob von Justi in his *Vollständige Abhandlung von denen Manufacturen und Fabriken* (Copenhagen, 1758–1761), but, as noted below, he later edited the publication that did provide detail.

Description des arts et métiers[13]

Perhaps only the French Academy of Sciences could have produced descriptions of technological processes sufficiently detailed to be acted upon. The plates in Diderot's *Encyclopédie*, published between 1762 and 1772, might be thought to belie that statement, but it has been demonstrated that they were extensively plagiarized from plates produced for the Academy.[14] The descriptions of the various arts were the result of collaboration between scientists and artisans and manufactures, and the prestige of the Academy was presumably crucial in obtaining their cooperation. In time the *Description des arts et métiers*, whose publication began in 1761, would

---

[13] The Academy of sciences edition used "Description" in the singular. The Swiss re-edition, to be considered, below employed the plural "Descriptions." Scholars have applied both forms to the Paris edition.

[14] Geraldine Sheridan, "Recording Technology in France: The *Descriptions des arts*, Methodological Innovation and Lost Opportunities at the Turn of the Eighteenth Century," *Cultural and Social History* 5 (2008): 348, n. 2, which cites an unpublished work of 1984 by Madeleine Pinault, and Jean-Pierre Seguin, "Courte histoire des planches de l'Encyclopédie," in *L'Univers de l'Encyclopédie* (Paris, 1964), 26–33.

consist of 73 or 81 parts, depending on how they are counted. The various parts totaled nearly 13,000 pages, with more than 1,800 plates.[15]

In content the parts ranged widely, some being devoted to objects of daily use, such as candles, pins, or soap, some to objects used in play (tennis rackets and playing cards), and some to luxury products, such as painted glass, decorated leather, pipes for smoking tobacco, or wigs. Mathematical and astronomical instruments were covered as were organs. Some of what we would call crafts were covered: book binding and carpentry, the latter extensively. Many of the parts were, however, devoted to industrial production: mining, iron production, anchor manufacture, coal mining, textiles, brick making, and various metal products. These were in folio format, and the large size, like that of the *Encyclopédie*, made possible clear renderings of manufacturing processes.

The idea for producing accounts of the various trades goes back to Colbert, who in 1675 requested the academy to work on a description of the mechanical arts, the goal being to benefit both French manufactures and the sciences.[16] Although work began in the seventeenth century, great progress was made when in 1709 René-Antoine Ferchault de Réaumur (1683–1757) took responsibility for the project, with the support of the regent Philippe d'Orléans (1674–1723). Large numbers of engravings were made, and much text accumulated; but after the regent's death, Réaumur's interest waned, and he turned to private projects. In 1757, the Academy divided up Réaumur's manuscripts among 20 of its members, and Henry-Louis Duhamel du Monceau (1700–1782) took de facto leadership of the project.[17] Publication began in 1761, with the firm of Desaint & Saillant.

[15] For an overview, see especially the pioneering work of Arthur H. Cole and George B. Watts, *The Handicrafts of France as Recorded in the* Descriptions des arts et métiers *1761–1788* (Boston: Baker Library, Harvard Graduate School of Business Administration, 1952, a 43-page work). A considerable quantity of work has appeared in recent decades, most of it focused on the plates. For some basic contributions, see especially Martine Jaoul and Madeleine Pinault, "La collection 'Description des Arts et Métiers,' Etude des sources inédites de la Houghton Library Université Harvard," *Ethnologie française*, NS 12 (1982): 335–360, and the companion article subtitled "Sources inédites provenant du château de Denainvilliers," *Ethnologie française*, NS 16 (1986): 7–38; and Madeleine Pinault-Sørensen, "La *Description des arts et métiers* et le rôle de Duhamel du Monceau," in *Duhamel du Monceau, 1700–2000: Un européen du siècle des Lumières*, ed. Andrée Corvol (Orléans: Académie d'Orléans, 2001): 133–55. A detailed list of the parts, arranged by the subject, is in *Les Publications de l'Académie royale des sciences de Paris (1666–1793)*, comp. Robert Halleux, et al. (Turnhout: Brepols, 2001), I: 485–550.

[16] "Cette Compagnie [l'Académie Royale des Sciences] étoit à peine formée qu'elle conçut le projet d'examiner & de décrire successivement toutes les opérations des Arts méchaniques, persuadée que cette entreprise pouvoit également contribuer à leur progrès & à celui des Sciences." – "Avertissement," of Duhamel du Monceau in *L'art du charbonnier* (1761), i. Cole and Watts cite Morand, *L'art d'exploiter les mines de charbon de terre*, who wrote that the Avertissement was separately published in 1759 and inserted in copies of the 1761 publication. See also Roger Hahn, *The Anatomy of a Scientific Institution: The Paris Academy of Sciences, 1666–1803* (Berkeley: University of California Press, 1973), 67–68.

[17] See Cole and Watts, *Handicrafts*, 4–10, and especially Pinault-Sørensen, "La *Description*."

Although there seems to be no account of the deliberations that led to the revival of the project in 1757, the timing coincides with the great upsurge in the production of economic literature – and particularly of practical literature – that has been described above. Indeed, the person who brought English farming to France also headed up the academy's project. Duhamel du Monceau and his scientific colleagues sought out as informants practitioners of the various trades and thus united science, best practice, and, at times, commercially relevant information in an attempt to produce works that could be acted upon and were so detailed as also to be a foundation on which to make further improvements. Their goal, stated in modern terms, was to present the trades with sufficient "tightness," or "thickness," or "density" that others would consider them sufficiently reliable to act on.[18]

Schauplatz der Künste und Handwerke

Not surprisingly, Justi recognized that the *Description des arts et métiers* was of monumental importance. Since the French parts were appearing in rapid succession, he perceived that the separate French parts could be translated and published in volumes that, through containing several of the parts, could be sold at a lower price; and in 1762 the first volume of a German translation, *Schauplatz der Künste und Handwerke*, came out under Justi's editorship.

Justi himself did not translate the first volume – that was the work of a so-called "translation factory" – but he did add notes. His interest in intervening editorially in the form of additions did, however, quickly wane, although the first four volumes (1762–1765) came out under his name. Then Daniel Gottlieb Schreber (1708–1777), a professor of Cameralwissenschaften and indefatigable author, translator, and editor, took over (vols. 5–12; 1766–1775). Volumes 14–20 (1780–1795) came out irregularly under different editors.

Swiss Revised Edition of Description

In 1771, 10 years after the first parts of the *Description des arts et métiers* were published, the Société typographique de Neuchâtel (STN), made famous by Robert Darnton, began publishing an edition that was part reprint, part translation of portions of the German, and part additions from elsewhere, along with original contributions. The editor was Jean-Elie Bertrand (1737–1779). He was one of the founders of the firm; and since publication began 4 years before the STN's edition of the *Encyclopédie*, it may be that the aim of publishing an edition of the *Description des arts et métiers* was a major impetus behind the firm's formation. Volume 1 appeared in 1771,

[18] These terms come from Joel Mokyr's *The Gifts of Athena: Historical Origins of the Knowledge Economy* (Princeton University Press, 2002).

and vol. 2, though dated 1774 on the title page, contained plates with the date 1775. Volume 3 appeared in 1775; vols. 4–6, 1776; vols. 7–8, 1777; vols. 9–11, 1779; vol. 12, 1780; vols. 13–15 and 18, 1781, though vols. 16–17 are dated 1780. The final volume, 19, is dated 1783. A volume 20 is recorded in an undated prospectus as "in press," and one other volume was promised, but neither of those ever appeared.

This edition, in form, is modeled on the German, in that it unites various parts into single volumes, though the German and Swiss editions differ in arrangement. The notes of Justi and Schreber are often translated from the German, but Bertrand, a professor and pastor, and one of the three founders of the firm, added material of his own, some of which appeared in volumes published after his death.[19]

Editions in Other Languages

In 1788, a Dutch edition began to appear. Not all of the texts were from *Description*, and there were many additions. Up through 1806, 23 volumes came out, with a final one appearing in 1820. In Denmark, a translation was begun in the late 1790s. This was part of the program of the Reiersen Foundation (Den Reiersenske Fond). Niels Lunde Reiersen, upon his death in 1796, had left a large fortune, the interest of which was to be applied to "promoting the national industry and manufactures."[20]

There was no other large-scale translating, but some parts were translated and published in Italian, Polish, and Spanish. At least one part appeared in English translation in Britain, and one was published in English in India. There may well have been other editions, but for a variety of reasons that is exceedingly difficult to determine.

The Place of the *Description* in Post-1750 Economic Literature

The *Description des arts et métiers* was considered to be highly important, although hyperbolic statements to that effect are not found other than in the prefatory statements to the German and Swiss editions. Justi called it "the most useful work that the world has ever seen" ("Ich finde gar kein Bedenken zu sagen, dass

[19] For detailed information on the contents, see the "Annexes" in Alain Cernuschi, "'Notre grande entreprise des arts': Aspects encyclopédiques de l'édition neuchâteloise de la *Description des arts et métiers*," in *Le Rayonnement d'une maison d'édition dans l'Europe des Lumières: la Société typographique de Neuchâtel 1769–1789*, ed. Robert Darnton and Michel Schlup (Neuchâtel: Bibliothèque publique et universitaire, 2005), 207–218. On the aim of publishing *Descriptions* being present from the beginning of the firm, see p. 185.

[20] "On the Present State of Manufactures in Denmark, Norway, and the Danish Dominions in Germany," *Commercial and Agricultural Magazine* I (Aug-Dec., 1799): 324. The foundation, which still exists, was responsible for some of the translations of economic literature that subsequently appeared in Danish; see Wikipedia.

dieses das allernützlichste Werk ist, das je in der Welt erschienen ist.").[21] He went on to say that it was a "Zeitpunct," opening up a new era in the "mechanical arts." Bertrand, the STN editor, used much the same language, and he then went on to justify his statement: it makes known with exactitude the tools and machines used by various artisans; it is so precise that a person with certain talents can carry out all the arts; that it is a work of such extreme difficulty that one despaired of ever seeing it appear.[22]

The fact that the work was the product of the French Academy of Sciences immediately gave it importance, but so did the format of the original edition. On the one hand, the fact of publication in parts, each available for purchase separately, emphasized that the descriptions were not theoretical, that, instead, they were directed to practitioners and intended for use. On the other hand, the parts were large folios, and folio was the format of theology, the mother of the sciences. It was the format for the books of greatest power and permanence and to publish in that format conveyed that the work was also worthy of inclusion in the grandest of libraries, just as did the *Encyclopédie*, with its folio volumes of plates depicting various occupations.

The German and Swiss editions were not folios, but they were very substantial. They were quartos, the next largest format, and they were thick volumes of hundreds of pages, with the apparatus that conveys learning, such as extensive notes and extended tables of contents. Each also used another paratextual element – dedications – to convey importance. Volume 1 of *Schauplatz* (1762) was dedicated to Peter II of Russia. That dedication, dated 1 June 1762, can be explained by the fact that Russian troops were then occupying Berlin, and its absence from most copies is explainable by the tsar's death before the month was out.[23] Volume 4 is dedicated to "E. Königl. Preussischen Hochverordneten Königsbergischen Krieges- und Domainen-Cammer" and contains a list of the officers and members of that body; volume 6 is dedicated to Stanislaus Augustus, king of Poland. The Neuchâtel edition also contained dedications to royalty. Volume 1 was dedicated to Frederick of Prussia, which implicitly gave permission to distribute within Prussia without

[21] "Vorbericht des deutschen Herausgebers," *Schauplatz der Künste und Handwerke* (1762), 9. I will subsequently refer to this work as "Schauplatz."

[22] "Depuis l'invention de l'Imprimerie, je ne crois pas qu'on ait formé de projet plus grand ni plus utile que celui de Messieurs de l'Académie Royale des Sciences. Donner une idée exact & detaillée des métiers, décrire avec netteté les opérations les plus dificiles [*sic*], faire connaître avec exactitude les outils & les machines emploïées par les divers artisans, qui travaillent pour nos besoins, nos commodités ou nos plaisirs, parler un langage intelligible aux plus ignorans, pousser la précision au point qu'un homme doué de quelques talens puisse, après une lecture attentive, exécuter lui-même les procédés de tous les arts; c'était un ouvrage l'extrême difficulté faisait désespérer de voir paraître. Les illustres Auteurs des Cayers des Arts et Métiers, ont prévu les obstacles, ils les ont bravé & le succès a passé leurs espérances. Leur entreprise fait une époque mémorable dans l'histoire des arts, elle illustre notre siécle, elle fait honneur à la France, où l'on a osé la former, elle rendra chers à la postérité la plus reculée, les noms des Savans, qui y ont généreusement consacré leurs talens & leurs travaux" – from the "Préface pour cette nouvelle édition."

[23] A copy of that dedication is in the copy in the Library Company of Philadelphia. It is entirely possible that some copies contain dedications other than those recorded in this essay.

interference from the publisher of the *Schauplatz*. Volume 2 (1774) was dedicated to Catherine the Great and volume 9 (1779) to the king of Denmark and Norway.[24]

Since the editions appeared over an extended period, they, at least the Parisian and German editions, were widely reviewed and noticed in the book-reviewing journals. The fact of the three different editions, each aimed at different though somewhat overlapping segments of the market, both with respect to language and class, means that Europe was substantially covered in a way that it would not have been, had there been only one edition. No records exist on sales of the Paris edition, but since the *Schauplatz* was a subscription book, it may be that a subscription list will be found in a copy. It should be possible, from the STN's records, to determine where copies of that edition were sold.

Although sales figures are lacking, it seems clear that these works were widely disseminated and acquired by individuals who saw them as important additions, even the most important, to the body of practical works being produced in Europe. Because, however, these works were each so impressive and so broad in their coverage of crafts and manufactures, they represent more than technology. They conveyed messages that transcended the specific texts they contained. They buttressed positions found in other practical works, but also in nonpractical texts aimed at changing policies and attitudes. In disseminating information about production processes, they implicitly supported abolition of the guilds. In holding up the importance of crafts and manufactures, they implicitly challenged the idea that the nobility could not engage in economic activity without loss of status; and in describing and depicting people at work, these publications upheld the dignity of work.

Guilds. Turgot's abolition of the guilds in 1776, an action that was soon reversed, followed a period of literature opposed to the guilds and their restriction on freedom. This is not the place to trace out bibliographically the history of that controversy, but to show that it engaged not just France but also Europe, it suffices to refer to *Chinki*, by the abbé Gabriel François Coyer (1707–1782). This work in the form of a dialogue went through at least six French editions as well as at least two in German and in Italian, and it was also translated into Croatian, Spanish, and Swedish. The *Description* both implicitly and explicitly made the point that know-how should not be a private good. In one of the early parts of the original series, *Art du tanneur* by Joseph Jérôme Le Français de Lalande (1764), is a statement about the history of the project, which attributes the slow progress of the arts to the secrecy of the workers and asserts that discoveries should be a common treasure.[25] Bertrand, who often

[24]On the implicit privilege inherent in a dedication, see Richard Yeo, *Encyclopaedic Visions: Scientific Dictionaries and Enlightenment Culture* (Cambridge: Cambridge University Press, 2001), 230. Yeo makes the point, p. 236, that encyclopedias were most appropriately dedicated to a sovereign or prince, but he does not deal with the *Description*, any more than do other of the extensive works on encyclopedias.

[25]"La principale cause de la lenteur qu'on observe dans le progrès des arts, est une crainte jalouse, une défiance intéressée de la part des ouvriers, qui cachent de leur mieux les pratiques & les ressources de leurs arts, de crainte de les partager. …Tout ce qui se découvre dans les arts comme dans les sciences, doit être un trésor commun à tous les peuples du monde" – iv. He goes on to write that "un secret dans les arts est une espece de monopole exercé par un particulier sur le reste des hommes" – v.

in the Neuchâtel edition, made explicit what was implicit, also emphasized that revealing secrets served the common good.[26] Even though it is not possible to assert that Bertrand's added comments had wide influence in France, they can be seen as reflecting conclusions that enlightened readers of the Parisian edition might have drawn. He noticed, as no doubt others did, that each of the parts concluded by printing regulatory documents. These were, he stated, directly contrary to good policy. [27] Could it be that that was precisely the conclusion the academicians wished to have drawn from including those documents? Without direct criticism, were they trying to make the point that freedom would lead to technological advances that would benefit all?

Nobility. The *Description* also had a role in the highly charged debate in France over whether engaging in economic activity meant derogation of noble status. The contrast with Britain is striking. Some sensitivity remained, as is shown by a section addressed to nobility in a prospectus for a mercantile academy, but in France such an appeal would have been unthinkable.[28] Again, it is a work of Coyer and the reaction to it that best reveals the intensity of the issue. In 1756, 5 years before the first volume of the Academy's series, *La noblesse commerçante* appeared. At least six French-language editions, some counterfeit, came out within the first year. The tie between the *Description* and those who wished the nobility to engage is best indicated by the fact that Justi, who was responsible for the *Schauplatz*, edited a German translation of Coyer, which he supplemented with an essay of his own.[29] To desire dissemination of technological knowledge meant you believed the nobility should engage in economic activity.[30]

The dignity of work and of workers. Although the widespread public debate was about the role of the nobility, the other side of the coin, the matter of deeper import, was the way work and workers were viewed. To see manual work as having

[26] "Tous les secrets des arts se dévoileront pour l'utilité commune" – I, vii.

[27] "Ces réglemens, comme plusieurs autres que l'on lit à la fin de chaque art, sont directement contraires aux principes d'une bonne police, puisqu'ils tendent manifestement à introduire le monopole dans le commerce des parchemins. On est bien étonné de voir presque tous les arts mécaniques tyrannisés en France par ces principes destructeurs" – III (1775), 365, n 20, a comment in *L'art du parchemin*.

[28] For example, Malachy Postlethwayt, in laying out a plan for a mercantile academy, *The British Mercantile Academy ... Shewing the Necessity of Young Merchants Being Bred to Trade with Greater Advantages than They Usually Are* (1750), included "Some considerations on the usefulness of this institution to the young nobility and gentry, and such who are intended for the study of the Law." It would seem that attendance by the sons of the nobility was not out of the question, though it would require some persuasion.

[29] *Der handelnde Adel dem der kriegerische Adel entgegen gesetzet wird, Zwey Abhandlungen über die Frage: Ob es der Wohlfarth des Staats gemäß sey, daß der Adel Kaufmannschaft treibe? aus dem Französischen übersetzet und mit einer Abhandlung über eben diesen Gegenstand versehen von Johann Heinrich Gottlob von Justi* (Göttingen, 1756). Russian, Italian, and Spanish translations also appeared.

[30] Those stances went hand in hand as well with opposition to the guilds, a topic on which the abbé Coyer also wrote a best-seller in 1768. *Chinki* had at least six French editions, at least two in German and Italian, plus translations into Croatian, Swedish, and Spanish.

dignity was inherent in the turn to practical literature after mid-century, but an earlier work, widely disseminated, had taken that stance. Cynthia J. Koepp in a most interesting article on *Le spectacle de la nature* (1732–1751) of Noël-Antoine Pluche (1688–1761) shows that he was a widely read proponent of the dignity of artisans and of the importance of the mechanical arts. Besides at least 57 editions in French and 22 in English, there were translations into Dutch, German, Italian, and Spanish.[31]

The technological publications referred to earlier also reinforced the idea that work itself, ordinary work, not just the brilliantly creative, should be viewed as possessing dignity. As the editor of the *Journal œconomique* put it:[32]

> …entre les occupations des hommes celles qui ne se présentent que sous des dehors modestes, sont aussi dignes de notre estime par le travail & l'industrie qu'elles exigent & par l'utilité qu'elles apportent, que les plus brillantes le sont de nos éloges par la beauté, la justesse & l'élévation d'esprit qu'elles demandent.

The Parisian *Description* did not explicitly assert the dignity of those who worked in the mechanical arts, but, as noted above, the paratext of the publications did so. Neither did the *Schauplatz* state explicitly that the producers of goods should be more highly esteemed, but Jean Bertrand, editor of the Neuchâtel edition, did:

> Si les Arts mécaniques avaient été estimés autant qu'ils sont estimables, il y a long-tems que tous leurs procédés auraient été décrits. Mais, il faut en convenir, nous avons trop avili dans nos vains préjugés ceux qui exercent les arts: Nous avons dédaigné de nous occuper sérieusement d'eux & de leurs travaux. Ce sont cependant ces ouvriers si ignobles au jugement borné de tant d'esprits superficiels; ce sont ces ouvriers trop injustement méprisés, qui pourvoient à nos besoins, multiplient en mille manières nos jouissances & nos plaisirs.

Bertrand was not content to view the workers as estimable solely because they supplied basic human needs. He stated that they multiply in a thousand ways our enjoyment and pleasure. Bertrand also argued that owners of manufacturing establishments, instead of being content with an assured profit, should master the details of the work in order to help bring the processes to perfection for the greater benefit of the state.[33]

> Il serait fort utile sans doute que chaque ouvrier joignant quelque théorie à la pratique, pût lire la description de son art; mais il l'est encore plus que les Manufacturiers soient bien instruits des pratiques de celui qu'ils font exercer. D'ordinaire le fabriquant est distingué des artisans; ceux-ci travaillent pour le compte de celui-là; ceux-ci agissent, forment, exécutent; celui-là fait travailler, paye & revend. Souvent le fabriquant content d'un ouvrage, qu'il est sûr de débiter, ne va point au delà & ne cherche pas mieux. Son profit est assuré, c'en est assez pour lui; il ne contribue point à la perfection de la manufacture, qu'il ne connait quelquefois que comme marchand, qu'il n'a point étudiée comme praticien. Que cet homme utile, qui communément a reçu quelque éducation, s'applique à connaître les détails du métier, bientôt les ouvriers mieux dirigées travailleront avec plus d'intelligence & la manufacture sera perfectionée au profit de l'Etat. Il conviendrait donc à tout fabriquant de lire les descriptions de l'art qui l'occupe.

---

[31] Cynthia J. Koepp, "Acknowledging Artisans and a New Social Order in Abbé Pluche's *Spectacle de la nature*," *Princeton University Library Chronicle* 68 (2007): 791–815.

[32] In "Plan du Journal," *Journal œconomique* (January 1751): 4.

[33] Vol I, vii–viii.

Mastering the details would truly be a sign of esteem.

Bertrand has often been quoted, because his statements help to demonstrate that the *Description des arts et métiers* was linked with various issues related to the economy. They, in fact, are similar to those of a much earlier scholar who worked on describing the crafts. Geraldine Sheridan's "Recording Technology in France," already cited, spells out that effort, which took place outside the Academy of Sciences. It began in 1692, when the abbé Jean-Paul Bignon (1662–1743) brought together three people to work on the project. One of them was Jacques Jaugeon about whom almost nothing is known. Sheridan states that his manuscript treatise on printing and binding (1704) in the library of the Bibliothèque de l'Institut de France is really a preface to the entire collection then projected. Jaugeon saw a natural progression in the crafts, from supplying "the necessary" to "the superabundant," which sounds very much like Bertrand's "jouissances" and "plaisirs." Jaugeon, states Sheridan, saw the crafts as the engine of "economic development and modernity." Jaugeon also emphasized the universality of the project which would make knowledge of the crafts a common good available for the benefit of all. That idea of universality was in fact carried out in all three editions through making available information from different cultures. It may well be, then, that these works were powerful statements about the path to "economic development and modernity."

Conclusion

As indicated earlier, we know little about who purchased these books and how they were used, but there are glimpses, as in the borrowing records of the Herzog August Bibliothek in Wolfenbüttel. Nine individuals borrowed 24 volumes of the *Schauplatz* between 1768 and 1779. One person took out six volumes, another person seven, one person the first two, but the others borrowed only one each, mostly volume 1, though in two cases a subsequent volume, thus indicating interest in a particular technology. Government officials were the largest group among the borrowers, but there was also a general.[34] Perhaps the most one can say is that there was a marked

[34] The details are that an Oberstleutnant, borrowed volumes 1 to 6 on October 25, 1769. Kommissar Alburg borrowed 4 volumes on March 15, 1769. A Herr Topp borrowed 7 volumes (1–2, 4–5, 6, 7–8) between September 14, 1778 and April 23, 1779. The other six borrowers took out only one volume each. These borrowers were also diverse and varied in what they borrowed. Cand. Jur. Berckhen borrowed v. 3 on November 28, 1772. Kammerkommissionsrat Greiner briefly borrowed v. 1 on September 13, 1768, and then General von Hoym took out that volume on September 19, 1768. Two "Schüler" borrowed: Zum Felde, v. 1, on September 28, 1770, and Mümler, v. 7, on April 20, 1771. Another official, Kommerzienrat Scharff borrowed v. 1-2 on February 4, 1775. The source of this information is Mechthild Raabe, *Leser und Lektüre im 18. Jahrhundert: die Ausleihbücher der Herzog August Bibliothek Wolfenbüttel 1714–1799*, 4 vols. (München: K. G. Saur, 1989). V. 3, "Alphabetisches Verzeichnis der entliehenen Bücher;" records these borrowings on p. 570; v. 4, "Systematisches Verzeichnis der entliehenen Bücher," does so on pp. 568–69.

tendency to borrow the initial volume, although a couple of borrowers show clear evidence of interest in a particular craft or manufacturing process.

The fact that the abbé Morellet, acting as an agent for the STN, had 13 subscribers for the Neuchâtel edition, is evidence of copies getting into the hands of important people.[35] We could, however, assume that to have been the case. Obviously, some were not interested. Thus, a bookseller in Prague, who ordered only one copy of the Neuchâtel *Descriptions* but six of the *Encyclopédie* in quarto and two in octavo, wrote on 7 March 1778, that the great lords do not concern themselves with these sorts of works, while those who could make use of them either do not understand French or already have the German translation.[36] The Netherlands, ever an entrepôt for French books, was, of course, a market for the *Descriptions*; and if STN claims are to be believed, 200 copies were sold there, but aristocratic Italy may not have been particularly responsive to the Swiss sales efforts.[37]

Some resistance clearly came from those who upheld agriculture, if not as the source of wealth, of nobility of the human spirit. A sign is "Die Wirthschaft eines philosophischen Bauers," which appeared in the first volume, 1761, of *Abhandlungen der Naturforschenden Gesellschaft in Zürich.* This work of Hans Caspar Hirzel (1725–1803) was immediately translated into French as *Le Socrate rustique* (1762). It was dedicated to the marquis de Mirabeau, the Physiocrat, whose *Ami des hommes* had been appearing in numerous French editions. Mirabeau subsequently added to the work, and it was republished in French in 1763, 1764, 1768, and 1777. German editions came out in 1774, 1785, and 1786, but they had been preceded by a Dutch translation in 1767. It was included in editions of Arthur Young's *Rural Oeconomy.* This work appeared in the United States in 1792 and 1800, and in Russian in 1789. Two Italian translations were published, one about 1782 and one in 1793. What it disseminated throughout Europe and the United States was an account of a Swiss peasant, simple but wise, so much so that he was a rural philosopher, a rural Socrates. The message was that agriculture could produce such men. Obviously, manufactures could not promise that.[38]

At the same time, the literature about manufactures grew. Through use of "The Making of the Modern World," the digitized collection of economic literature based on the Kress Collection and the Goldsmiths' Library, it is possible to show that the

---

[35] Importing the Swiss edition was illegal, but Morellet was able to avoid confiscation by customs authorities through having the books shipped to Turgot, controller-general of finances. See *Lettres d'André Morellet*, ed. Dorothy Medlin, Jean-Claude David, and Paul LeClerc, vol. 1 (Oxford, 1991), letter 113 and its note 4, as well as letter 140.

[36] Eric Berthoud, "Un commerce de librairie entre Neuchâtel et Prague de 1777 à 1789," *Musée neuchâtelois*, s. 3, v. 6 (1969): 135.

[37] The STN, in writing on August 5, 1773, to a bookseller in Bergamo, stated, in an effort to persuade him to take 30 copies of the *Descriptions*, that a Dutch bookseller had taken 200; see Anne Machet, "Clients italiens de la Société typographique de Neuchâtel," in *Aspects du livre neuchâtelois*, 170. For the order of Joseph Aubert of Livorno for 2 copies, in 1776 or 1777, see the illustration on p. 167.

[38] See Paul H. Johnstone, "The Rural Socrates," *Journal of the History of Ideas* 5 (1944): 151–75.

number of books using the word "manufactures" – obviously both French and English books – grew decade by decade from 1740: 1740–1749, 391; 1750–1759, 690; 1760–1769, 799; 1770–1779, 873; 1780–1789, 1289; and 1790–1799, 1707.

It is also evident that the *Description* continued to have life. Besides the Danish interest in a translation in 1799, the Dutch edition began publishing in 1788. A subscription list in volume 1 (1788) of the Royal Library copy in The Hague shows a work acquired by various segments of society. The list records 184 purchasers of 224 copies. That number would have been added to by subsequent subscriptions, but it was enough to go ahead, in contrast to the Dutch translation of Adam Smith's *Wealth of Nations*, which ended after part 1 in 1796. Booksellers were buying copies, perhaps on speculation, since some subscribed for multiple copies; hence the difference between the number of buyers and copies. Of others listed with an identification and not just a name are a number of military men, government officials, and merchants. There are lawyers, clergy, educators, physicians, druggists, carpenters, and others, plus 11 libraries, "Lesegesellschaften" to use the German word. If the military men represent those with a scientific interest and the government officials the policy makers, then one can say that the Dutch edition evinces interest in economic development through development of manufactures.

The Dutch edition and the Danish interest, when looked at in the light of some evidence from the United States, suggests that the *Description* took on new life at the periphery, where it pointed to economic development through manufactures.[39] The evidence from the United States comes in the form of documented interest by Benjamin Franklin and John Adams.

Benjamin Franklin wrote on 31 May 1788, to James Bowdoin II, the wealthiest man in New England, recently governor of Massachusetts: "Has your Society among its Books the French Work *sur les Arts et les Metiers*? It is voluminous, well executed, and may be useful in our Country. I have bequeath'd it them in my Will; but if they have it already I will substitute some thing else."[40] Evidently, the American Academy of Arts and Sciences did not have a copy, because in his will dated 17 July 1788, Franklin bequeathed them the folio edition. The second of the three works that he singled out in his will was the Neuchâtel quarto edition, and he bequeathed that to the Library Company of Philadelphia.[41] Franklin was not alone in placing a set in an important library. John Adams gave a partial set of the folio edition to the Harvard College Library in 1789.[42]

---

[39] The Netherlands was then underdeveloped; see Joel Mokyr, "The Industrial Revolution and the Netherlands: Why Did It Not Happen?" *De Economist* 148 (2000): 503–520.

[40] The text of this letter is available at http://www.franklinpapers.org/franklin/framedNames.jsp. Bowdoin replied on June 28, 1788, that the Society did not have a copy. It is today in the library of the Boston Athenæum.

[41] George Simpson Eddy, "Dr. Benjamin Franklin's Library," *Proceedings of the American Antiquarian Society*, NS 34 (1924): 206–07. The third work was the history of the Academy of Sciences; it was bequeathed to the American Philosophical Society.

[42] Cole and Watts, *Handicrafts of France*, 8, n. 2.

It is possible that Franklin received the Neuchâtel edition as a gift. Whether he or Adams purchased the Parisian edition is not known to me; but even if they did not, their making more widely available their sets is evidence that Franklin did, indeed, see the work as possibly "useful in our Country."

Some books are more than bodies of information. They convey messages, and those messages, it seems, can change over time. If initially, given the context at the center of Europe, the messages of the editions of *Descriptions* were about guilds, the role of the nobility, and the esteem to be granted to those who worked with their hands, later on the context in other locations on the periphery saw a different message: that a world of greater "jouissances" and "plaisirs" was possible through using technology to develop manufactures.

Chapter 3
The Technological Dynamics of Capitalism: A Note on Antiphysiocracy, Colbertism, and 1848 Moments

Erik S. Reinert

1848 Moments

Economics is a cyclical profession. Its cyclicality appears to follow the same type of mechanisms of "destabilizing stability" as described by US economist Hyman Minsky as leading up to financial crises.[1] When things are stable and improving over long periods of time, bank routines of risk evaluation grow increasingly lax, and in the end credit is given to people who are not even able to pay interest on the loans they are given ("Ponzi financing," as with subprime loans). Long periods of stability lead to increasing vulnerability, to Minsky's "destabilizing stability." This chapter argues that similar mechanisms are at work inside economics: long periods of economic progress in the core countries lead to increasingly abstract and irrelevant economic theories. Bad theories are allowed to dominate the discipline for long periods of time because the underlying economy is strong enough to withstand their poisonous influences, but, eventually, reality catches up and disaster ensues. This brings less abstract and more relevant economic theories and practices back; mindless *laissez-faire* is abandoned and more active economic governance again becomes acceptable. These turning points can, after their most famous manifestation, be referred to as "1848 moments," and they tend to be caused by economic crises, just as the 1848 turning point followed upon the severe financial crisis of 1847.

---

[1] Hyman P. Minsky, *Stabilizing an Unstable Economy*, New Haven: Yale University Press, 1986.

E.S. Reinert (✉)
President, The Other Canon Foundation, Norway, and Professor of Technology Governance and Development Strategies, Tallinn University of Technology, Estonia
e-mail: eriksreinert@gmail.com

J.G. Backhaus (ed.), *Physiocracy, Antiphysiocracy and Pfeiffer*, The European Heritage in Economics and the Social Sciences 10, DOI 10.1007/978-1-4419-7497-6_3,

In his 1848 *Principles of Political Economy,* John Stuart Mill describes such moments well:

> It often happens that the universal beliefs of one age of mankind – a belief from which no one *was*, nor without an extraordinary effort of genius and courage *could* at the time be free – becomes to a subsequent age so palpable an absurdity, that the only difficulty then is to imagine how such a thing can ever have appeared credible…It looks like one of the crude fancies of childhood, instantly corrected by a word from any grown person.[2]

The financial crisis in 1847 triggered a dramatic shift in economics starting in 1848. "If you went to sleep in 1846 and woke in 1850 you would wake into a different world" wrote an English university professor in his memoirs.[3] 1848 produced three important economics books, all critical of the economic order legitimized by Ricardian economics: Karl Marx and Friedrich Engels' *Communist Manifesto* (Marx was so radical that he was forced to flee Germany for England), Bruno Hildebrand's *National Economics in the Present and in the Future* (Hildebrand was a liberal who had to flee Germany for Switzerland in order to escape the death penalty), and John Stuart Mill's *Principles of Political Economy*. From completely different political angles, all three books attacked the mainstream economics of the day for suffering from the same weaknesses of which we accuse today's mainstream. By attempting to make economics a much more accurate science than it merits, it created economic disasters: both financial crisis and widespread poverty, initially in the periphery and gradually also in the core regions of the world economy. All three 1848 books understood that national wealth required industrialization, recanting Ricardo's trade theory, the very same theory which at present – in its most simplistic form – provides the basis of the world economic order that locks poor nations into a comparative advantage in being poor. In short: practical analyses based on real-world economic conditions, and particularly so in terms of the relationship between increasing and decreasing terms to scale, again came to the forefront.

The present financial crisis has given us a new such turning point, a new "1848" moment, a new wake-up call of the dangers of exceedingly simplistic and abstract economic ideas, and it is, in this context, worthwhile revisiting an earlier one, which occurred in France in the late Enlightenment. In the pendular dynamic of economics suggested here, Physiocracy may well have been the first school of excessively abstract and – in practice – harmful economic doctrine; Antiphysiocracy the first sensible, realist reaction to it. As such, the latter holds enormous heuristic value for our current attempts to rethink the nature and possibilities of economics and economic policy. This note aims to elucidate the technological dynamics of capitalism in light of this 1848 dynamic, and will draw on the legacy of economic governance bequeathed us by Colbertism and Antiphysiocracy to do so.

---

[2] John Stuart Mill, *Principles of Political Economy*, London: Longmans, Green, Reader, and Dyer, 1848, p. 3.

[3] In Richard Reeve, *John Stuart Mill: Victorian Firebrand*, New York: Overlook, 2007, p. 202.

Antiphysiocracy and Colbertism

This chapter focuses on one aspect of Antiphysiocracy, which in the eighteenth century drew on a variegated cluster of traditions (Cameralism, Colbertism, Mercantilism, Reason of State): the idea that different economic activities have different potentials for creating wealth and allotting relative power, and that the concept of "free trade" must be unpacked to reveal what is traded and how the structures of trade contribute to relative economic development. Physiocrats had argued, on the basis of a priori assumptions, that agriculture was the sole source of wealth in the world. As Schumpeter said about Physiocracy: "Its analytical merit is negligible, but all the greater was its success,"[4] Antiphysiocrats resisted this singular focus on agriculture by drawing on Europe's long and successful history of encouraging competitive manufactures and the synergies this created with other sectors of the economy, including agriculture.

This element of Antiphysiocracy is not chosen haphazardly, it was at the very core of the theoretical reaction to Physiocracy in Europe, uniting authors like Simon de Linguet, Abbé Mably, Accarias de Serrionne, Necker, Forbonnais, and Jean Graslin in France, Ferdinando Galiani – the Neapolitan envoy to Paris – and Pietro Verri from Italy,[5] and Johann Friedrich Pfeiffer (1718–1787) in Germany.[6] Two of Pfeiffer's book titles flag his Antiphysiocracy.[7]

To appreciate the origins of this tradition, one must reconsider the legacy of "mercantilism" in Europe, perhaps most symbolically represented in the figure of French finance minister Jean-Baptiste Colbert. As the pendulum of economics again moved towards more abstract levels – where all economic activities become qualitatively alike – the mere mention of Colbert's name was likely to have blood-pressures rising among most economists. His name has become shorthand for *dirigisme*, for government interventions, tariffs, bounties, prohibitions, and state-led attempts at economic development in general; in other words for mercantilism, the most vilified tradition in the history of economic analysis. One recent scholar argued that "mercantilists"

[4] Joseph A. Schumpeter, *History of Economic Analysis*, New York, Oxford University Press, 1954, p. 175.

[5] Sophus A. Reinert, 'The Italian Tradition of Political Economy: Theories and Policies of Development in the Semi-Periphery of the Enlightenment,' in Jomo K. Sundaram and Erik S. Reinert (eds.), *The Origins of Development Economics: How Schools of Economic Thought Have Addressed Development*, London: Zed Books, 2005, pp. 24–47.

[6] For a list of works by German antiphysiocrats, see Magdalena, Humpert, *Bibliographie der Kameralwissenschaften*, Cologne: Kurt Schroeder, 1937, p. 1031–1032.

[7] *Der Antiphysiokrat, oder umständliche Untersuchung des sogenannten physiokratischen Systems für eine allgemeine Freyheit und einzige Auflage auf den reinen Ertrag der Grundstücke*, Frankfurt: Schäfer, 1780 & *Grundriss der Finanzwissenschaft nebst einem Anhang über die Unausführbarkeit des physiokratischen Systems*. Frankfurt: in der Esslingerischen Buchhandlung, 1781. For a list of Pfeiffer's works, see Anton Felix, Napp-Zinn, *Johann Friedrich von Pfeiffer und die Kameralwissenschaften an der Universität Mainz*, Wiesbaden: Steiner, 1955.

merely sought to "appropriate the wealth of their subjects" by "preaching to coarse and drunken German princes," though generally it is portrayed simply as "very bad economics."[8] Nobel Laureate in economics, Paul Samuelson similarly and influentially dismissed it under the heading "grossly fallacious arguments for tariffs,"[9] and there can be no doubt that this still is the dominant view of his profession. Surveying the dismal historiography of the phenomenon, it seems hard to dismiss E.A.J. Johnson's verdict that "mercantilism" is an "unhappy word," often simply employed either as "an antonym for *laissez-faire* or a synonym for stupidity."[10] Both unhappiness and stupidity in fact come to mind when one notes that the Wikipedia for a while defined "mercantilism" as the "nigger school of economics."[11]

There is, however, a striking divergence in the scholarship separating the work of historians and economists on the matter. Whereas economists are prone to ridiculing the very idea that government interventions in the economy might be beneficial, historians have long produced thorough studies of precisely the opposite. Not only did France successfully develop through heavy-handed interventions, but so did England and all other great powers from the early modern period through the nineteenth century to the Asian Tigers.[12] Physiocracy made its name in explicit polemic with Colbert's industrialization programme, and Antiphysiocracy was largely the vindication of this maligned tradition of political economy.[13] The Storming of the Bastille, marking the start of the French Revolution, was triggered when news of the dismissal of the Antiphysiocrat Jacques Necker as Minister of Finance reached Paris. In addition to writing what are likely to be the best-selling economics books in any language during the eighteenth century,[14] Necker is also famous for his great *Eulogy of Jean-Baptiste Colbert*.[15]

---

[8] James W. Bell, 'Review of The Politics of Mercantilism by Philip W. Buck,' *The American Political Science Review*, 36, 3, 1942, pp. 575–576.

[9] Paul A. Samuelson, *Economics*, tenth edition, New York: MacGraw-Hill, 1976, p. 694.

[10] E.A.J. Johnson, *Predecessors of Adam Smith: The Growth of British Economic Thought*, New York: Prentice Hall, p. 3–4.

[11] The phrase is readable in the discussions section at http://en.wikipedia.org/wiki/Talk:Mercantilism. Last accessed 19/08/07.

[12] See recently Jeff Horn, *The Path Not Taken: French Industrialization in the Age of Revolution 1750–1830*, Cambridge, Mass.: The MIT Press, 2006 and William J. Ashworth, 'The Intersection of Industry and the State in Eighteenth-Century Britain,' in Lissa Roberts, Simon Schaffer, and Peter Dear (eds.), *The Mindful Hand: Inquiry and Invention from the Late Renaissance to Early Industrialisation*, Amsterdam: Koninklijke Nederlandse Akademie van Wetenschappen, 2007, pp. 349–377; Brian Balogh, *A Government out of Sight: The Mystery of National Authority in Nineteenth-Century America*, Cambridge: Cambridge University Press, 2009. See generally also Erik S. Reinert, 'The Role of the State in Economic Growth,' *Journal of Economic Studies*, 26, 4/5 (1999), pp. 268–326.

[13] On the politics of Physiocracy, see T.J. Hochstrasser, 'Physiocracy and the Politics of *Laissez-Faire*,' in Mark Goldie and Robert Wokler (eds.), *The Cambridge History of Eighteenth Century Political Thought*, Cambridge: Cambridge University Press, 2006, pp. 419–442.

[14] See Kenneth E. Carpenter, *The Economic Bestsellers before 1850*, Boston: Harvard Business School, 1975. Downloadable at www.othercanono.org.

[15] Jacques Necker, *Eloge de Jean-Baptiste Colbert*, Dresden: Freres Walther, 1780.

Carl Menger, the founder of the Austrian School of Economics, had the ambition that economics should be a "map of the forces at work." Today's standard textbook economics ("neoclassical economics") takes as its starting point a metaphor of "equilibrium," a choice inspired by the cutting edge of research in Victorian physics.[16] This force towards equilibrium is, however, only one of many forces at work. The most fundamental feature of capitalism in the real world is, however, change rather than stasis. Financial crises are just one of the many things that happen in real life, but cannot happen in the idealized world of neoclassical economics. From the standpoint of Joseph Alois Schumpeter – Austrian economist and Harvard economics professor who spent much time at Harvard Business School – "equilibrium" is the opposite of economic development. Equilibrium theory therefore fails to reflect many of the mechanisms of industrial and economic dynamics that create economic welfare. The recent, tragic failure of *laissez-faire* invites us to rethink some of these commonplaces and to revisit the world of Colbertism and Antiphysiocracy, a world in which political choices are not the enemy of material welfare but their very prerequisite.[17] What follows is an attempt to explain some of the technical reasons for the historical success of its economic policies at a time when intense competition rendered success in international trade vital for the continuing viability of nations; a time, in short, not unlike our own.[18]

Productivity Explosions

The numerous policies of Cameralism and Colbertism aimed to do several things. Most importantly perhaps, they sought to buttress state coffers in an age of intense interstate warfare and competition without undermining people's capacity to secure subsistence. The state had to grow wealthy on par with its citizens, not at their expense.[19] To do this, policy makers tapped into what, throughout early modern Europe, was known as a "*Paradox*" of policy. As an anonymous pamphleteer put it at the end of the seventeenth century, "*Mechanicks* prevent *Famin* in a nation," since "no places are more frequently afflicted with *Famin*, than those Countries which are employed in *Tillage*."[20] The record spoke clearly. Famines took place principally in

[16] Philip Mirowski, *More Heat than Light: Economics as Social Physics, Physics as Nature's Economics*, Cambridge: Cambridge University Press, 1989.

[17] As such, the ideological transition from 'Re-bonjour, Monsieur Colbert,' *The Economist*, 23 October 2008 to 'What went wrong with economics,' *The Economist*, 16 July 2009 is telling.

[18] On economic rivalries in the period see Istvan Hont, *Jealousy of Trade: International Competition and the Nation-State in Historical Perspective*, Cambridge, Mass.: Harvard University Press.

[19] On Physiocracy, Antiphysiocracy, and the legacy of Colbert, see Steven L. Kaplan, *Bread, Politics, and Political Economy in the Reign of Louis XV*, The Hague: Martinius Nijhoff, 1976.

[20] Anonymous, *A Discourse of the Necessity of Encouraging Mechanick Industry...* London: R. Chiswell, pp. 29–30.

agricultural economies, not in places like Venice, Holland, and England. Colbert's insight had been similar, and he actively sought to better France's subsistence through the active encouragement of infrastructure and manufacturing industries, from textiles to glass and metals. To do this, he harnessed one of the most advanced systems of information-gathering and processing in the world, through which he could rationalize the economic administration of the Kingdom.[21] To understand why his policies were successful, one must look at the differential capacities of economic activities to produce wealth.

What from a long-term perspective may look as relatively smooth curves of economic development are in reality is the result of explosive productivity changes in a small number of industries. A key to national economic wealth is to harness the economic activities where these "productivity explosions" are found. Figure 3.1 shows an early such "productivity explosion" form a breakthrough innovation: that of cotton spinning in the late 1700s when annual labor productivity rose with more than 25% annually for a brief period. At the time, the common sense of economics was for nations to attempt to get industries behaving like this inside their borders. Productivity explosions create a system of triple rents: profits are high, wages rise, and the government tax-base grows. In its essence, colonialism was a system that

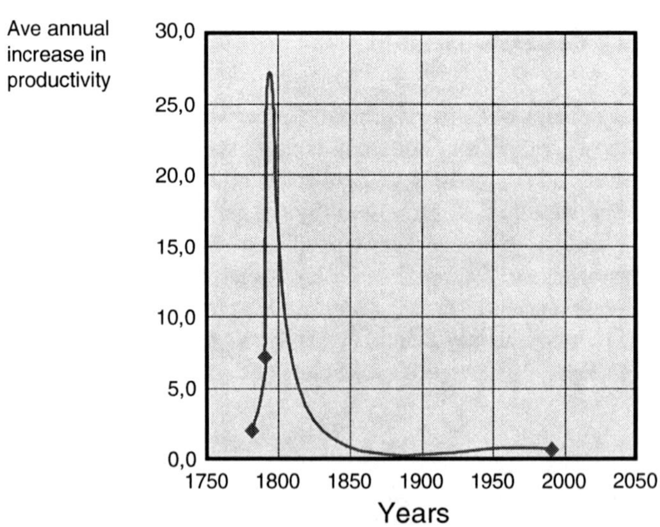

Fig. 3.1 An early productivity explosion. The mechanization of cotton spinning in the first paradigm
Source: Carlota Perez, Calculations from Jenkins 1994

[21] On this system, and its limits, see Jacob Soll, *The Information Master: Jean-Baptiste Colbert's Secret State Intelligence System*, Ann Arbor: The University of Michigan Press, 2009.

prohibited such production activities – industry in general – from being carried out in the colonies. At the time of this early productivity explosion, this prohibition of manufacturing was a main motive for the United States' independence in 1776.[22] Today we are experiencing a similar productivity explosion in the computer industry. Moore's Law tells us that, since the late 1970s, the capacity of the computer chips doubles roughly every 18 months, creating an upward curve like the one of the cotton industry in the 1700s. Also the activities, even technologically pedestrian ones, that are near the productivity explosion, may achieve triple rents. The task of cutting and preparing cables to the computer industry grew up geographically close to the computer industry itself when volume was low and prices not a big issue. Based on the growing demand, however, even low-tech industries may achieve economies of scale and run down the learning curve (see Fig. 3.2). We have to envision early European economic growth as learning curves existing in a large number of industries within the same labor market: the key to wealth was a large division of labor in increasing returns industries.[23] Colbert's genius was to enlarge the wealth-producing synergies that were found in Italian and Dutch city-states to a large national territory. One of the tools was to abolish internal trade barriers and erect external barriers, much in the same way Friedrich List recommended in Germany almost 200 years later.[24]

As List pointed out, English economists tended to explain economic progress as a result of free trade rather than as the result of "productivity explosions," thus

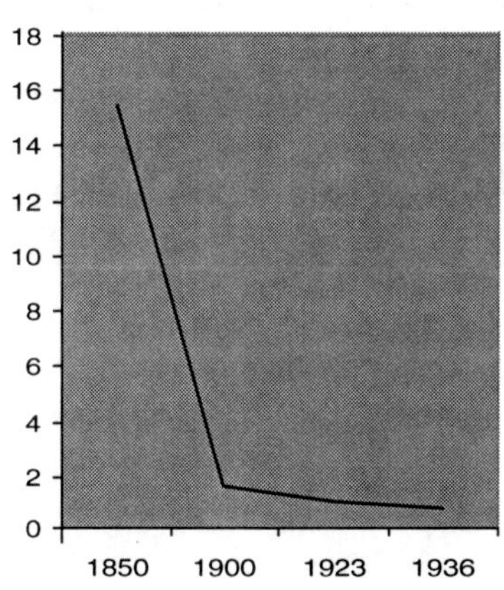

Man-Hours Required by Best-Practice Methods of Producing A Pair of Medium-grade Men's Shoes at Selected Dates in the U.S.

Year	Man-Hours Per Pair
1850	15.5
1900	1.7
1923	1.1
1936	0.9

Source: Reinert 1980

Fig. 3.2 Learning curve of best-practice productivity in medium grade men's shoes', United States 1850–1936

[22] T.H. Breen, *The Marketplace of Revolution: How Consumer Politics Shaped American Independence*, Oxford: Oxford University Press, 2004.

[23] As argued already by Antonio Serra, *Breve trattato delle cause che possono far abbondare li regni d'oro e argento dove non sono miniere...*, Naples: Lazzaro Scorrigio, 1613.

[24] Friedrich List, *Das nationale System der politischen Ökonomie*, Stuttgart/Tübingen: Cotta, 1841.

"confusing the carrier with the cause." Modern trade theory is not all that different, and can only benefit from a greater historical awareness of the complexities of economic development. History tells us that not only are production, entrepreneurship, and technological change important factors of growth, but also that these are not the automatic outcome of market mechanisms.[25] Sporadically, these insights are rediscovered, often in periods in which highly abstract economic theorizing has had tangibly catastrophic results.[26] The dynamic nature of historical capitalism, and what, in essence, Antiphysiocrats fought for, is clarified by studies of experience and productivity.

Learning Curves and Experience Curves

Colbertism was also a system of national learning. One classical article in *Harvard Business Review* is called "Profit from the Learning Curve." The learning curve is a productivity explosion seen from a different angle, measuring the explosive growth in labor productivity as a declining curve in labor units per unit of output (Figs. 3.2 and 3.3 middle).[27] Starting in the 1970s, Boston Consulting Group (BCG) developed the same concept using total costs, not labor hours, on the left axis, and called this an "experience curve."[28] Learning curves and experience curves have very important implications for competitive behavior between firms. Ray Vernon and Louis Wells, two professors at Harvard Business School, developed a life cycle theory of international trade.[29] One implication of this theory is that rich countries export when the learning curve is steep, but become importers when the learning curve flattens out. In other words, within the manufacturing sector poor countries tend to specialize where the learning curve is flat. Since the Terms of Trade (export prices compared to import prices) between rich and poor countries often have stayed the same, this means that the rich countries are able to take out as "triple rent" most of the fruits of technical change. Throughout the early modern period, when our current world system essentially took form, the industrial policy of leading nations was based on the idea that a nation was better off being slightly less efficient in an industry subject to a steep learning curve than specializing in industries with limited or no learning potential.

[25] Sophus A. Reinert, 'International Trade and National Security in Historical Perspective,' *On Track*, 15:2 (2010), pp. 12–15.

[26] Erik S. Reinert, *How Rich Countries got Rich... And Why Poor Countries Stay Poor*, London: Constable, 2007.

[27] W. Hirschmann, 'Profit from the Learning Curve,' *Harvard Business Review* (1964).

[28] Carl W. Stern and Michael S. Deimler (eds.), *The Boston Consulting Group on Strategy: Classic Concepts and New Perspectives*, 2nd ed., Hoboken: Wiley, 2006.

[29] Raymond Vernon, 'International Investment and International Trade in the Product Cycle,' *The Quarterly Journal of Economics* (1966); Louis T. Wells, *The Product Life Cycle and International Trade*, Cambridge, Mass.: Harvard Business School Press, 1972.

Industry Concentration

The number of firms in an industry goes through a cycle as technologies mature (Fig. 3.3, top). Initially the number of firms in the market grows: at one time there were more than 200 car manufacturers in the United States and more than a dozen

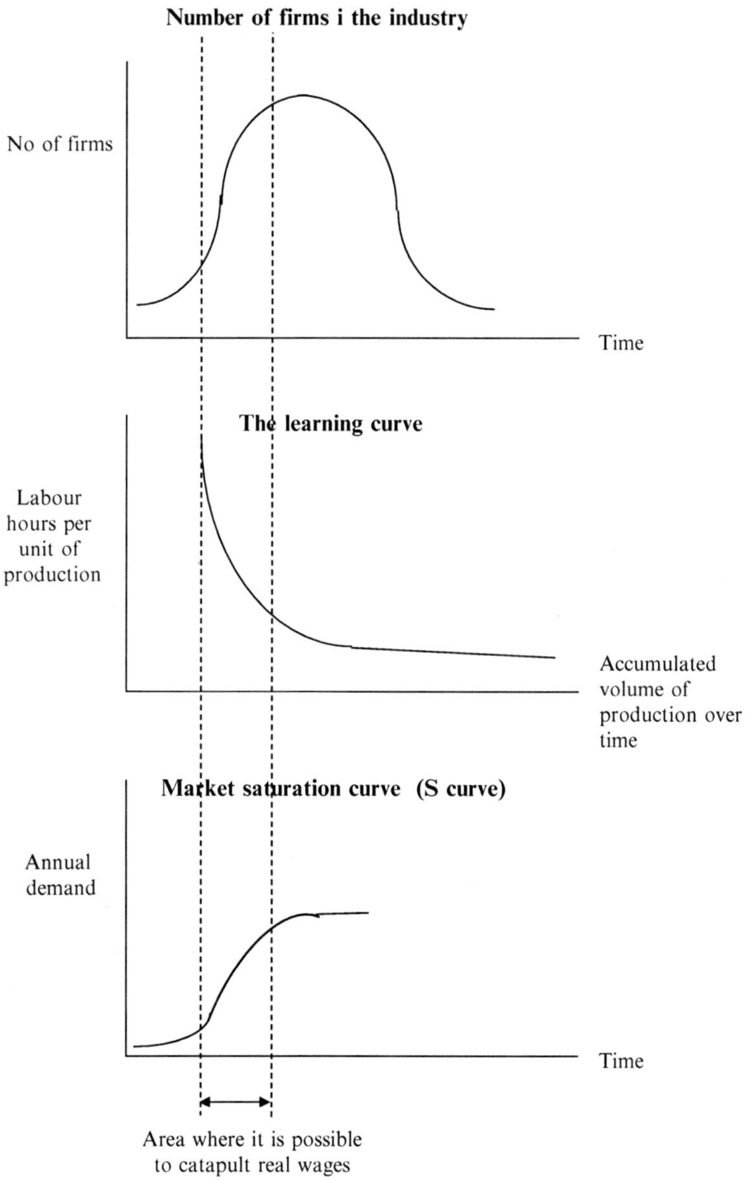

Fig. 3.3 The dynamics of industries

match factories in Norway. Some decades later there were four car manufacturers left in the Unites States and one match factory in Norway (today none).

Market Saturation Curve (S-Curve)

Normally, a steep learning curve is associated with a sharp increase in demand (Fig. 3.3, bottom). When the mobile industry starts growing no one has cellular phones and the market saturation curve takes on the form of an "epidemic curve" like in medicine. Flat to start with and flat towards the end, but with steep growth in the middle. When the curve flattens out the replacement market becomes the dominant segment, and product differentiation increases ("adding bells and whistles"). The close relationship between technical change and increasing demand is called Verdoorn's Law after a Dutch economist.[30]

The Quality Index of Economic Activities

Figure 3.4 attempts to make a fluid classification system for economic activities sorted according to their abilities to create triple rents (high profits, high wages, large tax-base). Black, on the top, marks a situation of temporary monopoly from a new innovation. White, at the bottom, marks a situation of "perfect competition" which is the "ideal" situation in neoclassical economics with "normal" or no profit. The problem is that economic theory only defines well pure black (monopoly) and pure white (perfect competition) while very few activities stay long in any of these positions. Industrial dynamics take place in the various shades of gray areas where theory has little precise to say.

The gravity in the system (from black to white) is produced by imitators of the original idea and general productivity developments, and under some circumstances – as when a patent expires – the fall can be very fast (the price of a medicine may suddenly fall by 90%). Some innovations, like the container, are born towards the white end, but the container was important to other industries because transportation costs were reduced.

Various factors that create gravity and gravity-resistance are listed in Fig. 3.4. The position of a nation's export activities, at what level (at what shade of gray, in Fig. 3.4) will be highly determinant for the real wages of that nation. Baseballs for the US national sport have not experienced innovation in the final assembly operations for a century. This is still 100% manual work. The world's most efficient baseball producers are in Haiti and Honduras, where their wages are between US

[30] Petrus Johannes Verdoorn, 'Fattori che regolano lo sviluppo della produttivitá del lavoro, '*L'industria* (1949), pp. 3–10.

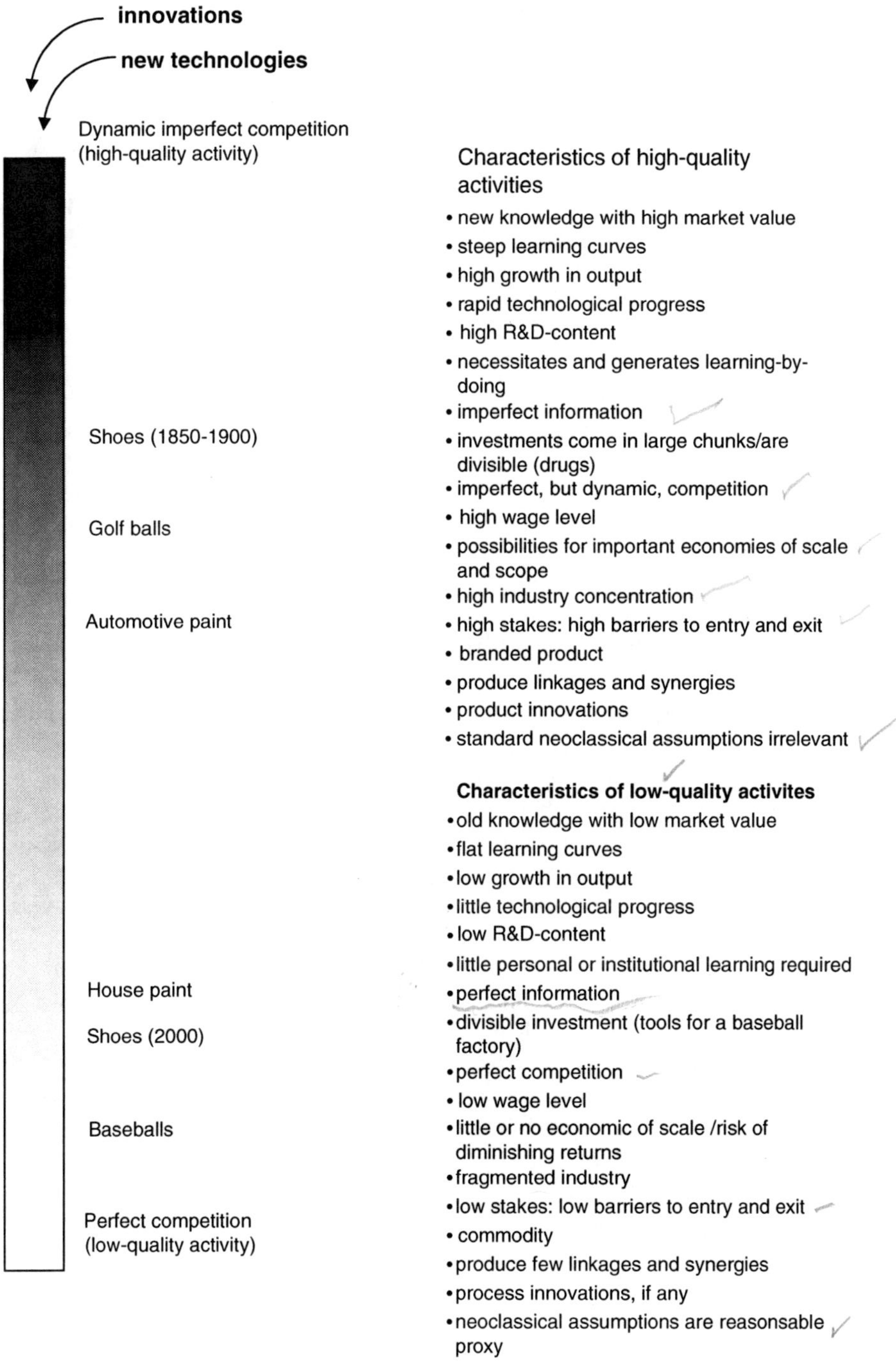

Fig. 3.4 The Quality Index of economic activities

Dollars 0.50 and 1.00 an hour. The wages in the national service sector, the librarians, or the firemen of Haiti, will have wages in line with the producers in the export sector. The world's most efficient producers of golf balls, on the other hand, are in New Bedford, Massachusetts, where the average industrial wage is US Dollars 14 per hour. Baseballs are a high-tech product that needs to be located near the engineers.

When Haiti exports baseballs to the United States and imports golf balls, the country exchanges 28 h of labor (at 50¢ an hour) for 1 h of labor in the United States (at 14$ an hour). These mechanisms are not captured in international trade theory, since this theory operates on the basis of bartering labor hours – all of the same quality – alone. The case of baseballs and golf balls is an extreme one, but the very same forces are at work with France's relationship to the rest of the world under Colbertism. Businesses – and nations – stay wealthy only through continuous innovation; the welfare state must be a Schumpeterian welfare state in order to survive. Remaining at the same level of profits or real wages requires continuous innovations. Or, as one of the characters in Alice in Wonderland says: "This is how fast you have to run here in order to stand still."[31]

The Gestation Period for Innovations

An updated Colbertism, from which Antiphysiocracy generally drew its inspiration, would have to accommodate today's high-tech industries. Technologies differ on a variety of axis, and accordingly what US economist Moses Abramowitz called "the factor bias of economic growth" also varies. The building of railroads was extremely intensive in "capital without skills." The coming science-based techno-economic period is likely to be extremely extensive in "knowledgeable capital."

The factor bias of technologies also shows other peculiarities. The Fordist mass production paradigm made national catching up with the leader nations through reverse engineering (the Japanese pulling a US car apart and creating an improved version) a viable option. The coming science-based paradigm will be dominated by patents and copyrights and will make reverse engineering impossible or illegal. Since few nations have positive balances of payments in patents, royalties, and copyrights, this is likely to worsen world income distribution.

The gestation period from invention to innovation (i.e., when the invention reaches the market) also varies considerably from one techno-economic paradigm to another. The IT-paradigm made relatively short time-lags possible between a conceptual idea and a "killer application." The coming science-based paradigm will require large amounts of skilled and patient capital, as in Fig. 3.5. A typical product takes 15 years from inception to positive cash flow. Here, various forms of capital are

[31] Lewis Carroll, *Alice's Adventures in Wonderland and Through the Looking Glass* (London, 2003), 143.

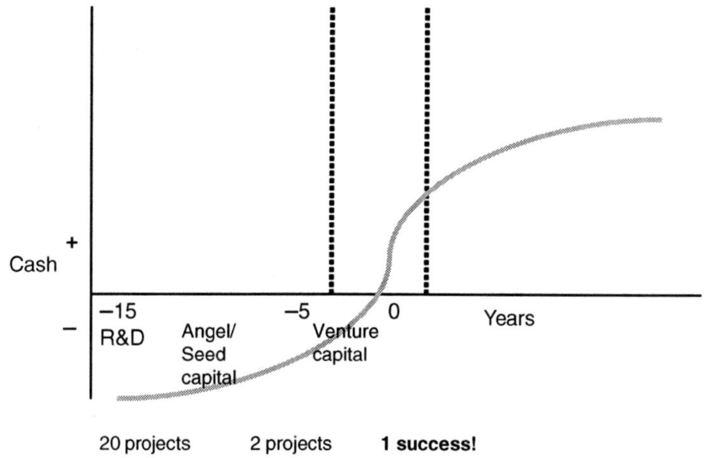

Fig. 3.5 The time-lags of the coming paradigm

needed, R&D capital, angel capital, seed capital, and venture capital. Out of an initial pool of 20 projects, only one is likely to be a success after 15 years. Venture capital typically enters only 5 years before positive cash flow, when there are two projects left of the original 20, when the success rate is 50% vs. the 5% for the investor who starts in year 0 (positive cash flow) minus 15. Observers of US industrial policy noted that a growing public participation in the national innovation system started already several years ago. Sovereign Wealth Funds as well as the huge financial reserves that many nations have accumulated are likely to become heavily involved in this new version of capitalism. The state will no longer be the enemy it used to be seen as during the Cold War years, but more like economic historians describe early capitalism in Venice 500 years ago: Venetian wealth was built on a symbiotic relationship between private entrepreneurship and the activities of the state. And as with Venice, national hegemonies are unfortunately still going to be decided by "economies of scale in the use of force" as Venice's foremost historian, Frederic Lane put it.[32] Economic power and military power will continue to be two sides of the same coin, something which Antiphysiocrats knew all too well.

Conclusion: Strategies in a Turbulent Capitalism

In all its simplicity, Boston Consulting Group's "Product Portfolio Matrix," Fig. 3.6, provides a navigational map, a résumé of the forces at work, which can be used by companies and nations alike. It was a key tool when this author, as part of US consulting group Telesis, advised the Irish Prime Minister's Office on the country's

[32] Frederic C. Lane, *Profits from Power: Readings in Protection Rent and Violence-Controlling Enterprises*, Albany: State University of New York Press, 1979.

Fig. 3.6 BCG product portfolio matrix

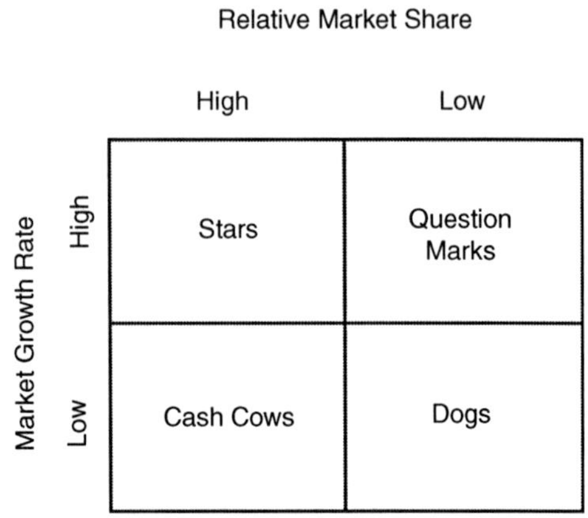

industrial policy in 1980. The core strategic element consists of the flow of funds from the lower left corner, the "cash cows," to the potential new winners, the "question marks" of the upper right hand corner. Early industrialization – both in Europe, the United States and Japan – has relied on agriculture as a kind of "cash cow," a sector from which funds flowed in order to finance industrialization. This was also the case of Colbertism, and Physiocracy may be explained as a reaction to an excessively aggressive strategy of industrialization; the landowner's revenge against Colbertism.[33] As one Italian Antiphysiocrat wrote about the Physiocratic system: "had this been generally adopted it would again have submerged Europe in the barbarism of the feudal centuries," into "feudal anarchy."[34] The Physiocracy vs. Colbertist Antiphysiocracy controversy was – both from an economic and a political standpoint – not unlike the industrialization vs. free trade strategy that was such an important issue during the US Civil War. The South represented free trade Physiocracy and the North represented industry-building Antiphysiocracy. The same axis can be found in many countries. Yet, there can be no doubt: Antiphysiocracy was the movement of technological development and successful capitalism as we know it, the tradition from which our most cherished achievements have emerged. It is high time that the economics profession realizes and accepts its true heritage.

History, of course, cannot provide a blueprint for the future. Ireland managed to ride down the steepest learning curve of recent times, harnessing the productivity explosion of the IT-revolution. The next one will be different. Figure 3.5, the former figure, represents a description of what will be going on *inside* the upper right hand corner in the next techno-economic paradigm. It is important to understand the many forces of capitalism. To a large extent, the wealth and poverty of nations are formed

[33] Elizabeth Fox-Genovese, *The Origins of Physiocracy: Economic Revolution and Social Order in Eighteenth-Century France*, Ithaca: Cornell University Press, 1976.

[34] Paolo Vergani, *Della importanza e dei pregi del nuovo sistema di finanza dello Stato Pontifico*, Rome, 1794, p. 77.

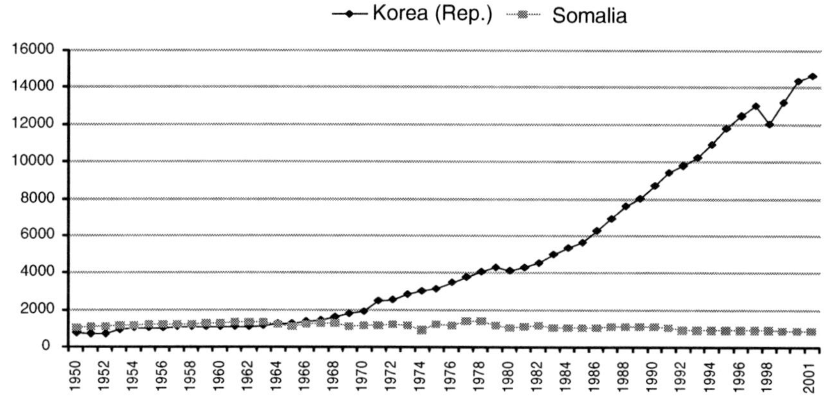

Fig. 3.7 Somalia vs. Korea. Korea (Rep.)-Somalia, GDP per Capita 1950–2001
Source: original data extracted from Angus Maddison, OECD, Paris, 2003

by the "forces at work" – using Menger's term – depicted in the graphs in this chapter. In the tradition of Carl Menger and UK economist Nicholas Kaldor, this note sees "degrees of imperfect competition," caused by technological change and increasing returns, to be a determining element in explaining differences in national wealth. If we wish to explain the difference in GDP per capita between Somalia and Korea – where Somalia was a richer country than Korea until this writer was a teenager (Fig. 3.7) – the main explanatory variables are found in these same forces. Historically, they can also help explain why France, though for centuries following the exact opposite policies to those preached by neoclassical economics, nonetheless industrialized to become one of the world's leading economies. The legacy of Colbertist capitalism in France was centennial, and may yet again provide insights for successful political economy.[35] But we must not forget the words of Colbert's greatest acolyte in the Enlightenment, and, against what many scholars still think, an ardent Antiphysiocrat on all central points, the *Intendant du Commerce* Vincent de Gournay. "It amounts to insulting the great Colbert," he warned,

> to think that, because he set a few limits to our trade, he intended them to last forever; it was enough to have drawn our commerce out of nothing and let it to the point where he left it. He probably reckoned that it would be easy to take it further after him, and to make sure that there would be no province in the Kingdom that would not benefit from it, and that could not one day communicate with all the nations of the world with its shipping and output.[36]

[35] Philippe Minard, *La fortune du colbertisme. Etat et industrie dans la France des Lumières*, Paris: Fayard, 1998.

[36] Jacques-Clause-Marie-Vincent de Gournay, 'Mémoire' [1753], in Henry C. Clark (ed.), *Commerce, Culture, & Liberty: Readings on Capitalism Before Adam Smith*, Indianapolis: Liberty Fund, 2003, 371–391, p. 387.

This chapter has attempted to describe the Schumpeterian-Colbertian mechanisms behind successful capitalism. The economy is dynamic, and so must economics be. But of the many things neoclassical economics abdicated from studying, freeing theory from context was one of the most serious ones. Keynesianism was a context-sensitive theory and – in the very same way – so was Antiphysiocracy. Colbertism, Cameralism, Mercantilism, and the Antiphysiocratic tradition offered the economic theories that built nation-states, a task still unfinished in many Third World nations. For all the globalization of recent decades, our current 1848 moment amply demonstrates that "national" economic structures still very much matter and that we again must learn to appreciate the roles of context, governance, and industrialization in economics.

Chapter 4
Another Grand Tour: Cameralism and Antiphysiocracy in Baden, Tuscany, and Denmark–Norway

Sophus A. Reinert

During the summer of 1784, the Danish statesman Peter Christian Schumacher (1743–1817) decided to go on a Grand Tour. It would not be his first such tour, but whereas he before had ventured out to learn "languages, politics, and statistics," he now wished to study the nature and causes of the wealth of nations.[1] In terms of current scholarship on the Grand Tour, Schumacher's general sentiment is less surprising than his proposed itinerary. For rather than heading for Paris, Bordeaux, London, or Birmingham, along the principal arteries of the European economy, he resolutely went south, across Germany, Switzerland, and northern Italy, making purposeful stops in the reformist states of Baden, Venice, and Tuscany. The current Anglophone narrative of the Grand Tour privileges British and French travelers questing for Arcadia in Italy and continental observers spying on British technological achievements. The ways in which travel contributed to the emulation of economic and administrative practices between the minor states of Northern, Central, and Southern Europe are therefore seldom explored. Yet Schumacher sought practical guidance for reforms in Italy, not picturesque rusticity. For in the shadow of the ruthless imperial rivalries between the age's great powers, another Grand Tour existed, one on which emissaries from smaller states visited each other for insights into the best strategies for securing their precarious political existences in the face of overpowering international competition. This world, which the administrative and intellectual tradition of Cameralism helps define, in turn helps puts the fate of the specific doctrine of economic reform known as Physiocracy in a new

This chapter develops material from chapter 5 of Sophus A. Reinert, *Translating Empire: Emulation and the Origins of Political Economy*, Cambridge, Mass.: Harvard University Press, 2011.

[1] Peter Christian Schumacher to Ove Høegh-Guldberg, 12 August 1784, in *Ove Høegh Guldbergs og Arveprins Frederiks brevveksling med Peter Christian Schumacher 1778–1807*, ed. J.O. Bro-Jørgensen, Copenhagen: Nyt Nordisk Forlag Arnold Busck, 1972 (hereafter GFS), pp. 288, 291.

S.A. Reinert (✉)
Gonville and Caius College, University of Cambridge, Cambridge, CB2 1TA, UK
e-mail: sar62@hermes.cam.ac.uk

J.G. Backhaus (ed.), *Physiocracy, Antiphysiocracy and Pfeiffer*, The European Heritage in Economics and the Social Sciences 10, DOI 10.1007/978-1-4419-7497-6_4,

perspective. Whereas the rapid fall from grace of Physiocracy in France, as its radical policy implementation precipitated a human disaster during Turgot's ministry in the 1770s, is well known, the fate of Physiocratic reforms in the two other areas in which it is thought to have been influential, the Margravate of Baden and the Grand Duchy of Tuscany, is less so.[2] Yet there too Physiocracy was a short-lived experiment.[3] Schumacher's travels uniquely allow us to qualify the reception in the semi-peripheries of the Enlightenment of what, historiographically speaking, was the greatest doctrine of political economy at the time, but also to reconceptualize the reform culture of small Cameralist states in a world increasingly dominated by violent competition between global empires.

Reconnaissance and Recreation

In his essay "Of Travel," Francis Bacon laid down the principles by which early modern voyagers should approach their endeavor. It was important, he wrote, to observe and take note of "whatsoever is memorable" abroad. Yet, the point was not for a gentleman to adopt foreign customs indiscriminately, "but only prick in some Flowers of that he hath learned abroad, into the Customs of his own Country."[4] As it developed in the seventeenth and eighteenth centuries, the European institution of the Grand Tour would adhere closely to Bacon's principles. But, since memory could be put to many uses, so did the intensifying practice of espionage, a capacious term for conveying the widespread and more or less covert emulation of agricultural,

---

[2] Joseph A. Schumpeter, *A History of Economic Analysis*, Oxford: Oxford University Press, 1954, p. 223.

[3] On the fate of Physiocracy in Germany, see Richard T. Gray, *Money Matters: Economics and the German Cultural Imagination, 1770–1850*, Seattle: University of Washington Press, 2008, pp. 109–169; Keith Tribe, *Governing Economy: The Reformation of German Economic Discourse 1750–1840*, Cambridge: Cambridge University Press, 1988, pp. 119–31; id., "The Reception of Physiocratic Argument in the German States," in B. Delmas, T. Demals, and Philippe Steiner (eds.), *La diffusion internationale de la physiocratie*, Grenoble: Presses Universitaires de Grenoble, 1995, pp. 331–44. On Physiocracy in Tuscany see, among many others, Mario Mirri, "Per una ricerca sui rapporti fra 'economisti' e riformatori toscani: L'abate Niccoli a Parigi," *Annali del Istituto Giangiacomo Feltrinelli*, 2, 1959, pp. 55–115; id. "La fisiocrazia toscana: un tema da riprendere," in *Studi di storia medievale e moderna per Ernesto Sestan*, 2 vols., Florence: Leo S. Olschki, 1980, vol. II, pp. 703–60; Antonella Alimento, "La réception des idées physiocratiques à travers les traductions: le cas toscan et vénetien," in Delmas, Demals, and Steiner (eds.), *La diffusion internationale de la physiocratie*, pp. 297–313. On Tuscan economic policy in the eighteenth century generally, see Hermann Bühi, *Finanzen und Finanzpolitik Toskanas im Zeitalter der Aufklärung (1737–1790) im Rahmen der Wirtschaftspolitik*, Berlin: Emil Ebering, 1915; Luigi dal Pane, *La finanza toscana dagli inizi del secolo XVIII alla caduta del granducato*, Milan: Banca commerciale italiana, 1965.

[4] Francis Bacon, *The Essays, or Councils, Civil and Moral*, London: H. Herringman et al., 1696, pp. 47–8. On this tradition of writing on travel, see Justin Stagl, *A History of Curiosity: The Theory of Travel 1550–1800*, London: Routledge, 2004.

industrial, and political technologies in early modern Europe.[5] As such, there existed a clear tension between the enlightened ideals of international travel – education, toleration, and cultural commerce – and it is often more insidious aims of espionage and emulation. A key for understanding this lies in the continuation and exasperation of economic inequalities between competing nations in an age which can be fruitfully considered one of "globalization," an age in which the exigencies of international trade to an ever greater extent came to influence domestic life and politics.[6] In a seminal essay, Melissa Calaresu has in effect demonstrated the paradoxical extent to which the institution of the Grand Tour eventually came to undermine the very principles from which it had first emerged, as undeniable economic and political disparities between kingdoms like Britain and Naples gave rise to cycles of prejudice (in the North) and consternation (in the South).[7]

These economic differences have affected later historians just as they affected the inhabitants of eighteenth-century Europe, almost parodical stereotypes having become entrenched in the idealized geography of the Grand Tour in relation to what, in Bacon's terminology, was considered "memorable." On the one hand there was Britain, to which travelers usually were drawn by the marvels of modernity, by Lunar Clubs and industrial furnaces, by shipyards and experimental technologies. On the other hand there was Italy, offering art, culture, climate, and the abiding lure of antiquity. It was, supposedly, a "museum" and "a theme-park of the past," an adult wonderland of the senses, catering to the most refined connoisseurship of art and the most demanding venereal exigencies alike; just as one did not go to Birmingham for pies and joviality, so one no longer visited Italy for insights into political and economic problems.[8] There is, of course, a grain of truth in this. There can be no doubt that the Marquise de Sade encountered a more heteroclite carnal commerce in Naples than in Rotterdam, and nobody would be surprised that it was

---

[5] See, for particularly enlightening examples, John Raymond Harris, *Industrial Espionage and Technology Transfer: Britain and France in the Eighteenth Century*, Aldershot: Ashgate, 1998 and Paolo Preto, *I servizi segreti di Venezia: Spionaggio e controspionaggio ai tempi della Serenissima*, Milan: Il saggiatore, 2004. For earlier cases of such "economic espionage" see Alan Marshall, *Intelligence and Espionage in the Reign of Charles II, 1660–1685*, Cambridge: Cambridge University Press, 2003, pp. 136–7.

[6] For useful caveats see Paul Cheney, *Revolutionary Commerce: Globalization and the French Monarchy*, Cambridge, Mass.: Harvard University Press, 2010, p. 3.

[7] Melissa Calaresu, "Looking for Virgil's Tomb: The End of the Grand Tour and the Cosmopolitan Ideal in Europe," in Jaś Elsner and Joan-Pau Rubiés (eds.), *Voyages and Visions: Towards a Cultural History of Travel*, London: Reaktion Books, 1999, pp. 138–161.

[8] George B. Parks, "The Decline and Fall of the English Renaissance Admiration of Italy," *The Huntington Library Quarterly*, vol. 31, no. 4, 1968, pp. 341–357, especially p. 356; Franco Venturi, "L'Italia fuori d'Italia," in *Storia d'Italia*, vol. III: *Dal primo Settecento all'Unità*, eds. Ruggiero Romano and Corrado Vivanti, Turin: Einaudi, 1973, 987–1481, pp. 1070–1071; Jeremy Black, *Italy and the Grand Tour*, New Haven: Yale University Press, 2003, pp. 3, 7, 14. On Birmingham and industrial espionage there, see Peter M. Jones, *Industrial Enlightenment: Science, Technology and Culture in Birmingham and the West Midlands, 1760–1820*, Manchester: Manchester University Press, 2008.

not in Greece but in England that the industrial spy Duke François La Rochefoucauld lamented "the jealousy of the majority of manufacturers, who refuse all entry to strangers."[9] Yet, it must be remembered that Adam Smith eulogized the potato-eating Irish prostitutes of London as the "most beautiful women perhaps in the British dominions," and that, when the "Friends of the Fatherland" set up a school of political economy in Zaragoza in 1784, they settled on a Neapolitan textbook for their course.[10] England and Italy developed along very different trajectories in the early modern period, but this must not blind us to the very real historical conditions in which London could be known for whores as well as finance, Naples for both harlequins and economic analysis.

Although recent historiography has been supremely aware of social and economic differences in Europe and their cultural consequences (to which an enormous literature on British encounters with Southern sensuality, street-life, and bucolic bliss testifies), there is often a tendency to partition and analyze only a very limited set of economic factors traditionally held to be relevant for cultural history. Yet, an interpretative category like "the material culture of Italy" can quickly become counterproductive if it is understood to merely encompass antiques, souvenirs, and trinkets bought on the Grand Tour. There was certainly a "marketplace of the Grand Tourist," and the Tour probably "generated" a "geography of desire," but said markets and desires catered to a far broader array of passions and interests than those often considered. The "material culture" of Enlightenment Italy also included some of Europe's busiest ports and its premier producers of silk, oil, and wine, as well as one of the richest traditions of reformism in all of Europe, all deeply inflected by the memory – institutionalized through architecture, art, and historical traditions – of Italy's lost economic *grandezza*.[11]

The enormous weight of the past affected practical matters in Europe just as much as it did literary tropes and nostalgic sentiments, and at the time few political economists, not to mention casual observers, dared ignore the historical dynamics of international competition and the fleeting nature of national greatness, even when secured through modern commerce rather than ancient conquests.[12] As such, it is

---

[9] Donatien-Alphonse-François de Sade, *Opere complete*: *Viaggio in Italia*; *Viaggio in Olanda*, ed. Bruno Cagli, Translated by Pietro Bartalini Bigi, Rome: Newton, 1993, pp. 273–4; Norman Scarfe, *Innocent Espionage*: *The La Rochefoucauld Brothers' Tour of England in 1785*, Woodbridge: Boydell, 1995, p. 40. See, on jealousy at the time, Istvan Hont, *Jealousy of Trade*: *International Competition and the Nation-State in Historical Perspective*, Cambridge, Mass.: Harvard University Press, 2005.

[10] Adam Smith, *An Inquiry into the Nature and Causes of the Wealth of Nations*, ed. Edwin Cannan, 2 vols., Chicago: University of Chicago Press, 1976, vol. I, p. 179; Pietro Paolo Celesia *ai Serenissimi*, 5 October 1784, Archivio di Stato di Genova, Genova, Italy, *Archivio Segreto* 2482.

[11] Barbara Ann Naddeo, "Cultural Capitals and Cosmopolitanism in Eighteenth-Century Italy: The Historiography and Italy on the Grand Tour," *Journal of Modern Italian Studies*, vol. 10, no. 2, 2005, 183–199, p. 189.

[12] Sophus A. Reinert, "Lessons on the Rise and Fall of Great Powers: Conquest, Commerce, and Decline in Enlightenment Italy," *The American Historical Review*, vol. 115, no. 5, 2010, pp. 1395–1425.

not surprising that Italy, which uniquely in Europe had declined twice from the very pinnacle of material greatness, continued to offer pertinent lessons of political economy. This was not, however, simply a matter of Italy representing an imperial *memento mori*, a geographical reminder that all terrestrial greatness passes, though this sentiment too affected Enlightenment travelers.[13] The temporal vicissitudes of Italy were also a source of far more practical knowledge about the consequences of policies and the developments of manufacturing and administrative techniques in small states, an aspect of the Enlightenment Grand Tour which has gone almost entirely unnoticed, not only because of our incessant focus on élite Brits abroad – rather than on visitors from areas politically and economically closer to Italy – but also because of the cultural legacy of the Tour itself. As material differences continued to widen during the first century of the Industrial Revolution, the later evolution of the Grand Tour came to emphasize some aspects of the eighteenth-century experience at the expense of others. After Goethe, the Romantics, and the Burkean ideal of the sublime captured the hearts and minds of Europe, Italy's decline was reevaluated and what once inspired strategies for reform came to convey only esthetic sentiments. The eighteenth century was a transitional period that looked backwards to William Thomas's 1549 *History of Italy*, written at a time when Italy taught the world everything, and also forwards to Henry James' 1909 *Italian Hours*, when Italy taught only melancholy.[14] Nonetheless, the tendency of historiography is to approach the Enlightenment Grand Tour more in the spirit of the latter than the former, rather influenced by Aby Warburg's "psycho-historical" escapism from the modern condition than by his contemporaries, like Gustav von Schmoller, Werner Sombart, and Alfred Doren, who turned to the Italian archives as a means of grasping the mysteries of long-term economic competition and development.[15]

[13] See again Reinert, "Rise and Fall" and, similarly, Louisa Shea, "Rousseau's Ruins," in Christie McDonald and Stanley Hoffmann, *Rousseau and Freedom*, Cambridge: Cambridge University Press, 2010, pp. 193–206.

[14] William Thomas, *The History of Italy (1549)*, ed. George B. Sparks, Ithaca: Cornell University Press, 1963; Henry James, *Italian Hours*, ed. John Auchard, London: Penguin, 1995.

[15] Compare, for example, Aby Warburg, *Die Erneuerung der heidnischen Antike: Kulturwissenschaftliche Beitrage zur Geschichte der europäischen Renaissance*, eds. Horst Bredekamp and Michael Diers, Berlin: Akademie Verlag, 1998 to Alfred Doren, *Studien aus der Florentiner Wirtschaftsgeschichte*, 2 vols., Stuttgart: Cotta, 1901–8 and Werner Sombart, *Der moderne Kapitalismus: Historisch-systematische Darstellung des gesamteuropäischen Wirtschaftslebens von seinen Anfängen bis zur Gegenwart*, 3rd ed., 3 vols. in 6 parts, Munich and Leipzig, 1928; See, on the interests of German Renaissance historians at the time, Perdita Ladwig, *Das Renaissancebild deutscher Historiker, 1898–1933*, Frankfurt am Main: Campus Verlag, 2004. On Warburg see José Emilio Burucúa, *Historia, Arte, Cultura: De Aby Warburg a Carlo Ginzburg*, Buenos Aires: Fondo de Cultura Económica, 2002; on his dislike of Schmoller and Doren, see Bernd Roeck, *Florence 1900: The Quest for Arcadia*, New Haven: Yale University Press, 2009, pp. 71–2. On the German Historical School generally see Erik Grimmer-Solem, *The Rise of Historical Economics and Social Reform in Germany, 1864–1894*, Oxford: Oxford University Press, 2003 and Yuichi Shionoya, *The Soul of the German Historical School*, Berlin: Springer, 2005.

Again, the point is not to substitute one monochrome vision of the Enlightenment Grand Tour with another, only to return some lost color to our historiographical palette. During his travels to Florence in 1817, Stendhal was famously enthralled in "ecstasy" by the city's "sublime beauty" and its "many streets full of grandeur and melancholy," a condition now recognized as the "Stendhal Syndrome."[16] His experience doubtlessly encapsulated a principal quality of the Grand Tour for many. Yet, dysphoric rapture was not the only lure of Italy, and it might be worthwhile to explore a different quality as well, one more attuned to what Italian reformism offered eighteenth-century travelers; another Grand Tour, the olfactory goal of which was not orange blossom, Chianti, and fried *trippa*, but rather fresh hemp, leathery libraries, and the hematic scent of iron nails. For this too was a widespread sentiment at the time. Entering Florence only 3 decades before Stendhal, for example, the well-traveled Prussian officer, historian, and publicist Johann Wilhelm von Archenholz, who defined himself as a "restless man of the world," felt less "sanguine" about the tropes of the time. He had heard many praise the city as heaven on earth, but "such a gasconade," he thought, could only have been justified "in the sixteenth century, when Italy saw the arts in the cradle in all neighboring countries, and the finest towns in Europe were filled with wooden houses." The streets of Florence could no longer compete with those of London, there were "no splendid palaces," and its statues were "injudiciously placed." All in all, Florence exemplified the condition of Italy itself, which not only had "declined," but "in the eighteenth century plunged… into the barbarism of the middle ages." Italy's greatness during the Renaissance had rested on an economic superiority that had proven impossible to maintain in the face of aggressive competition from larger, unified territorial states north of the Alps. "The times," he noted, "are materially changed."[17]

And Archenholz was an astute observer indeed. Whereas Genoa once was "the Peru of Italy," it had abandoned trade in favor of "money concerns." The problem, of course, was that "money" was "no wealth with respect to state-economy, but only a token of wealth," a token which quickly left Italy as soon as the underlying activities producing real wealth moved abroad. From Genoa to Venice, the story was the same. Decline had set in to the point where the greatest resource at times was tourism.[18]

[16] Stendhal, *Rome, Naples et Florence*, 2 vols., 3rd. ed., Paris: Delaunay, 1826, vol. II, pp. 102, 107. For a famous example of the syndrome's impact on modern popular culture, see Dario Argento's *La sindrome di Stendhal*, Cine 2000 and Medusa Produzione, 1996. See, on the Florence we have gained, Roeck, *Florence 1900*. On the evolution of the Grand Tour to Italy more generally, see Edward Chaney, *The Evolution of the Grand Tour*, London: Routledge, 2000.

[17] Johann Wilhelm von Archenholz, *England und Italien*, 5 vols., Carlsruhe: Christian Gottlieb Schmieder, 1787, parts of which were translated as Johann Wilhelm von Archenholtz [sic], *A Picture of Italy*, trans. Joseph Trapp, 2 vols., London: G.G.J. and J. Robinson, 1791, quotations from vol. I, pp. 135–8, 21, 27, 59–60, 136–8, 192. On Archenholz and his self-image, see Boris Bovekamp, *Die Zeitschrift "Minerva" und ihre Herausgeber Johann Wilhelm von Archenholz (1743–1812) und Friedrich Alexander Bran (1767–1831): Ein Beitrag zur Kompatibilität, Aufklärung und Liberalismus*, Kiel: Ludwig, 2009, p. 32. See also Ute Rieger, *Johann Wilhelm von Archenholz als "Zeitbürger": eine historisch-analytische Untersuchung zur Aufklärung in Deutschland*, Berlin: Duncker & Humblot, 1994. On his tour of Italy, see Venturi, "L'Italia fuori d'Italia," pp. 1107–8.

[18] Archenholtz, *A Picture of Italy*, vol. I, pp. 21, 135–8.

In short, the smaller states of Italy, Germany, and Scandinavia came to share common problematics in international competition, allowing for the possibility of mutual observation, learning, and emulation. Archenholz's praise of Tuscan economic reforms is therefore all the more interesting. The "Florentine nobles" had become impoverished as the commercial culture of the Renaissance, "which alone had brought the state to such a pitch of greatness," had been overturned by the courtly ethos of the Medici Grand Duchy.[19] It was in order to "remedy this evil" that the present Grand Duke Leopold set about changing the economic imagination of his compatriots, encouraging nobles to "show their splendor in encouraging arts, manufactures, agriculture, and in performing good actions." Change was in the air, and "under the present government" Tuscany was "the happiest country in Italy," with "wise laws, a flourishing commerce, and an increasing cultivation under a fair climate." They had "more improved in agriculture" than anywhere else in Italy, and it was Leghorn, not London, which "convinces us what wonders may be performed, in a short time, through wise politic measures."[20] In effect, what Archenholz liked the most about the port-city of Leghorn was precisely what later Grand Tourists like Henry James would enjoy the least: "Leghorn is a new city, neither antiquities, nor modern works of architecture, such as magnificent churches and palaces, nor galleries, nor collections of statues, must be looked for here: they are reserves for future times. Instead of them the traveler will find great industry, manufactures, and shipping."[21] It was a sentiment reminiscent of John Adams' contemporary letter to his wife Abigail, in which he set down the principles by which civilizations developed:

> I must study politics and war that my sons may have liberty to study mathematics and philosophy. My sons ought to study mathematics and philosophy, geography, natural history, naval architecture, navigation, commerce, and agriculture in order to give their children a right to study paintings, poetry, music, architecture, statuary, tapestry, and porcelain.[22]

What Archenholz in effect was saying about Italy, within parameters of Enlightenment historiography and political economy he shared with the likes of John Adams, was that the peninsula was not merely a "museum" or a "theme park" after all, but a living society actively mediating the vicissitudes of time, that there was art

[19] Archenholtz, *A Picture of Italy*, vol. I, p. 138. See, on the emergence of this ethos, Marcello Fantoni, *La corte del Granduca: Forma e simboli del potere mediceo fra Cinque e Seicento*, Rome: Bulzoni, 1994.

[20] Archenholtz, *A Picture of Italy*, vol. I, pp. 133–4, 139, 171. On Arhenholz' comparisons of England and Italy, usually in England's favour, see Rieger, *Johann Wilhelm von Archenholz*, pp. 39–42. So well known was Archenholz for his negative treatment of Italy that Goethe made fun of him while travelling there, see Johann Wolfgang von Goethe, *Italian Journey*, London: Penguin, 1970, p. 116.

[21] Archenholtz, *A Picture of Italy*, vol. I, p. 173. Emphasis added. Cf. Henry James, *Italian Hours*, ed. John Auchard, London: Penguin, 1995, pp. 272–3.

[22] John Adams to Abigail Adams, no date but 1780, in *The Letters of John and Abigail Adams*, ed. Frank Shuffelton, London: Penguin, 2004, p. 378. For context see David McCullough, *John Adams*, New York: Simon & Schuster, 2001, pp. 236–7.

for those who cared for it, survivals from its former state of economic greatness, but also fresh forms of reformism offering pertinent lessons in statecraft. Italy represented several historical stages simultaneously, each of which conveyed unique insights to a wide array of visitors. Late eighteenth-century British travelers, hailing from the economic hegemon of the age, might feel only "sympathy" for their poor neighbors on the continent, but other Grand Tourists chose to observe and engage with a much richer material culture of armaments, agriculture, and industry as well as trinkets and souvenirs in the small states of Europe.[23] Around the year 1900, Florence would be known as "the world's capital of Bric-a-bracdom," with a market for art "as inexhaustible as the coal mines of England."[24] This observation, and the rich world of prejudice and material differences it betrays, need not overshadow the fact that the line was less clearly drawn in the eighteenth century between culture and the economy, between Italy and England, nor that travelers continued to visit Italy for reconnaissance as well as for recreation. A key for appreciating this other Grand Tour lies in the widespread tradition of European political economy known as Cameralism, a technology of material administration quite different from the contemporary imperialist strategies of England and France.

Cameralism and Great Power Imperialism

Though generally considered a unique Germanic tradition, the academic and administrative discipline of "Cameralism" was influential across Spain, Northern Italy, and Scandinavia.[25] Etymologically, it derived from the German *Kammer* (a word itself derived from the Latin *camera*), which was first used to denote the prince's private apartment, and then by extension the locus of his administration. The same root survives today in *Kammermusik* as a form of musical expression, lionized by the likes of Haydn and Mozart, proper for performance within a princely chamber and thus distinct in form and origins from sacral and later orchestral compositions.[26] Sweden was not Saxe-Gotha any more than Denmark–Norway really was as a political community free from conflicting patriotisms, but they all shared, through tradition, emulation, translation, and itinerant university professors, a common discourse of Cameralism, known as such, which, though conversant with other

[23] On British "sympathy" see Jeremy Black, *The British Abroad: The Grand Tour in the Eighteenth Century*, Stroud: The History Press, 2003, pp. 230–60.

[24] In Van Wyck Brooks, *The Dream of Arcadia: American Writers and Artists in Italy, 1760–1915*, New York: E.P. Dutton & Co., 1958, p. 79.

[25] Ernest Lluch, "Cameralism beyond the Germanic World: a Note on Tribe," *History of Economic Ideas*, 5: 2, 1997, pp. 85–99.

[26] Tribe, *Governing Economy*, p. 6.

traditions of economic thought, represented a more or less coherent cluster of theories, practices, and preoccupations. Far more than a mere economic theory, Cameralism was a technology for governing men and nature alike, as much a science of forestry and metallurgy as of statecraft. In terms of faith in the information-processing faculties of the administrative apparatus and the trenchant idioms of reason of state, Cameralism had much in common with the sensitivities of Colbert's legacy of governmental practices in Europe more generally, but it drew uniquely on its spatial relation to Europe's economic geography.[27]

The 1648 Peace of Westphalia, which brought the horrors of the Thirty Years' War to an end, had recognized more than 300 German principalities occupying the territories between Poland and France, between the Baltic and the Alps. Historians of urbanization agree that a hierarchical network of urban centers developed in Germany in the absence of a unified state or metropolis as several cities competed to assume the functions and responsibilities of the emerging economic order. Numerous smaller urban districts thus emerged in the German territories where one single larger city tended to develop in the larger unified territories like France and England, also partly a consequence of the very tangible rivalry between German absolutist princes. Compared to London's 675,000 and Paris' 570,000 inhabitants in 1750, Berlin, the largest Germanic city, was on a different demographic scale entirely with only 113,000.[28] That said, the numerous princes of Germany were decidedly less "absolute" than often acknowledged, for myriad obligations to God, to the Holy Roman Empire, to their neighbors, and, sporadically, to their people, "clipped," as Isabel Hull has eloquently put it, "the wings of their heraldic eagles."[29] This mosaic of pseudo-absolutist princedoms competing among themselves and with the more unified powers of Western Europe gave birth to a neo-Aristotelian tradition of administrative theory and practice that conceived of the prince as a patriarch or *Hausvater*, responsible for the material and spiritual wellbeing of his children-subjects.[30] Thus born from the small states' need to safeguard and muster their limited resources in light of rivalry with Britain, France, and Holland,

[27] On Colbertism see Philippe Minard, *La fortune du colbertisme: État et industrie dans la France des Lumières*, Paris: Fayard, 1998.

[28] Jan de Vries, *European Urbanization 1500–1800*, Cambridge, Mass.: Harvard University Press, 1984, pp. 116, 153; Paul Bairoch, Jean Batou, and Pierre Chévre, *La population des villes européennes de 800 à 1850 – The Population of European Cities from 800 to 1850*, Geneva: Droz, 1988, pp. 4, 28, 33.

[29] Isabel V. Hull, *Sexuality, State, and Civil Society in Germany, 1700–1815*, Ithaca: Cornell University Press, 1996, p. 155.

[30] On this tradition see Jürgen Backhaus, "The German Economic Tradition: From Cameralism to the Verein Für Socialpolitik," in Maria Albertone and Alberto Masoero (eds.), *Political Economy and National Realities*, Turin: Fondazione Einaudi, pp. 329–357 and Volker Bauer, *Hofökonomie: Der Diskurs über den Fürstenhof in Zeremonialwissenschaft, Hausväterliteratur und Kameralismus*, Vienna: Böhlau Verlag, 1997.

Cameralism developed in synergy with the emerging science of natural history, latent resources of the land requiring discovery, observation, and understanding in order to be harnessed fully, economically as well as scientifically.[31]

Already in the eighteenth century, it was generally accepted that the statesman Veit Ludwig von Seckendorff had codified the "science" of Cameralism in the 1665 *Additions* to his 1656 *Princely State* after observing the flourishing Dutch economy first hand during his travels with Duke Ernest the Pious of Gotha. The principles of political economy he laid down were still believed to be relevant for developing small states threatened by more powerful international rivals, including the importance of surveying, cataloging, and harnessing the resources of the land, of encouraging emulation, industry, and the proliferation of useful knowledge.[32] His emphasis on these elements found its most central policy implication in import substitution, in the political support for planting manufactures to supply domestic needs as a means of escaping poverty and dependence on foreigners. The problem in the early modern period, for the unfortunate imperialist powers of Scandinavia as for the largely landlocked German states, was thus one of competitive development in the face of far superior English, French, and for a while Dutch imperial technologies. Not only could the great powers routinely conquer the overseas colonies of the Cameralist states and interrupt their trades on the seas, but they could also actively intrude in their internal affairs and attempts at development.[33] This insight echoed throughout the Cameralist tradition and was developed further by men like Carl von Linné, better known as Linnaeus, who brought the discourse of "planting" to a whole new level of both theory and practice.[34]

[31] On these aspects of Cameralism see Marc Raeff, *The Well-Ordered Police State: Social and Institutional Change through Law in the Germanies and Russia, 1600–1800*, New Haven: Yale University Press, 1983, p. 100; Alix Cooper, "'The possibilities of the land': The Inventory of 'Natural Riches' in the Early Modern German Territories," *History of Political Economy*, vol. 35, Annual Supplement, 2003, pp. 129–153; id., *Inventing the Indigenous: Local Knowledge and Natural History in Early Modern Europe*, Cambridge: Cambridge University Press, 2007, pp. 96–8; Jürgen Backhaus and Richard E. Wagner, "From Continental Public Finance to Public Choice: Mapping Continuity," in Steven G. Medema and Peter Boettke (eds.), *The Role of Government in the History of Economic Thought*, Durham: Duke University Press, 2005, 314–332, pp. 317–318.

[32] Veit Ludwig von Seckendorff, *Additiones oder Zugaben und Erleuterungen zu dem Tractat des Teutscher Fürsten-Staats*, Frankfurt: Thomas Matthias Göken, 1665. For his current relevance in the eighteenth century see Johann Friedrich von Pfeiffer, *Berichtigungen berühmte Staats-, Finanz-, Policei-, Cameral-, Commerz- und ökonomischer Schriften dieses Jahrhunderts*, 6 vols., Frankfurt am Main: Esslingersche Buchhandlungen, 1781–1784, vol. I, p. 387. On Seckendorff see Sophus A. Reinert, "Cameralism and Commercial Rivalry: Nationbuilding through Economic Autarky in Seckendorff's 1665 *Additiones*," *European Journal of Law and Economics*, vol. 19, no. 3, 2005, pp. 271–286.

[33] Richard L. Gawthrop, "The Social Role of Seventeenth-Century German Territorial States," in A. C. Fix and S. C. Karant-Nunn (eds.), *Germania Illustrata: Essays on Early Modern Germany Presented to Gerald Strauss, Sixteenth Century Essays and Studies*, vol. 18, 1992, pp. 243–258; Reinert, "Cameralism and Commercial Rivalry."

[34] Carl von Linné, "Principes de l'Oeconomie, fongés sur la Science naturelle & sur la Physique," *Journal Oeconomique*, May 1752, pp. 40–65; on this article see Philippe Steiner, *La "science nouvelle" de l'économie politique*, Paris: Presses Universitaires de France, 1998, pp. 13–17.

Not only were foreign industries to be domesticated, but the fruits of foreign soils too would be forcibly transplanted and "acclimatized" to the small Cameralist states of Germany and Scandinavia. In its most extreme manifestation, this penchant for autarky, for political and economic independence, led to extraordinary efforts to reproduce the perceived benefits of tropical imperialism enjoyed by the great maritime powers in the temperate and arctic territories available to the Cameralist project. It is easy, in hindsight, to ridicule such attempts to domesticate exotic growths in hostile climates, and the idea of enormous plantations of tea spanning the arctic tundra is wondrous at best.[35] Yet, the introduction of New World crops like tobacco, potatoes, and the tomato had indeed revolutionized the foundations of Old World agriculture and consumption habits, and the immense wealth produced by the cultivation of sugar, coffee, tea, and even cotton at the time were understood to result from conscious acts of strategic planting in key colonies, whether coffee in St. Helena, sugar and coffee in Brazil and Martinique, or cotton in the American South.[36] Simultaneously, Central and Northern Europeans too had bought into the contemporary craze for colonial goods, habits which were poignantly debilitating in light of the contemporary theory of the balance of trade. As a result, the impossibility of competing for colonial markets and resources directly funneled many of the energies driving Englishmen and Frenchmen across the hemispheres in a more local direction, ideals of self-sufficiency informing the administrative choices of small states from Italy to Scandinavia.

Admittedly, the northern Cameralist states fared better in the colonial race than their largely landlocked southern brethren. One of the great powers of the seventeenth century, Sweden controlled a veritable Baltic Empire, covering parts of present-day Finland, Russia, Estonia, Latvia, Poland, and Germany. Building on this, a succession of Swedish monarchs established a presence in Africa, the so called Swedish Gold Coast, already in the seventeenth century, but it was soon lost to the Dutch and later to the English. Its imperial misadventures in the Western Hemisphere were only moderately more successful. New Sweden enjoyed a short-lived existence along the Delaware River from 1638 to 1655, by which time it was captured by the Dutch and, 9 years later, by the English. In the eighteenth century, Sweden similarly annexed the Caribbean islands of Saint-Barthélemy – the name of its current capital Gustavia still recalls its complex colonial history – and even Guadeloupe for some time, but it never acquired the sort of intercontinental empire Swedes had dreamed of in the seventeenth century.[37] The Kingdom of Denmark–Norway similarly claimed

[35] Lisbet Koerner, *Linnaeus: Nature and Nation*, Cambridge, Mass.: Harvard University Press, 1999.

[36] See among others Richard Drayton, *Nature's Government: Science, Imperial Britain, and the "Improvement" of the World*, New Haven: Yale University Press, 2000; Londa Schiebinger, *Plants and Empire: Colonial Bioprospecting in the Atlantic World*, Cambridge, Mass.: Harvard University Press, 2004, pp. 1–12 and *passim*.

[37] Kristina Söderpalm, "Handel och sjöfart: Svenska Ostindiska Kompaniet," in Pontus Grate (ed.), *Solen och Nordstjärnan: Frankrike och Sverige på 1700-talet*, Stockholm: Nationalmuseum, 1993, pp. 172–175.

Iceland, the Faroe Islands, and Greenland in the icy North Atlantic, which Hans Egede in 1741 stated had as strong an economic potential as "anywhere else," but also the Caribbean islands of St. Thomas, St. John, and, after purchasing it from the French in 1733, St. Croix, in addition to Tranquebar in India, seat of the Danish East India Company. This latter colony, administering a number of smaller trading posts on the Indian subcontinent, would only be bought by the British in the nineteenth century, while Denmark's Levant company succumbed to poor management and what an envoy referred to as the "Envy, Jealousy, and Opposition of certain Nations," who sought to monopolize the "work and industry" of the Eastern Mediterranean.[38] Both Denmark and Sweden also expanded northwards, acquiring vast possessions in "Lapland," the northernmost stretches of present-day Norway, Sweden, Finland, and Russia. Even where their empires were formally established, however, Scandinavians simply lacked the administrative capacity and economic power to maintain and expand their influence. Indeed, the failure of Scandinavia to unify and become a world power in the early modern period, when it controlled the key strategic resources of timber, tar, hemp, and metals, in addition to vast fisheries, remains one of the enigmas of global history, but can only be understood, as Einar Maseng argued, in light of the centennial diplomatic and military campaigns of great powers to break Nordic alliances at crucial junctures and hinder the emergence of a centralized monopoly on northern raw materials.[39]

A report prepared for King Frederick IV by the Danish Board of Police and Trade in 1716 tellingly suggests the radical measure of accepting the de facto liberty of Caribbean colonists to trade with other colonial powers. The islands were administered to produce sugar and cotton rather than foodstuffs, and constant warfare rendered it impossible for supply ships of the Danish East India Company to reach St. Thomas more often than once every other year.[40] The English city of Bristol alone sent out an average of 83 ships yearly to the West Indies in the period 1713–1717.[41] The Danish colonist's new-found freedom from Company oppression, however, was Janus-faced. As the Governor of St. Thomas, Erik Bredal, wrote to the

[38] Hans Egede, *Grønlands Beskrivelse*, Oslo: A.W. Brøggers Boktrykkeris Forlag, 1926, p. 140. On Dano-Norwegian colonial history see particularly Kay Larsen, *De Dansk-Ostindiske Koloniers Historie*, 2 vols., Copenhagen: Centralforlaget, 1907–1908; Yngvar Ustvedt, *Trankebar: Nordmenn i de Gamle Tropekolonier*, Oslo: Cappelen, 2001; Michael Bregnsbo and Kurt Villads Jensen, *Det Danske Imperium: Storhed og Fald*, Copenhagen: Aschehoug, 2004. On its botched efforts in the Levant see C.F. Wandel, *Danske Handelsforsøg paa Levanten i det Attende Aarhundrede*, Copenhagen: C.A. Reitzels Forlag, 1927. For Sigurd Wilhelm de Gähler's account of 15 June 1754, see pp. 21–24.

[39] Einar Maseng, *Utsikt over de Nord-Europeiske Staters Utenrikspolitikk*, ed. Lars Mjøset, 3 vols, Oslo: Universitetsforlaget, 2005, vol. I, pp. 32–3.

[40] Reproduced in Waldemar Westergaard, *The Danish West Indies Under Company Rule (1671–1754) with a Supplementary Chapter, 1755–1917*, New York: Macmillan, 1916, pp. 306–314.

[41] Kenneth Morgan, *Bristol and the Atlantic Trade in the Eighteenth Century*, Cambridge: Cambridge University Press, 1993, p. 14.

Directors of the Company on 25 May 1719, their liberty of trade as a result of Denmark–Norway's failure to administer its empire had made them slaves of another kind: "The English nation is the one that does us the most good, and from which we have most to fear, for truth to say, they hold our very lives in their hands."[42] Failing to provide for the welfare of its overseas citizens and employees, Denmark–Norway allowed them the freedom to trade for their own provisions. This freedom not only bought them food, but also the anxieties of dependence on the goodwill of a competing and often hostile power. Once dependent by the ancient rights of conquest, liberty continued to elude the inhabitants of the Danish West Indies as they became dependent through the modern rights of commerce. It was a vice embedded in the contemporary structures of international trade, whereby specialized colonies produced raw materials for the rich rather than developing healthy holistic economies for themselves.

In the grand scheme of things, however, if Denmark and Sweden were no great powers and no great Nordic State materialized, Scandinavia fared better in the imperialist game than the smaller states occupying the lands east of the Rhine. Yet, even these looked with envy at the riches of empire, seeking ways in which to emulate the flourishing colonies of Western Europe. But, it was hardly a Cameralist conceit to compete out of one's league. It is easy to forget the legion of political communities engaged in early modern imperialism, but in 1608–1609 even Medici Tuscany planned colonies in Sierra Leone and off the coast of Latin America.[43] And the tiny Cameralist Duchy of Courland, a vassal of the Polish–Lithuanian Commonwealth nested on the Baltic Sea, established colonies on two continents, settling the St. Andres Island near the Gambia River in 1651, and Tobago in 1654 after James I of England "conceded" it, seemingly with no particular authority, to his godson James Duke of Courland.[44] By 1666, however, all its overseas dominions had been lost to the great powers.[45] German states had not fared any better. The Brandenburger Gold Coast, later the Prussian Gold Coast, was settled in 1682 but bought by the Dutch already in 1721, the same year in which Brandenburg's colony at Arguin, on the west coast of Mauritania, was taken over by the French. It is tempting to think, in light of current historiography, that Enlightenment notions of "sweet commerce" gradually would have attenuated this imperialist impulse, but it is useful to remember that even the French political economist Jean François Melon, famous for dichotomizing the ancient world of conquest and the new one of commerce,

[42] Governor Erik Bredal to the Directors of the West India Company, 25 May 1719, in Westergaard, *The Danish West Indies*, pp. 315–317.

[43] Giorgio Spini, *Michelangelo politico e altri studi sul Rinascimento fiorentino*, Milan: Edizioni Unicopli, 1999, p. 86.

[44] Jean-J. Dauxion Lavasse, *A Statistical, Commercial, and Political Description of Venezuela, Trinidad, Margarita, and Tobago…* London: G. And W.B: Whittaker, 1820, pp. 344–345.

[45] David Kirby, *Northern Europe in the Early Modern Period: The Baltic World 1492–1772*, London: Longman, 1990.

insisted on the necessity of securing ultramarine colonies.[46] Barred from the seas, it became ever clearer that the Cameralist empire would have to be realized inwards, in the heartland and on the Northern periphery of Europe, precisely as Seckendorff had suggested in his 1665 *Princely State*. And generations of Enlightenment Swedes would find succor, if not greatness, in referring to Lapland as "The Swedish West Indies."[47]

Influential architects of British Empire like the Bristol merchant and political economist John Cary predatorily pushed for ever greater conquests, for literal looting and pillaging, for ever-intensifying extraction, manufacturing, and even burning valuable raw materials in order to play the international market. The world was their oyster.[48] For Cameralists, whose worlds at times were the size of oysters, such reckless adventurism might have been lucrative in the short run, were they to find a fish small enough to fry, but it offered no prospects of sustainability. These limitations gave birth to an extensive and too-often ridiculed literature on the management and conservation of natural resources, on river-fisheries, forestry, and mining. "It is always a bad principle of state," the Norwegian commentator John Christian Bie wrote in 1770, in the first pamphlet to be published in the short period of freedom allowed to the press in the Kingdom of Denmark–Norway, "to look at the present time and advantage alone. A righteous Statesman must have his goals expanded to [include] posterity" in the same way that "a farmer" sells his fruit but not his trees, thus achieving long-term welfare by carefully managing his estate, by "planting," rather than by rapaciously capitalizing his resources.[49]

Not only the production, but also the circulation of ideas in the Cameralist world was inflected by this preoccupation with international competition and internal development. In a period of increasing exchanges of works on political economy through translation, the German language was comparatively the most receptive to foreign texts in all of Europe, enjoying a vertiginous deficit in the balance of

---

[46] This tradition of interpretation is famously rendered in Albert O. Hirschman, *The Passions and the Interests: Political Arguments for Capitalism before its Triumph*, 2nd edition, Princeton: Princeton University Press, 1997. Cf. Jean-François Melon, *Essai politique sur le commerce*, revised edition, no place: no publisher, 1736.

[47] On this trope, see Karin Johannisson, *Det Mätbara Samhället: Statistik och Samhällsdröm i 1700-Talets Europa*, Stockholm: Norstedts Förlag, 1988, p. 98 and more at length Sverker Sörlin, "Guldet från Norden: Norrlandsvisioner från Olaus Magnus till Johan Galtung," in Sune Åkermann and Kjell Lundholm (eds.), *Älvdal i norr*, Umeå: Universitetet i Umeå, 1990, pp. 83–147, particularly pp. 109–22.

[48] John Cary, *An Essay on the State of England*, Bristol: W. Bonny, on which see Sophus A. Reinert, "Traduzione ed emulazione: La genealogia occulta della *Storia del Commercio*," in Bruno Jossa, Rosario Patalano, and Eugenio Zagari (eds.), *Genovesi economista*, Naples: Istituto italiano per gli studi filosofici, 2007, pp. 155–192, and more at length in id., *Translating Empire*.

[49] J.C. Bie, "Philopatreias trende Anmærkninger. 1. Om de dyre Tider og Handelens Svaghed. 2. Om Rettergang. 3. Om Geistlighedens Indkomster," in Kjell Lars Berge (ed.), *Å beskrive og forandre verden: En antologi tekster fra 1700-tallets dansk-norske tekstkultur*, Oslo: Norges Forskningsråd, 1998, pp. 103–122, particularly p. 107.

translations on the subject.[50] Just as attempts to "plant" foreign crops and industries in Cameralist lands were more common than attempts to export reindeer and cloudberries to the Spice Islands, efforts to "plant" translations could be justified without fear of imbalance. As the German theologian Friedrich Schleiermacher in hindsight argued in his 1813 lecture "On the Different Methods of Translating" delivered to the Royal Academy of Sciences in Berlin:

> Just as our soil itself has no doubt become richer and more fertile and our climate milder and more pleasant only after much transplantation of foreign flora, just so we can sense that our language, because we exercise it less owing to our Nordic sluggishness, can thrive in all its freshness and completely develop its own power only through the most many-sided contacts with what is foreign. And coincidentally our nation may be destined, because of its respect for what is foreign and its nature which is one of mediation, to carry all the treasures of foreign art and scholarship, together with its own, in its language, to unite them into a great historical whole, so to speak, which would be preserved in the centre and heart of Europe, so that, with the help of our language, whatever beauty the most different times have brought forth can be enjoyed by all people, as purely and perfectly as is possible for a foreigner. This appears indeed to be the real historical aim of translation in general, as we are used to it now.[51]

This was only one of the more explicit examples of a wide-ranging and long-lasting tradition. The Swedish statesman Johan Westerman's 1768 inaugural lecture to the Swedish Academy of Sciences on how to emulate foreign manufactures in Sweden encapsulated the process well. Its frontispiece, framed by palm-trees on one side and pine-trees on the other, depicts a radiant classical building – presumably the Academy itself – enlightening a bearded man in the act of planting a small palm in a temperate Scandinavian terrain, with the words "För Efterkommande" written underneath him, literally meaning "for those who come after," or for posterity. In this spirit, Westerman's argument bewailed the lack of industry in Sweden compared to the wealthier powers of Europe and emphasized the role the Academy could play in helping it catch up, among other things by domesticating foreign growths and emulating English "tools and machines" to introduce new industries and improve work-efficiency. The Academy's official answer to his pamphlet brought the discourse of planting full circle. Traveling around Europe, other members of the institution had also noticed not only that the Swedish language lacked the word which "Frenchmen call *Industrie*," but that Swedes lacked the very "quality" of industry itself, and praised Westerman's efforts to remedy the situation.[52] Welfare required the translation, the bringing across and planting, not only of languages

---

[50] Sophus A. Reinert, "The Empire of Emulation: A Quantitative Analysis of Economic Translations in the European World, 1500–1849," in Sophus A. Reinert and Pernille Røge (eds.), *The Political Economy of Empire in the Early Modern World*, Basingstoke: Palgrave Macmillan, forthcoming 2011.

[51] Friedrich Schleiermacher, "On the Different Methods of Translating," in Daniel Weissbort and Astradur Eysteinsson, *Translation – Theory and Practice: A Historical Reader*, Oxford: Oxford University Press, 2006, p. 209.

[52] Johan Westerman, *Inträdes-Tal, om Svenska Näringarnes Undervigt emot de Utländske, förmedelst en trögare Arbets-drift*, Stockholm: Lars Salvius, 1768, pp. 30, 33.

but of growths and industries, of economic cultures. It was in this spirit of *ersatz* imperialism that Cameralists such as Peter Christian Schumacher would embark on Grand Tours not of France and England but of the small states of central and southern Europe, not to learn how best to conquer foreign lands territorially and economically, but how to make the most of one's natural resources in a world of ruthless international competition. And in this context, there was far more to learn from the reform-experiences of contemporary small states than from the imperialist great powers.

A Grand Tour of Political Economy

Though today largely forgotten, Schumacher was one of the more powerful figures of his time. "Kammerherre" to the King of Denmark–Norway, formerly long-time consul to Morocco and later St. Petersburg, he was an important architect of the 1780 League of Armed Neutrality and one of Europe's greatest practical Cameralists.[53] His successful career doubtlessly owed much to him being a close friend and protégé of the powerful Danish statesman and scholar Ove Høegh-Guldberg (1731–1808), the prime minister and mentor to the young illegitimate Prince Frederick of Denmark–Norway. Høegh-Guldberg is remembered best for his ruthlessness, being among those most responsible for the fall and ghastly execution of Johann Friedrich Struensee, a German physician to the schizophrenic king Christian VII and, for a while, de facto ruler of the country. Yet, he was also a principal architect of Denmark's successful continuation as a sovereign polity in the late eighteenth century, in precise opposition to Struensee's programme of cultural and political Germanification.[54] During the War of American Independence, Count Andreas Peter Bernstorff, minister of foreign affairs from 1773 to 1780, feared that England would emerge too weak from the conflict, thus upsetting the world's balance of power. Instead of following Bernstorff's orders during the negotiations with Russia, however, Schumacher adhered to secret dispatches from Høegh-Guldberg demanding a harder Anglophobic line.[55] Forced to retire from explicit power-politics

[53] Aage Friis, *Andreas Peter Bernstorff og Ove Høegh Guldberg: Bidrag til den Guldbergske Tids Historie (1772–1780)*, Copenhagen: Det Nordiske Forlag, 1899, pp. 200–206. On the 1780 armed neutrality see Isabel de Madariaga, *Britain, Russia, and the Armed Neutrality of 1780: Sir James Harris's mission to St. Petersburg during the American Revolution*, New Haven: Yale University Press, 1962. For his correspondence see Rigsarkivet, Copenhagen, Denmark, 06312, *Schumacher, Peter Chr., 1762–1817.*

[54] Jens Glebe-Møller, *Struensees vej til Skafottet: Fornuft og Åpenbaring i Oplysningstiden*, Copenhagen: Museum Tusculanums Forlag, 2007.

[55] Robert Nisbet Bain, *Scandinavia: A Political History of Denmark, Norway and Sweden from 1513 to 1900*, Cambridge: Cambridge University Press, 1905, pp. 408–410; P. Vedel, "Schumacher, Peter Christian," in C.F. Bricka (ed.), *Dansk Biografisk Lexikon… XV. Bind, Scalabrini-Skanke*, Copenhagen: Gyldendalske Boghandels Forlag, 1901; Madariaga, *Britan, Russia, and the Armed Neutrality*, p. 233.

by the new King in 1784, Høegh-Guldberg helped Schumacher go on a Grand Tour to "the Southern Parts of Europe" before taking on political office again.[56]

Ostensibly traveling for reasons of health, escaping the harsh northern winter in favor of Italy's more welcoming climate, Schumacher was on a bibliographical expedition for Høegh-Guldberg, who instructed him to buy books for the princely sum of 100 *Riksdaler*, half in incunabula and half in recent publications, as well as on an explicit mission of economic espionage.[57] As is obvious from their subsequent correspondence, the Enlightenment Grand Tour was a capacious institution able to incorporate vastly different projects, from the salutary (warm climate, good food) and the esthetic and cultural (old books, fine art) to the pragmatic and pedagogical (political and economic espionage). The last time he had ventured out on a Tour, 14 years earlier, Schumacher wrote, his purpose had then been to learn "languages, politics, and statistics." Now, he explicitly set out to better understand the principles of the wealth of nations. His "main application" would be to study "agriculture," the riches of the land, and the means of harnessing them, fields in which he hoped to serve his country after his diplomatic career was over. Høegh-Guldberg was enthusiastic about Schumacher's decision to study "national economy" abroad, and hoped he would send him reports and observations on the matter from the continent; "the wise traveller," he instructed him in a Baconian manner, "sees what he can, and learns what he wants."[58] It is striking, given the aim of observing and emulating political economy, that he never encouraged Schumacher to visit France or England, but this makes eminent sense in the context of Cameralist *ersatz* imperialism. British models of development had been circulating relentlessly for decades, but there were pertinent limits to how useful their model was for laggards in the game of imperialism. Faced with the impossibility of competing directly with the great powers of the age, Cameralist statesmen found there was more to learn from studying the successful practices of other small states, a practice which deeply problematizes the contemporary stereotypes about the Grand Tour and its geographical division of labor: Stygian industry in the north, Arcadian idyll in the south.

The "fatherland" required all the help it could gain through espionage and emulation, and Schumacher's correspondence with Høegh-Guldberg highlights the problems of *ersatz* imperialism with striking clarity. Denmark–Norway had suffered, Schumacher wrote from Leipzig, from having tried too hard, from having "always wanted to try more, than what we were capable of executing." Danish statesmen cared about "generalia," when the key to worldly happiness lay in the "Details," and this was above all true in the realm of political economy. The former led one to throw "great sums" away to establish "colonies and factories [colonial outposts]," the latter

[56] Peter Christian Schumacher to Ove Høgh-Guldberg, 28 June 1784, in GFS, p. 281.

[57] Ove Høgh-Guldberg to Peter Christian Schumacher, 19 November 1784, in GFS, p. 304.

[58] Peter Christian Schumacher to Ove Høegh-Guldberg, 12 August 1784 and Ove Høegh-Guldberg to Peter Christian Schumacher, 31 August 1784, in GFS, pp. 288 and 291 respectively.

assured that expenses in fact were "useful" to the country. "Actually," Schumacher wrote after years of dedicated foreign service, from Russia to Morocco:

> I believe that Denmark never should think about playing a role abroad; it is not powerful enough for that, and such plans are bound to make it very unhappy. To be governed in that manner, which Denmark has been over the past 12 years [the period of Høegh-Guldberg's rule], to ensure Denmark's peace and the common and householdly happiness of all subjects, this is the Only thing which a Prime Minister must work towards [*beskjeftige seg med*]... Denmark's situation and the great powers which now have appeared in the North, will certainly not allow us to become conquerors.[59]

Schumacher had taken deep draughts from the bitter cup of realism. By comparison, on the eve of Sweden's disastrous attack on Russia in 1741, one of its noblemen had urged his country to favor a bid for "honourable participation in the general motions of the world" to its current "ignominious quiescence."[60] Its far more ignominious subsequent defeat taught Scandinavians a lesson in humility, and the cruel dynamics of greatness and decline would haunt Schumacher through Germany, Switzerland, and Italy, directing his travels as he sought remedies for Denmark–Norway's precarious situation in other small states which, like his homeland, had to brave competition with greater powers. So in addition to marveling at the Venetian Carnival, wondering about the mysteries of magnetism and electricity, and making fun of the Pope, as Protestant travelers were prone to do, Schumacher shaped his Grand Tour around the ideals of political economy.[61] Conspicuously, he avoided Naples, one of the premier destinations of the Grand Tour itinerary as it was institutionalized through travel books and the actual establishment of physical networks of inns, way-stations, and specialized personnel in Enlightenment Europe, dismissing it in rather cruel terms: "it holds so little influence in the European system that it cannot be of particularly dire importance [*magtpaaliggende*] what system they have."[62] Instead, on his way to Italy, he visited Karlsruhe, on Baden's border with France, for no other reason than to see "whether the Physiocratic system, which the Marquis of Baden himself has been greatly carried away by and sought to introduce in some of his lands, has been successful." This was an extremely important question. Baden had actually sought to implement the basic building-blocks of Physiocracy, "laying all Taxes solely on the Ground alone," the notorious "single

[59] Peter Christian Schumacher to Ove Høegh-Guldberg, 1 September 1784, in GFS, p. 293.

[60] In Michael Roberts, *The Age of Liberty*: *Sweden 1719–1772*, Cambridge: Cambridge University Press, 1986, p. 35.

[61] For another Grand Tour bringing together interests in economics and electricity, see Paola Bertucci, *Viaggio nel paese delle meraviglie*: *Scienza e curiosità nell'Italia del Settecento*, Turin: Bollati Boringhieri, 2007.

[62] Peter Christian Schumacher to Ove Høegh-Guldberg, 2 April 1784, in GFS, p. 329. On the institutionalization of itineraries, see Calaresu, "Looking for Virgil's Tomb." On the connection between economic destitution and Naples' negative image in Europe, see Nelson Moe, *The View from Vesuvius*: *Italian Culture and the Southern Question*, Berkeley: University of California Press, 2006, p. 52.

tax [*impôt unique*]" which by 1784 long since had been ridiculed by luminaries such as Voltaire and Ferdinando Galiani.[63]

Upon the unification of the two separate branches of the Margravate of Baden in 1771, Karl Friedrich of Baden-Durlach (1728–1811), soon Elector and then Grand Duke of Baden, had inherited a number of territories along the East bank of the fertile Rhine basin and its mostly mountainous hinterland, including parts of the Black Forest, stretching as far in its South-East corner as Lake Constance. Its rugged terrain held both a wide variety of mineral resources and, along the Rhine, lush agricultural lands. Francis Russell, the Duke of Bedford, traveled through the region a few years after Schumacher, wrote lyrically of the "truly romantic vale" of the Rhine basin, the exquisite wine, the "vast number of manufacturies" in a town he visited, the excellent universities, the Elector's wisdom at requiring a wide university education of all his civil servants. Yet, so alien was the Cameralist ideology to him that he had no word for its curriculum, which he noted included not only "the Sciences" but also "the Laws of Nature and the Country, Eloquence, Farming in all its branches, Politics, Commerce, Knowledge of Trades and Manufactures, &c. &c." [64] This was the context in which Physiocracy first came to be implemented in Germany.

There, Physiocracy emerged from, and gave scientific validity to, an explicitly "feudal reaction" against the rise of commercial and manufacturing interests and the complex phenomenon known as the rise of the bourgeoisie.[65] And even if Karl Friedrich of Baden is often mentioned as one of the principal exponents of "Enlightened Despotism," alongside Frederick the Great, Joseph II, Leopold of Tuscany, and Catherine of Russia, and though he moved towards ending serfdom in his territories, it is not surprising that he, the "Enlightened Despot" most interested in Physiocracy, to the extent that he even wrote a treaty on it himself, would also pass a law excluding bourgeois councilors such as Schumacher himself from holding high office in his state.[66] "Nobility," as Karl Friedrich wrote, was simply "a purer race."[67] It was, therefore, not surprisingly his last bourgeois minister, Johann Jakob Reinhard,

[63] Peter Christian Schumacher to Ove Høegh-Guldberg, no date but around New Year's Eve 1784, in GFS, p. 306; Voltaire [Francois Marie Arouet], *L'Homme aux Quarante Ecus*, Paris: no publisher, 1768; Ferdinando Galiani, *Dialogues sur le commerce des bleds*, London: no publisher, 1770. See also Nuçi Kotta, *L'Homme aux Quarante Écus*: *A Study of Voltairian Themes*, with a foreword by George R. Havens, The Hague: Mouton & Co., 1966, pp. 38–83 and particularly Steven L. Kaplan, *Bread, Politics, and Political Economy during the Reign of Louis XV*, The Hague: Martinius Nijhoff, 1976.

[64] Francis Russell, Duke of Bedford, *A Descriptive Journey Through the Interior Parts of Germany and France*, London: G. Kearsley, 1786, pp. 9, 39, 44–6.

[65] Helep P. Liebel, "Enlightened Bureaucracy versus Enlightened Despotism in Baden, 1750–1792," *Transactions of the American Philosophical Society*, New Series, vol. 55, No. 5, 1965, pp. 1–132, p. 14; Gray, *Money Matters*, p. 119.

[66] Karl Friedrich von Baden, "Kurzer Abriss von den Grundsätzen der politischen Oekonomie," *Archiv für den Menschen und Bürger*, 4, 1782, pp. 234–63; Jeremy Black, *Eighteenth-Century Europe*, Basingstoke: Palgrave Macmillan, 1999, p. 136.

[67] Liebel, "Enlightened Bureaucracy," p. 22.

who laid the groundwork for Baden's economic policies in the second half of the eighteenth century, instituting wide-ranging agricultural and industrial reforms already in the 1750s and 1760s. The problem he had identified, not unlike Seckendorff a century earlier, was that of fully harnessing the possibilities of the land and putting untapped resources – land, labor, raw materials – to productive use. The Seven Years War furthermore put an enormous strain on the state's finances, inspiring numerous policies to intensify Baden's productive and thus taxable capacity. Reinhard's solution was to introduce and plant new crops, such as potatoes, tobacco, flax, and mulberry trees to set up a domestic silk industry, breeds of livestock, and import-substituting industries. Reinhard's policies would continue to influence Baden's political economy long after Karl Friedrich's turn to Physiocracy, explaining the uninterrupted encouragement of industries there and continuing survival of tariffs and bounties at a time of ostensibly free trade. Similarly, where Physiocracy never cared much for technological development per se, many of Reinhard's reforms stressed the importance of precisely this, and would continue to inflect government policies after his death.[68]

The Margrave decided to implement Physiocracy around 1768, and initiated a correspondence with Mirabeau, François Quesnay's right hand, over how to render it useful in practice. The tendency of the epistolary was clear. Karl Friedrich repeatedly asked detailed questions about real economic reforms and the precise means of calculating the "single tax" in an agricultural context of very small-scale and subdivided cultivation like that characterizing most of Baden; Mirabeau responded with slogans about "eternal truths" and the "law of nature."[69] In the absence of more concrete guidelines, the Physiocratic experiment began with the simultaneous liberalization of trade and implementation of a single tax in the northern Baden towns of Dietlingen, Theningen, and Bahlingen in 1770. Yet, since the "single tax" de facto was superimposed on already existing structures of taxation, the reforms were hard to swallow for many in the poorer areas. And neither did it work miracles in wealthier regions such as Dietlingen, where the community's debt more than doubled in the first decade of the experiment. Farmers quickly petitioned to return to the old way of doing things, but the final vestiges of the Physiocratic system were only

[68] Liebel, "Enlightened Bureaucracy," pp. 36–47. On the economic consequences of eighteenth-century warfare in Baden, see also Carl Friedrich to Mirabeau, 22 September 1769, in Carl Friedrich of Baden, *Brieflicher Verkehr mit Mirabeau und Du Pont*, ed. Carl Knies, 2 vols., Heidelberg: Carl Winter's Universitätsbuchhandlung, 1892, vol. I, pp. 3–5.

[69] See Karl Friedrich to Mirabeau, 22 September 1769, 13 October 1769, and no date [1770], in *Brieflicher Verkehr mit Mirabeau und Du Pont*, vol. I, pp. 3–5, 10, 18–20; Mirabeau to Karl Friedrich, 4 October 1769, no date [probably 1769], 31 March 1770, in *Verkehr mit Mirabeau und Du Pont*, vol. I, pp. 5–9, 10–17, 20–38. But see, for Mirabeau's more practical side and the differences between his "public" and "private" opinions of the Margrave and the success of Physiocratic reforms in Baden, Vieri Becagli, 'Il'"Salomon du Midi" e l'"Ami des Hommes." Le riforme Leopoldine in alcune lettere del marhese di Mirabeau al Conte di Scheffer', *Ricerche storiche*, VII, 1 (1977), 137–195, p. 163.

overturned in the early nineteenth century.[70] The experiment was first initiated under Reinhard, then taken over by the Weimar economist Johann August Schlettwein in 1772, a complex thinker who, though embracing many of Quesnay's teachings, nonetheless refused to consider manufacturing activities as "sterile" and was opposed to a wholehearted implementation of doctrinal Physiocratic doctrines because of the sharp contextual differences between France and Baden. Importantly, he also agreed with Reinhard on the importance of encouraging technological developments to increase agricultural productivity. Where Quesnay was understood in Baden to have argued that capital investments in technology could slow down growth by derailing resources which otherwise could have been put to use clearing new lands, the Cameralist insistence, in light of international rivalries with more powerful states, on improvement rather than expansion inflected the actual application of Physiocracy in Germany. And Schlettwein's work in Baden was, as Helep Liebel put it, "more cameralist than physiocrat." As such, it was only after his dismissal the following year, when the post of Finance Minister was taken up by none other than Du Pont de Nemours, that a bona fide Physiocrat became involved directly in the reforms.[71]

Du Pont de Nemours was a rather typical Physiocrat, cultivating a sectarian infatuation with Quesnay and preaching his doctrines as if they were Messianic revelations. Yet, he readily admitted in his autobiography that "to control [his] theory, while verifying its consequences and applying them to the facts," he relied only on chatter with "a few carters who worked beside the road" and with "the only person whom I knew who had any rural notions, *my Father's Cook*!"[72] His tenure as Baden finance minister was, not surprisingly, a failure, and he returned to Paris only a year later, at which point the Physiocrat and mesmerist Charles de Butré stepped in as his replacement. Though Mirabeau presented him as "the only man in Europe truly admirable and infallible in this genre," he too proved singularly inept, and was away from Baden on private business from 1770 to 1786 before being finally banished from the lands. Some positive reforms did, however, occur in this period, the best known being Karl Friedrich's partial abolition of serfdom in 1783, initiated in emulation of Joseph II's similar policies in his neighboring lands the year before. Between this and the planting of new fields, crops, breeds, and technologies in "The Palatinate, Baden and the Swabian circle," agricultural productivity increased "some eight to tenfold" in the later part of the eighteenth century. This was largely a consequence of Cameralism, however, not Physiocracy, and even Karl Friedrich himself would continue to encourage "sterile" domestic industries into the 1780s.[73]

---

[70] A. Emminghaus, "Carl Friedrich von Baden physiokratische Verbindungen, Bestrebungen und Versuche, ein Beitrag zur Geschichte des Physiokratismus," *Jahrbücher für Nationalökonomie und Statistik*, vol. 19, 1872, pp. 1–63, p. 36.

[71] Liebel, "Enlightened Bureaucracy," pp. 48–9, 74–7.

[72] Du Pont de Nemours, *Autobiography*, ed. Elizabeth Fox-Genovese, Washington, Del.: Scholarly Resources, 1984, pp. 226, 231–2.

[73] Mirabeau to Carl Fredrik Scheffer, 16 October 1784, in Becagli, 'Il'"Salomon du Midi"' pp. 194–5; Liebel, "Enlightened Bureaucracy," pp. 53–4, 96, 98, 100; Derek Beales, *Joseph II*, 2 vols., Cambridge: Cambridge University Press, 1987–2009, vol. II.

In effect, Physiocracy was never established in Baden in any meaningful sense, and the verdict of the principal historian of these events is remarkably damning: Karl Friedrich was "an absolute prince who preferred his own pet theories and his own infallibility to the advice of his ablest councillors. It was in this spirit that he tried to introduce the physiocratic system into Baden, also against the counsel of his ministers, and it was because of this mentality that the experiment failed."[74]

There can be no doubt that the Physiocratic experiment in Baden was a failure, as it indeed soon was known to be so internationally. The widely translated British agronomist and political economist Arthur Young, for example, looked at Dietlingen and could only marvel at "what a curse upon the agriculture of a country" Karl Friedrich's adoption of Physiocracy had been.[75] Somewhat ironically, the debate over Physiocracy in Germany would nonetheless only take off in 1778, after the doctrine already had failed spectacularly in practice in France as well as in Germany, and been criticized even in German journals for its wrongheaded assumptions with regards to the capacity of farmers to carry the state's fiscal burden and the ostensible "sterility" of commerce and manufactures.[76] Ferdinando Galiani's "famous" *Dialogues on the Grain Trade* had even been translated into German in 1777, the translator including a history of the text's influence in the French polemic over Physiocracy.[77] Schumacher was aware that other travelers before him, particularly the publisher Christoph Friedrich Nicolai, had recently reported negatively on the practical application of Physiocracy in Baden, but he wanted to see the results with his own eyes and speak to the actual statesmen in charge about the true worth of this new doctrine of political economy and of its consequences.[78] "Nicolai," he wrote to Høegh-Guldberg, had "expressed, against Schlettwein, that his Plan was unrealizable

[74] Liebel, "Enlightened Bureaucracy," p. 13.

[75] Arthur Young, *Political Arithmetic…* London: W. Nicoll, 1774, pp. 252–3. This is not to say that other parts of Baden were praised more highly on the Grand Tour. As late as the early twentieth century, D.H. Lawrence noted the "big, fat, rather gloomy fields" of Southern Baden, "damp and unliving," in *D.H. Lawrence and Italy*, ed. Tim Parks, London: Penguin, 2007, p. 101.

[76] Gray, *Money Matters*, p. 109–113. See, for example, *Anmerkungen über die französische Schrift*: *Moyens d'arrêter la misère publique*, Frankfurt, 1772 and later Wilhelm Dohm, "Ueber das physiokratische System," *Deutsches Museum*, no. 10, 1778, pp. 289–324. On Dohm, see Paolo Bernardini, "Aufklärung e Beamtentum: I. Metodo storiografico e teoria dell'economia in C.W. Dohm (1773–1779)," *Annali della Fondazione Luigi Einaudi*, vol. XXIII, 1989, pp. 371–470. The Baden-Durlach experiment would remain fundamental to the Physiocratic debate in Germany. See Anonymous, *Die Kontribuzion oder Uibersicht des Kontribuzionstandes in Beziehung auf das phisiokratische Sistem*, Vienna: No publisher, 1780, [iv] and Georg Andreas Will, *Versuch über die Physiokratie…* Nuremberg: Kaspe, 1782, pp. 30–34.

[77] Ferdinando Galiani, *Dialogen über die Regierungskunst vornemlich in Rucksicht auf den Getreydehandel*, Lemgo: Meyerschen Buchhandlung, 1777, pp. 1–10.

[78] Friedrich Nicolai, *Beschreibung einer Reise durch Deutschland und die Schweiz im Jahre 1781*, 12 vols., Berlin and Stettin, 1783–1796, vol. I, pp. 265–6. On Nicolai see Pamela Eve Selwyn, *Everyday Life in the German Book Trade*: *Friedrich Nicolai as Bookseller and Publisher in the Age of Enlightenment, 1750–1810*, Philadelphia: Pennsylvania State University Press, 2000.

[*uudførlig*]," and dismissed it on the basis of the "bad outcome" of its implementation, which, he added, had led to a famous and public debate. So who was right? Unlike most travelers, Schumacher was a powerful Cameralist whose connections counted, and when he arrived in Baden he had no troubles seeing the Margrave and his remaining ministers personally to hear their side of things. They too, he learned, had

> found the Plan unrealizable, and the Marquis himself, who previously has been greatly carried away by the Physiocratic System, [and] even written a piece to explain it, admitted to me, that though he still believed the introduction of this system was [a] happy [occurrence] for his subjects, there still existed too many Difficulties in introducing it that he had simply had given up on it.

So "soon," Karl Friedrich had confessed to Schumacher, the "Emperor" would enforce new regulations overturning Physiocratic reforms, for his "subjects" were "so heavily burdened by it, that he necessarily must give up on it."[79] Around this time, Mirabueau wrote in private correspondence that he hoped Gustav III of Sweden would visit Baden and learn some "able lessons" from the Physiocratic experiment there. He would, needless to say, not have approved of Schumacher's contemporary dispatches, which had their natural effect. Høegh-Guldberg's reply left little doubt as to the relevance of Physiocracy or the possibility of its acceptance in Denmark–Norway: "Everything which you write is important to me. *The Physiocratic System will never be mine*."[80]

And neither would Schumacher's travels onwards through the land of Physiocracy change his initial impression of the doctrine's value for small state reformism. After visiting Baden, he headed southwards to the second region outside France in which Quesnay's doctrine was thought to have been cultivated and indeed found its ideal manifestation: Leopold's Tuscany.[81] While Florence and the Tuscan hills were perennial linchpins of the Grand Tour, Schumacher's reason for visiting defied custom. It was not the Uffizi, nor Brunelleschi's dome, which drew him there, but Tuscany's unique history of economic policies. Economic decline had set in centuries before Schumacher visited, and a rich culture of political economy had developed in Tuscany, as it had in the rest of Italy, to come to terms with the vicissitudes of time. When Peter Leopold (1747–1792), later Holy Roman Emperor, moved there from Austria to take over the Archduchy in 1765, he officially drew Tuscany into the Cameralist sphere of influence. Not surprisingly, the political economy of his reign shared many preoccupations, not only with the centennial indigenous tradition of reformism and economic legislation, but also with Cameralist concerns with the

---

[79] Peter Christian Schumacher to Ove Høegh-Guldberg, no date but around New Year's Eve 1784, in GFS, p. 306; Nicolai, *Beschreibung*, vol. III, pp. 86–87.

[80] Mirabeau to Carl Fredrik Scheffer, 16 October 1784, in Becagli, 'Il'"Salomon du Midi,"' pp. 194–5; Ove Høegh-Guldberg to Peter Christian Schumacher, 17 March 1785, in GFS, p. 324. Emphasis added.

[81] Tuscan ministers were well aware of the Baden experiment before they embarked on their own reforms, see Becagli, 'Il'"Salomon du Midi,"' p. 140, n13.

harnessing of natural resources. Relatively protected from the great imperialist gambits of the time for reasons of geography and dynastic politics, Leopold could turn his attention to reforming the economy, and, under his watch, Tuscany in effect became one of the most minutely surveyed lands in the world. And as part of a general preoccupation across Italy with reforms and the emulation of more successful foreign models in the 1750s and 1760s, Tuscan political economists turned to a number of ultramontane authors for inspiration, among which were Quesnay and Mirabeau.[82] As late as 1781, Mirabeau's envoy to Baden, de Butré, proclaimed that Tuscany was realizing the Physiocratic ideal, and it has been argued that Tuscans "naturally had a physiocratic mentality."[83] But were Leopold's reforms strictly Physiocratic, and was the Tuscan economy primarily "agricultural?"[84] Gian Francesco Pagnini had declared in 1765 that the historical success of Tuscan manufactures had come to an end and that future reforms would have to focus on the agricultural sector, and historians have tended to take his utterance seriously.[85] Using official data in 1757, however, Gianrinaldo Carli had calculated that the region exported 372,000 *scudi* worth of agricultural produce versus 1,267,000 worth of manufactures.[86] As it turns out, actual historical conditions were indeed somewhat less than black and white, mercantilist industrial protectionism versus libertarian Physiocracy.

18 September 1767 saw the first law freeing the internal circulation of grain from most of its barriers, and a number of other laws soon followed, revoking myriads of regulations. Much has been made of the supposedly Physiocratic inspiration for the abolishment of corporations on 1 February 1770, yet the relevant law justifies itself as a means of "increasing the manufactures" of the state, not its agriculture, and in their place Leopold instituted a "Chamber of Commerce, Arts, and Manufactures." Taxes on domestic manufactures were seriously curtailed a few days later to ensure "that honest liberty, which gives birth to the good of commerce," and on 5 February

[82] Eric Cochrane, *Florence in the Forgotten Centuries 1527–1800*, Chicago: University of Chicago Press, 1973, pp. 429, 435–7, 447.

[83] Charles de Butré, *Loix naturelles de l'agriculture et de l'ordre social*, Neuchatel: Imprimérie de la société typograhique, 1781, pp. 144–57, discussed in Becagli, 'Il'"Salomon du Midi,"' p. 170; Norbert Jonard, "Le Problème du luxe en Italie au XVIIIe siècle," *Revue des études italiennes*, 15, 1969, pp. 295–321, on which see Till Wahbaeck, *Luxury and Public Happiness*: *Political Economy in the Italian Enlightenment*, Oxford: Oxford University Press, 2004, p. 131.

[84] See for example George Holmes, *The Oxford Illustrated History of Italy*, Oxford: Oxford University Press, 1997, p. 137: "Tuscany became a model state in the European Enlightenment debate when Peter Leopold put into practice physiocratic doctrines." On the supposedly entirely "agricultural" nature of the Tuscan economy, see Wahnbaeck, *Luxury and Public Happiness*, p. 84.

[85] Gian Francesco Pagnini, *Della Decima*, Lisbon and Lucca: G. Bouchard, 1765, for a conscientious reading of which see Mario Mirri, "Fisiocrazia e riforme: il caso della Toscana e il ruolo di Ferdinando Paoletti," in Manuela Albertone (ed.), *Governare il mondo*: *l'economia come linguaggio della politica nell'Europa del Settecento*, Milan: Fondazione Giangiacomo Feltrinelli, 2009, 323–441, p. 360. For an extreme case of reliance on Pagnini on this, see Wahnbaeck, *Luxury and Public Happiness*, p. 84.

[86] Gianrinaldo Carli, "Saggio politico ed economico sopra la Toscana," in id., *Delle opere…*, Milan: Nell'Imperial Monistero di S. Ambrogio Maggiore, 19 vols., 1784–94, vol. I, 323–368, pp. 337–8.

all taxes on the export of manufactured linen, hemp, and cotton were removed. Simultaneously, however, the law introduced a uniform tax on their equivalent imports, and measures in those years focused on centralizing and homogenizing the Tuscan economy, not dissolving its territoriality. They sought to "facilitate commerce," but not through *laissez-faire*. "Arbitrary" street selling was, for example, banned and strict geographical delineations of commercial spaces were introduced on 23 June 1770. The grain trade was liberalized, but the export of certain raw materials was prohibited to ensure the development of domestic manufactures. And neither were they isolated atavisms. New tariffs on imported leather goods and textiles followed, and the vocabulary of legislation in the 1770s is replete with calls both for "liberty" and the "protection of industry." Leopold and his advisors were pragmatic, not doctrinaire; when an efficient market for wolf-hunting failed to materialize upon the abolition of patents on it, they simply renewed privileges for hunters willing to take the job.[87]

Freedom of domestic and international grain trade was granted in 1775, and a new tariff-code was established in 1781.[88] Industrial activities continued to be encouraged during this period; subsidies were given to exporters of silk manufactures, successful synergies were established between governments and individual entrepreneurs, and, with time, a ban on the export of raw materials was even reintroduced. Furthermore, many of the agricultural reforms embarked upon – such as arriving at a Montepulciano wine able to travel as far as England – were not technically Physiocratic in origin. As Eric Cochrane aptly puts it, "Florentines were too well read in their own history to believe that manufacturing was really unproductive." The important reformist minister Francesco Maria Gianni even concluded that the Physiocratic "single tax" was only "so much hot air," and that its inventors, though "beloved names in the subject of political economy" were "the ingredients of charlatanry," authors of a "destructive system." The true source of wealth was "human industries," not the soil per se.[89] This was really a typical stance even among the most ardent Tuscan "Physiocrats."[90] Agronomist Ferdinando Paoletti, for example, embraced Quesnay's emphasis on agricultural improvement but adapted Physiocracy to Tuscan conditions and insisted on government encouragements for

[87] Lorenzo Cantini, *Legislazione toscana*, 32 vols., Florence: Fantosini, 1800–1808, vol. XXIX, pp. 46–55, 325, 335–7, 339–40; vol. XXX, pp. 34–8, 69, 83, 92–3, 107–8, 151–3, 244–5, 255; vol. XXXI, pp. 109–15.

[88] On the debates surrounding these new tariffs, see Vieri Becagli, *Un unico territorio gabellabile:La riforma doganale leopoldina. Il dibattito politico 1767–1781*, Florence: Università degli studi di Firenze, 1983.

[89] Cantini, *Legislazione toscana*, vol. XXXI, p. 73; Francesco Maria Gianni, *Scritti di pubblica economia*, 2 vols., Florence: Niccolai, 1848–9, vol. I, pp. 12, 28–9; Cochrane, *Florence in the Forgotten Centuries*, pp. 435–7, 445, 448, 450–2.

[90] Renato Mori, *Le riforme leopoldine nel pensiero degli economist Toscani del '700*, Florence: Sansoni, 1951, p. 28; Schumpeter, *History of Economic Analysis*, p. 374n; Eric Cochrane, *Tradition and Enlightenment in the Tuscan Academies, 1690–1800*, Chicago: University of Chicago Press, 1961, pp. 232–48.

exports of refined goods.[91] That said, agricultural investments were made, also under Physiocratic influence (a law allowing for the temporary freedom to export linen seed might be one example), including, just as in Baden, the widespread planting of new crops such as tobacco as a means of supplying domestic demand for colonial goods. Uniform weights and measures were introduced, Leopold inaugurated one of the most advanced information-systems in Europe, and his new Tuscan Penal Code, inspired by Beccaria, Enlightened the world entire.[92]

By the early 1780s, and particularly from the time Schumacher visited, the principal Tuscan Physiocrats were dead, measures were taken to curtail elements of the reforms which had been "too liberal" and been found counterproductive to economic development, and the divergence between ideal and reality became ever clearer. There had been *buona fede* Physiocrats in Tuscany, but Physiocracy had been one influence among many in Tuscan reformism, and was, in spite of the assurances of propagandists like Mirabeau, never wholeheartedly realized there.[93] So did Schumacher draw any positive lessons of political economy on his travels there, and did he find any rare books in this unique land of tradition and renovation? As it turns out, he did both and at the same time. After fruitlessly spending weeks on end browsing used bookshops and consulting with "antiquarians" around Northern and Central Italy, he developed an astute sense of contemporary bibliography. First of all, he reasoned, incunabula were impossible to come by, no matter how much money one brought. Secondly, modern works were usually published in Italian, not, as previously, in Latin, the very change from a hierarchical to a horizontal system of European languages which characterized the rise of regional economic discourses communicating through translations at the time.[94] The Tuscan publishing industry,

[91] Ferdinando Paoletti, *I veri mezzi di render felici le società*, Florence: Stecchi and Pagani, 1772, p. 231. On Paoletti as one of the more coherent Tuscan Physiocrats, see Mirri, "Fisiocrazia eriforme," pp. 406–21.

[92] See on these reforms, and from different perspectives, also Furio Diaz, *Francesco Maria Gianni: Dalla burocrazia alla politica sotto Pietro Leopoldo di Toscana*, Milan: Ricciardi, 1966, p. 90; R. Burr Litchfield, *The Emergence of a Bureaucracy: The Florentine Patricians, 1530–1790*, Princeton: Princeton University Press, 1986, pp. 297–8; Bernardo Sordi, *L'amministrazione illuminata: Riforma delle comunità e progetti di costituzione nella Toscana leopoldina*, Milan: Giuffrè, 1991; Emmanuelle Chapron, *"Ad utilità pubblica": Politique des bibliothèques et pratiqued du livre à Florence au XVIIIe siècle*, Geneva: Droz, 2009.

[93] Luigi del Pane, *Industria e commercio nel Granducato di Toscana nell'età del Risorgimento*, vol. I: *Il Settecento*, Bologna: Pàtron, 1971, p. 260; Becagli, 'Il'"Salomon du Midi,"' p. 155; for an extremely careful reading of Physiocracy in Tuscany and the polyvalence of sources considered there see Mirri, "Fisiocrazia e riforme," particularly pp. 360–370. For a very different kind of reading, see Wahnbaeck, *Luxury and Public Happiness*, passim.

[94] See Karlheinz Stierle, "Translatio Studii and Renaissance: From Vertical to Horizontal Translation," in Sanford Budick and Wolfgang Iser (eds.), *The Translatability of Cultures: Figurations of the Space Between*, Stanford: Stanford University Press, 1996, pp. 55–67, particularly p. 65; Anthony M. Cinquemani, "Milton Translating Petrarch: *Paradise Lost* VIII and the *Secretum*," in Carmine G. Di Biase (ed.), *Travel and Translation in the Early Modern Period*, Amsterdam: Rodopi, 2006, pp. 65–88, particularly p. 79.

Schumacher noted, had in particular devoted itself to books on "the stewardship of the land and the economy of states [*Landhuusholdningen og Staaternes Oeconomie*]."[95]

> I am currently creating for myself a collection of books on politics and state economics, which always will be at Your Highness' command. It is with extreme pleasure that I am reading the famous Genoesi's [sic] writings on the economy. I find some new observations in them, of which some must be greatly applicable to Denmark. This book has particularly served as blueprint to the Grand Duke of Tuscany for some good devices which this Duke is introducing in his land, and their consequences will soon have proven the truth of the author's sentences everywhere. Tuscany is truly mounting in wealth, and if this good Duke lives, it will become, from a fallen land, as it was in the time of the Grand Duke's father, one of the happiest States in Europe.[96]

Again comparing his studies of European political economy with the paradigm of Physiocracy, Schumacher concluded that the Grand Duke of Tuscany had "adopted from the Physiocratic System everything which was proven advantageous, and let go everything which rested only on pure political speculations."[97] The key to wealth for small states was not conquest or utopian schemes, but the full employment of existing resources, intelligent agriculture, and flourishing industry. This depended, as Archenholz too had observed in Florence, on the encouragement of the "middle class," on meritocracy and subsidies for economic activity and research alike. Tuscany had freed tradesmen from guild regulations, created great projects of public infrastructure, and encouraged the free export of grain, though Schumacher felt they might have wavered too far from the "English example" in this case, not understanding properly the role of the government in instilling trust and avoiding food-shortages in lean years.[98] In this, he was agreeing with the assessment of the great Cameralist Johann Friedrich von Pfeiffer, in a passage noticed by contemporaries, that "the Physiocratic system has not been accepted and put into practice by a single European state."[99] Aspects of it might have made its way into policy, but agricultural reformism did not straightforwardly equate with Physiocracy.

---

[95] I here follow Grith Lerche, *The Royal Veterinary and Agricultural University: Its Contribution to Rural Education and Research in Denmark*. Frederiksberg: KVL, 1999, p. 21: "In Danish the word "landhusholdning" did in fact encompass the whole economy of the country, including trade and not just the household of farmers."

[96] Peter Christian Schumacher to Ove Høegh-Guldberg, 2 April 1785, in GFS, pp. 327–328. Cochrane, *Florence in the Forgotten Centuries*, p. 446 noted the reliance of Tuscan reformers on John Cary and other foreign authors in the 1750s and 1760s, also through Antonio Genovesi's mediation. On this extraordinary work of interventionist English economics and its inflection by Genovesi see Reinert, "Traduzione ed emulazione."

[97] Peter Christian Schumacher to Ove Høegh-Guldberg, 2 April 1785, in GFS, pp. 327–328. See similarly the more general and methodological caveat about the dangers of abstraction in Ove Høegh-Guldberg to Peter Christian Schumacher, 7 May 1787, in GFS, p. 394. Schumacher's verdict on the nature of Tuscan emulation is echoed very closely by Cochrane, *Florence in the Forgotten Centuries*, p. 446.

[98] Peter Christian Schumacher to Ove Høegh-Guldberg, 14 May, in GFS, pp. 340, 343.

[99] Johann Friedrich von Pfeiffer, *Natuerliche, aus dem Endzweck der Gesellschaft entstehende allgemeine Polizeiwissenschaft*, 2 vols., Frankfurt am Main, 1779, vol. II, p. 62; Will, *Versuch über die Physiokratie…*, p. 35.

"The government of Paris alone," Schumacher noted in awe, provided more yearly taxes for the Sovereign than did "Denmark, Sweden, and Sardinia all three together." All this led him to conclude that a "Country is not happy because it is big, but only because it is administered well," which he realized was easier said than done in a world in which the great commercial powers deployed troops for economic advantage. His experiences in Venice, in particular, where he discussed the politics of international trade with the reformist patrician and political economist Andrea Tron at length, underlined the fragility of Cameralism in the face of jealousy of trade. Small states needed policies and peace to catch up, but this was difficult when "The Dutch, in a very despotic manner, have sought to *prescribe laws to the Republic*," a contemporary idiom for establishing an empire, by sabotaging its trade and decimating its navy.[100] It was the same reign of economic terror which led Høegh-Guldberg to detest the Turks, "because they, in the same way as the Spaniards in Mexico and Peru, and the English in India, have everywhere made deserts in lands which had been lovely in the past."[101] The insight that liberty in the modern world had come to depend on economic superiority in a world of warlike competition again reared its head, and great thinkers and statesmen again looked to old books for answers. Symbolically, after weeks of searching, Schumacher finally came across incunabula for Høegh-Guldberg as well. From the "Antiquarii" of Sienna, he happily got hold of 1481 edition of Ephraim's sermons and a 1482 Horace, whose "sapere aude!" or "dare to know!" would be equated with Enlightenment by Immanuel Kant only a few months later.[102]

As Schumacher made his way back to Denmark, he stopped again in Leipzig to organize the translation into German of some works he had brought with him from Italy. He and Høegh-Guldberg came to an agreement with the noted publisher Johann Samuel Heinsius to print books for them, locate texts that might interest them as well as important catalogs, and send them to Denmark, and for their translational needs they turned to one Christian August Wichmann, something of a political economist in his own right whose earlier translations of Physiocratic texts must have interested the two Danish Cameralists deeply. Not only did Wichmann translate and Heinsius publish a manuscript account, by an anonymous Italian nun, of the "new St. Catherine of Siena" which Schumacher had discovered in that city, but the

[100] Peter Christian Schumacher to Ove Høegh-Guldberg, 23 April 1785, in GFS, p. 334. On Tron see Sophus A. Reinert, "Blaming the Medici: Footnotes, Falsification, and the Fate of the English Model in Eighteenth-Century Italy," *Journal of the History of European Ideas*, vol. 32, No. 4, 2006, pp. 430–455.

[101] Ove Høegh-Guldberg to Peter Christian Schumacher, 1 April 1788, in GFS, p. 412.

[102] Peter Christian Schumacher to Ove Høegh-Guldberg, 23 April 1785, in GFS, p. 338; Immanuel Kant, "An Answer to the Question: What is Enlightenment? (1784)," in James Schmidt (ed.), *What is Enlightenment? Eighteenth-Century Answers and Twentieth-Century* Questions, Berkeley: University of California Press, 1996, pp. 58–64. On the history of "*sapere aude*!" see Carlo Ginzburg, "The High and the Low: The Theme of Forbidden Knowledge in the Sixteenth and Seventeenth Centuries," in id., *Clues, Myths, and the Historical Method*, translated by John and Anne Tedeschi, Baltimore: Johns Hopkins University Press, 1989, pp. 60–76; Franco Venturi, *Utopia e riforma nell'illuminismo*, Turin: Einaudi, 1970, p. 16.

two also produced the German edition of Antonio Genovesi's 1757–1758 translation of George-Marie Bûtel-Dumont's 1755 translation of John Cary's 1695 *Essay on the State of England.*[103] More than any of the observations made by Schumacher, his choice of book to bring back from Italy and translate speaks volumes about the lessons of the other grand tour, and about the economic policies which, in the 1780s, were found most conducive to the development of small states unable to compete directly with the major powers of the age. In the spectrum of contemporary European political economy, it would be hard to identify a book further distanced from Physiocracy than Cary's forgotten but extraordinarily influential volume. Though its several cumulative translations certainly had inflected its message, it remained one of the most powerful arguments for government-led industrialization circulating in eighteenth-century Europe, and a succinct statement of the synergies between industrial and agricultural development.[104]

The book which Wichmann "handed over to the German public" had first been brought to his attention by a friend of his who had traveled in Italy, "Peter Christian von Schumacher, a statesman and businessman," "Kammerherr" for the King of Denmark. Returning from a visit to Cameralist Tuscany, then under the rule of the Austrian Grand Duke Leopold II, Schumacher had recommended Genovesi's works to Wichmann to "render them available for translation and circulation [*Bekanntmachung*]." Why? Because, as Schumacher also had written to Høegh-Guldberg, the policies they suggested worked in small states struggling against more powerful competitors. The book he had brought was a "quartet" of political economy, to which British, French, Italian, and now German authors had contributed, it was a distillation not only of economic theory but also of Europe's economic history in the eighteenth century, and the Grand Duke of Tuscany himself had

> constructed his economic system of government [*ökonomische Regierungs-System*], on the basis of which he maintains his own state for the welfare of his own subjects and to the common happiness of all friends of good in Europe, primarily on the principles of this doctrine of political economy [*Staatswirthschaft*].[105]

Ersatz imperialism had found its theoretical justification, but it was not in Physiocracy. Rather, because of Schumacher's experiences of its implementation, it was in its antithesis.

---

[103] See Christian August Wichmann, *Die entlarvte Heilige oder die neue Katharina von Siena in der Geschichte einer Nonne…* Leipzig: Heinsius, 1786; Ove Høegh-Guldberg to Peter Christian Schumacher, 10 October, 21 November 1786, and 22 December 1786, in GFS, pp. 375, 379, and 382 respectively. See Schumacher's correspondence with Wichmann in Rigsarkivet, Copenhagen, Denmark, 06312, *Schumacher, Peter Chr., 1762–1817 Breve, kopibøger, optegnelser m.m.*, 7: *Breve fra private V-Æ*, A. I. 3: *Breve fra Christian August Wichmann, Leipzig*.

[104] Reinert, "Traduzione ed emulazione."

[105] Christian August Wichmann, *Anton Genovesi, ökonomisch-politischer Commentarius zu Johann Carys historisch-politischen Bemerkungen über Grossbritanniens Handel und Gewerbe*. Leipzig: Johann Samuel Heinsius, 1788, pp. iv, viii.

Wichmann himself, as one of Germany' most ardent Physiocrats, had sought to convince Schumacher of his mistakes.[106] His surviving letters to Schumacher tell an intriguing story. Not only did he defend "Physiocracy" against "errors" of interpretation, but he criticized Pfeiffer's *Antiphysiocrat* and admitted that though Pfeiffer was "greatly superior" in "style of writing and rendering," he preferred the Baden Physiocrat Schlettwein also for his leading an "exemplary life." The latter had furthermore visited him, and the two were "completely convinced" that Schumacher had been misinformed when told that "the Grand Duke [of Tuscany] rules not according to purely Physiocratic principles but according to Genovesian principles. Genovesi has adopted much, very much from Physiocracy," and it was not for lack of "good will" that he had not accepted it fully, but because he had not "grasped the entire system." Finally, his "commentary on Cary" contained ideas which he had "put down" in his later works, in which Genovesi was

> far closer to Physiocracy – and I believe he will be ever closer than before. I am looking for the opportunity to bring him a letter to ascertain this point. Enough – Peter Leopold has given more than one prescription which is not drawn from Genovesi, but ever more, with the passing of time, from Physiocracy; and in this he goes further every day.[107]

Genovesi never gave any indication of knowing Physiocracy existed, and anyway failed to adhere to its most central tenets; he believed in the multiplying effects of manufactures; he preferred small-scale to large-scale landowning; he believed in tariffs to structure international trade. His basic proposals never wavered; and he had been dead for 17 years.[108] Yet, Wichmann insisted on drawing him, and Leopold's varied policies, into a Physiocratic mold some historians still see them as occupying. Schumacher's personal experiences inoculated him against these arguments, and Wichmann's introduction to his translation of Genovesi's edition of Cary in the end told the exact story the Dane wanted told: Physiocracy had been an intermezzo in the eighteenth-century Cameralist experience. It had been tried and found wanting.

Schumacher's Grand Tour, and the world of small-state emulation which it represents, provide us with two important historiographical caveats. First of all, the differential economic geographies of the Grand Tour must be respected. Franco Venturi was quite right, in his magisterial "Italy out of Italy," that the economic, social, and political discrepancies unveiled by foreign visitors to Italy galvanized reformist movements on the peninsula and inspired "emulation" in the eighteenth

[106] On Wichmann's fame as a Physiocrat, see Will, *Versuch*, pp. [1], 28–30, 71–2; Karl Steinlein, *Handbuch der Volks-wirthschafts-lehre*, Munich: in Commission der literarisch-artistischen Anstalt, 1831, p. 77.

[107] See Christian August Wichmann to Peter Christian Schumacher, 25 April 1786, f. 3v and "undated fragment," f. 2r in Rigsarkivet, Copenhagen, Denmark, 06312, *Schumacher, Peter Chr., 1762–1817 Breve, kopibøger, optegnelser m.m.*, 7: *Breve fra private V-Æ*, A. I. 3: *Breve fra Christian August Wichmann, Leipzig*. I am grateful to Reinhild Spiess and her family for invaluable assistance in deciphering these letters.

[108] See Sophus A. Reinert, "John Cary and the Emulation of English Political Economy in Eighteenth Century Europe," PhD Dissertation, University of Cambridge, 2009

century.[109] Yet, one must not forget that Italy attracted visitors not only from France and England, but from the small states of central and northern Europe as well, states in situations close enough to those of Italy to allow for learning rather than condescension. Furthermore, Schumacher's journey emphasizes the need to distinguish carefully between agronomy, and the Enlightenment obsession with rendering agriculture more productive on the one hand, and the numinous doctrine of Physiocracy on the other. The global importance of the Physiocratic movement was noteworthy in the 1770s, but its international reception was ever modulated by local conditions, and individual inflections often affected even its analytical core. Steven Kaplan put it well, "the test of adherence" to Physiocracy was less "a simple litmus" than "a difficult rorschach."[110] It was a test at which the vast majority of European political economists, even the most agriculturally inclined, failed in one way or another. Just as Physiocracy itself had.

---

[109] Venturi, "L'Italia fuori d'Italia," p. 999.

[110] Kaplan, *Bread, Politics*, p. 116.

Chapter 5
Johann August Schlettwein (1731–1802): The German Physiocrat

Helge Peukert

Introduction

In Germany, physiocracy never had a lasting influence. This is also true for Schlettwein, the most important German physiocrat of the eighteenth century. Their approach became one of the shortest and weakest episodes of any school of economic thought in Germany. Some argue that the main ideas of French physiocracy (Meek 1962; Oncken 1902; Gömmel and Klump 1994) could simply not be transmitted to the very different German circumstances (Priddat 1998, 49). Nevertheless, as Schumpeter noted, the French physiocrats found ardent supporters only in Germany (1965, 290). In fact the anti-physiocratic movement (e.g. Dohm, Pfeiffer, Ch. Rüdiger, Schmohl, and Will) had more proponents than the physiocrats themselves (I. Iselin, Margrave of Bade-Durlach, Jung-Stilling, Chr. Springer, Chr. Wichmann).[1]

The practical proposals to implement a physiocratic policy failed even when they were implemented on a small scale. Schlettwein advised the Margrave of Baden-Durlach to implement a single tax (land tax) according to the physiocratic creed in the Baden villages of Dittlingen, Theningen, and Bahlingen (Liebel 1965; Zimmermann 1983, 170ff.). But the experiment failed. Nevertheless, Schlettwein never gave up his basic ideas even when they became more and more discredited in France.

The literature on Schlettwein is rather limited (see the dissertations of Krebs 1909 and Specht 1929). But a bibliography of his writings exists (Schlettwein 1981). The negative image of Schlettwein is largely due to Schumpeter's brief but rather

[1] See e.g. Braunreuther 1955; Blaich 1983; Borel 1923; Freyseng 1925; Muhlack 1982; Tribe 1988 (Chap. 6).

H. Peukert (✉)
Krupp Chair in Public Finance and Fiscal Sociology, University of Erfurt, Nordhäuser Str. 63, 99089 Erfurt, Germany
e-mail: helge.peukert@uni-erfurt.de

J.G. Backhaus (ed.), *Physiocracy, Antiphysiocracy and Pfeiffer*, The European Heritage in Economics and the Social Sciences 10, DOI 10.1007/978-1-4419-7497-6_5,

negative remarks (bad economist, lunatic of one simple idea see Schumpeter 1965, 294). In the following, we will show that Schlettwein was more interesting as Schumpeter suggests. As Priddat points out, he tried to combine a physiocratic value theory (he was one of the first to expose a consistent value theory on an axiomatic basis) with major tenets of German cameralism which included a strong support of liberal personal rights (Priddat 1998, 53–59). It will be highlighted that his main achievements belong to what may be called "gouvernementality" (government and mentality, according to Foucault 2004).

Schlettwein was born in 1731 in Groß-Obringen near Weimar, his family lived in modest origins. Since 1749 he studied law and cameralism in Jena. Very early he started to write on many diverse subjects (including religious, philosophical, but they also dealt with topics of the natural sciences), he was sometimes called a polyhistor in a negative way. From 1763–1773 he worked for Markgrave Carl Friedrich von Baden-Durlach as a Privy and executive councilor (*Kammer- and Polizeirat)*, where he wrote a couple of expert's opinions on money, the establishment of schools etc. and he also helped to introduce the physiocratic experiments.

In 1771, he went with the Margrave to Paris to meet Mirabeau and Du Pont. While the Margrave was deeply impressed by Du Pont, Schlettwein disagreed on diverse points (e.g. on the possibility to fix exactly the net product of the small peasant holdings in Baden) with him which was one of the reasons why he left the Margrave, besides his strong self-confidence and uncompromising sense for telling the truth, he had many enemies at the court. He mainly changed from cameralism to physiocracy under the influence of *Mirabeau's L'amie des hommes* and his *Philosophie rurale*. During the practical experiment to institutionalize a single tax, he fell in disgrace mainly due to his disagreement with Du Pont and so he went to Vienna and Freiburg to get an appointment, but he failed. With the help of I. Iselin, he had a part time appointment to lecture economics in Basle in 1776. One year later he was appointed professor of politics, cameralism, and finance at the University of Gießen where he taught until 1785. The economic faculty, a part of the general financial reform in the state, was founded in 1777 by a decree of Landgrave Ludwig IX of Hesse-Darmstadt. Schlettwein was also appointed privy councilor and permanent dean of the faculty (Klippel 1994). Again he had some trouble with the ministry, e.g. because he did not establish the faculty as fast as possible and the faculty could not attract many students (on average less than five), and because he planned to lecture on too many subjects (for all the details of his career see Krebs 1909, 7–55). When his wife made an inheritance and after a new dispute, he handed in his notice and went to the estates of his wife in Mecklenburg where he tried to start physiocratic reforms again. After the divorce with his wife in 1789, he was paid a pension. In the following, he had no more appointments but held some lectures in Greifswald. He died in 1802 in Dahlen (Mecklenburg) at 71 years of age.

He wrote incessantly, especially monographs and articles, e.g. in his own journal archive for the man and citizen. In the last years of his lonely life he made the proposal to discuss with I. Kant the refutation of his system but Kant refused. In the following we will analyze two main contributions of Schlettwein which contain all major elements of his thinking. They show that physiocracy does not have a narrow economic focus but is an encompassing theory of society, including the conditio humana, the social, the cultural, and the political spheres as subsystems of an integrated architecture.

The Nature of Man, Natural Rights, and the Just Community

In his book on the rights of mankind or the only true reason of all laws, orders, and constitutions (Schlettwein 1980, [1]1784) Schlettwein lays down his basic paradigmatic approach on man and society. As usual he does not cite any other contemporary source. But we know that he did not consider Quesnay's contribution and that he thought the English R. Cantillon to be the founder of the physiocratic system (Krebs 1909, 57–58). He starts with the nature of man and the peculiarities of human action. Man is split up into two parts: the body and the accompanying drives of man which constitute the animal part of man (mainly food, drink and sex, 1980, 100–101).

Besides this and distinguished from all other species he has intelligence, reason, understanding and mind, and the power to form intellectual ideas. In so far, man is a spiritual being (1980, 4–5). The animal and the reasoning part both make up the human being; he does not dismiss the animal part as inferior or negative.[2] His epistemological position is not easy to detect because he does not further highlight the relationship between the two basic segments. It can e.g. not be decided if he shared a Lockean empiricist or a Descartian epistemological point of view, although it seems evident that his position is closer to the latter.

But he is a child of the early unitary and balanced enlightenment in so far as we should fulfill our material needs and passions under the guidance of reason. He shared the point of view of the moderate enlightenment sensualist Charles Bonnet and not the more radical position of, e.g., the encyclopedists or Rouseeau's. Like him, Schlettwein seemed to believe in a persistent ethereal body which enables the soul a remembrance of the life on earth in heaven (Krebs 1909, 59). Another aspect is foresight: Humans are able to combine past, present, and future and to anticipate probable consequences of our actions. Further, Schlettwein presupposes that his capacities for reasoning coincide with his character as a moralizing being. In so far, he has a unitary conception of the human mind and the conditio humana. A side aspect of this unitarism is that the existence of god is without doubt: God is the ultimate anchor of man and society; he is also the last origin of the natural rights.

[2] Man is able "die äußerlichen Dinge sich mit Bewustseyn vorzustellen, in ihrem Innern zu fühlen, oder zu empfinden, durch geistige, höhere, übersinnliche Vorstellungsfähigkeiten, das ist, durch Verstand und Vernunft, allgemeine, geistige, oder intellektuelle Ideen, die durch die Empfindungsorgane des Körpers nicht so empfindbar sind, zu bilden, Gründe und Folgen, das Gegenwärtige, Vergangene und Zukünftige zu verbinden …" (1980, 4). In the following we will leave out the numerous special emphases.

But it is interesting to note that Schlettwein does not start with the ultimate originator but with the self-conscious human actor, i.e. the modern autonomous self-conscious individual. His concept is balanced insofar as the spontaneous reflecting actor is not on top of the pyramid but (s)he is embedded in a material and transcendental social environment. The real essence of man is to liberate himself from the immediate passions and drives by thinking and also by omission. The greater the moral freedom the more independent it is from sensual impressions and bodily impulses (1980, 8–9); again reflection and morality coincide.

Schlettwein does not dig deeper and ask in how far freedom of choice as an uncaused cause is possible. But we can also interpret this as a deliberate neglect because the main function of his book is to develop a new field of the sciences of the state and society and not to present an (new) epistemology. Surprisingly, he presents major abstract aspects for the analysis of human action: the actor, the circumstances, the motives, and the consequences (1980, 15). These aspects are not spectacular but they largely coincide with the aspects of human action in T. Parsons (1937) early writings where it was meant as a summary of the main theories of action of the founding fathers in sociology.

Schlettwein seems to suggest that the four aspects also should be present in the mind of the actor to act rationally, i.e. to take all relevant aspects (aims, consequences, etc.) into consideration. The organizing center of our actions is called the I, the personality is focused in the soul. In the following he sharply distinguishes the material outward aspect of action which can be prevented by force and the motivational inner aspect of action, the moral principal on which the action is based and which cannot be suppressed externally (1980, 37). A person is (also in the legal sense) to be held the more responsible for his actions the less they may be induced externally (sensual impressions, force, etc., 1980, 82–83).

But this is not to say that actors could choose any course of action they like. He goes on to argue that natural duties and obligations exist, dictated by reason (and our consciousness, 1980, 25). First of all, the decision rule is that man (because he can only be present at one place in time) should do the greatest good and then continue with the second best, he therefore formulates a formal maximizing rule (1980, 30).

As a general rule people should try to make themselves perfect and complete, they should live according to their nature, to their major drives (1980, 43).[3] This is a natural law and all natural laws are ultimately given by god (1980, 44). The evidence of natural rights is without doubt for him. He never discusses how we can discern a correct interpretation of the natural rights and distinguish them from wrong or erroneous reasoning. For him the language of reason always speaks out in a clear-cut and evident way (1980, 119). The question is, if we should accumulate riches and goods or cultivate our reasoning?

[3] "Mache dich vollkommen, thue das, was dir wahrhaftig gut ist, lebe deinem Wesen gemäs, folge deinen wesentlichen Trieben. Dies ist also das allgemeinste Naturgesetz für den Menschen" (1980, 43).

In Schlettwein we find both: On the one hand, we should consume what corresponds to our drives (we should extend our *Genießungskreiß*, 1980, 59 and develop a *vergnügtestmögliche Existenz*, 1980, 132). On the other hand, we should make us more perfect in our ability to act morally and with conscience to serve the perfection of humanity (1980, 104). He does not see a trade-off relationship between the two orientations, just the contrary: We may pursue material goals but with much foresight which corresponds with our specifically human faculty to reason. He often mentions an extension of want satisfactions as an aim but he as well mentions a qualitative upgrading and ennobling (1980, 105). Sometimes the animal aspects should be subordinated to the more spiritual aspects (1980, 123), sometimes they should complement each other (1980, 135). In sum, our life should be pleasurable and elucidated (1980, 151–152).

His ideal person has an innerworldly orientation (M. Weber) but a maximum of riches and consumption goods is definitely not his main target function and as will become obvious in the following, standards of benevolent behavior and finally god's laws draw a clear boundary of human actions which preclude a primarily self-interested, egotist, and (in the sense of new institutional economics) opportunist behavior. Positive should never contradict natural laws (1980, 46). Part of these natural laws or rules concerns our social behavior. Schlettwein strongly rejects a tit-for-tat strategy. When other people persecute or denigrate us we should not retaliate but our civil and positive behavior should be upheld and the other person should be elucidated verbally of his misbehavior. Human reason includes as a moral standard the love for mankind (1980, e.g. 52–53, 72–73).

In Schlettwein, we often find a tendency of general societal improvement in the sense that humans and society should always try to improve their general level of humanness and coincidence with natural rights. This could include the proposition that a higher developed person should (more or less) force another person to change his behavior to bring it in accordance with the superior level. But Schlettwein rejects this allegation because no person has the right to force one's will upon the will of another person, he defends the principal rights of negative freedom (I. Berlin) whatever the aims of a person in the confines of the law may be (1980, 63).

We are also not allowed to force an owner to manage his property in a better way; we are only allowed to argue with him and point out a better disposal (1980, 211). But if a person plans to do an obvious bad thing we have the right to forcefully prevent the deed (1980, 329) but only if the badness is absolutely obvious. We also have the right for self-defense but even in the case of potential murder as morally high standing persons, we should prefer to be killed instead of killing the aggressor (1980, 33–335). This principle of quasi-liberal rights of freedom is also underlined by his thesis that self-love (which is not identical with moral egotism) is a constituent aspect of man (1980, 94). The liberation of this drive out of the animal world takes place when it is accompanied by a love to humankind. As mentioned, we can detect the principles of natural rights by using our mind. Human reason is unique and indivisible.

Therefore, Schlettwein argues, the natural rights are the same for everybody, irrespective of estate or class to which a person belongs (1980, 113). This is obvious for every person with a sane mind (1980, 161). He transcends the feudalist and other hierarchically based arguments for differential natural rights (like e.g. Aristotle's plea for just slavery).

But his societal approach is nevertheless based on a hierarchy of different societies: those of the marital, the parental, the master–servant, the civil society, and finally the state as the combination of families (1980, 115). These roles are associated with different positive rights but the elementary natural rights are valid for all of them (1980, 116), especially the right (and duty, suicide is forbidden and against god's will, 1980, 126ff.) to maintain and save our life (1980, 123). Every person was created as an autonomous individual, he or she is independent from each other and free (1980, 161). No person has the right to curtail the freedom of other persons if they act in the confines of the laws (1980, 163). Schlettwein's argument for liberal autonomy and freedom therefore has a religious basis.

In the natural state no private property exists. But humans have the right to appropriate material or natural things of the environment if they serve his needs to drink, eat, etc. and when they have not been apprehended by other people before. If he invests some effort (e.g. to collect apples) or transforms a material object, it is his legitimate possession (1980, 137ff.). The simple declaration of will is not sufficient. Property is for him an indispensable necessity for personal development and freedom (1980, 178). A couple of natural objects cannot become private property because they can never be used in their totality by a single actor, his examples are rivers, the atmosphere, lakes, etc. (1980, 145). But the right of disposal has definite limits: things or objects should not be abused or destroyed. Their use is only legitimate if it supports human life.

Man also has the right to occupy land for residence and for production. Schlettwein comes close here to Locke's theory of property because we are allowed to appropriate as much land as we are able to cultivate. Land is the ultimate source of all production and surplus. This is the first time where his physiocratic basis becomes obvious.[4] Nature is the basis for all human happiness (1980, 176).

But there are limits to the appropriation of goods and land which depend on the state of other fellowmen. If one person possesses goods in abundance and he becomes aware of another person with a disposal of goods beyond the social minimum, this person has the right to ask for being given the necessary minimum and the richer person has the duty to give away (1980, 167–169). This is according to his love for mankind and in line with the tendency of self-perfection; otherwise the person acts in line with doggish egotism ("egoistisches Hundegefühl," 1980, 171). He should even share if he would sink beyond the poverty line 1980, 173.

Somewhat unconnected the duty for truth follows (1980, 153ff.). This originates from his duty vis-à-vis god, his creator (1980, 157). Language is the bond by

[4] "... kommen alle aus einer gemeinschaftlichen Quelle, nämlich aus der Erde, welche durch ihre von dem Urheber der Natur erhaltene produktive Kraft sämmtliche Bedürfnisse des animalischen Lebens erzeuget ..." (1980, 149).

which humans are intimately connected. The signs he uses should never be used not to tell the truth. We should not deceive, cheat, lie, or dissemble (1980, 184). Schlettwein comes close to Habermas theory of communication and language and the mode of communicative action based on truthfulness. Truth is the basis and the precondition of all good. In a long part, he gives examples why truthfulness is so important and a value in itself.

His theory of property is relatively easy to comprehend. Most nonpossessed objects can be appropriated. They belong to us as long as long as we hold them in our hands or on our land (1980, 214). Objects can belong to us by tradition (past events, but in the natural system testaments and inheritance are unnatural, 1980, 256–257), by occupation (if hitherto nonpossessed), and by force (1980, 227). The importance of property becomes evident in the long debate of debatable cases (e.g. when a river changes, the effects of storms, wild game, etc.) which must be neglected here. The next part deals with contracts (1980, 263ff.). He describes the voluntary and reciprocal relationship of contracts which usually involve the transference of property rights. He differentiates many forms of contract. Even in wars the usual contracts and the property of the enemy should be respected as much as possible (1980, 341). Wars for defense, restitution, and punishment are in accordance with natural law (1980, 339).

Schlettwein now changes from the state of nature to society, i.e. the law of society. Societal law can never contradict or restrict the human or natural rights which have been described so far (1980, 355). This is a very strong statement in favor of the basic negative rights. What is good for the private individual should never be moved back in favor of some social good (he calls it the *Privatbeste* vs. the *gemeine Beste* 1980, 356–357). He forcefully rejects any conception of a common good separated from the individual well-being. In so far, he follows the individualist stance of the cameralist tradition (but see Peukert 2005 for some nuances). The main aim is to guarantee the rights of the people (198, 362). He then distinguishes different social or constitutional contracts, e.g. according to the principle one man one vote and the majority rules. A majority should not decide on questions which concern e.g. personal or religious affairs (1980, 367). He distinguishes the three powers of the legislative, the executive, and the protective (military).

It is surprising that Schlettwein only discusses very practical questions and differences among possible constitutions (like an egalitarian vs. a stratified constitution). He never discusses the character and more theoretical aspects of the constitution he has in mind (an ideal, a real proposal, a thought experiment, how is the first constitution established, by whom etc.?). This part of the book may be the weakest what the analytical depth is concerned. Very quickly he goes on to describe the three elementary societal forms on which a society or state is based, first comes the marital relationship which is based on the strong sexual drive but which has the function of the reproduction of the species (1980, 380ff.). He utters some rather paternalistic ideas: Since the man occupies the organs in sexual intercourse he confiscates the woman with consequences for the legal status of the offspring which belong to the man (as long as he lives); but this also implies duties for the man to nurture the children. The man is also the owner of the body of the woman (the *Eigenthumsherr ihres Leibes*, 1980, 408). But sexual intercourse is only acceptable when both sides agree (1980, 388).

He develops very peculiar theories: Intercourse with a virgin necessitates in any case a permanent relationship. Intercourse with other women also allows temporary relationships even if they become pregnant and do already have children. In this case, he has only to take care for the child materially (1980, 396). A (sexual) community of a couple of men and women is against nature because the property relationships cannot be discerned (who is the father?). In contrast, under certain conditions one man and many women or the reverse is not against nature in principle. It cannot even be proven that monogamy is superior (1980, 405). Divorce is in accordance with nature in so far as both parties agree or some facts like incapability for sexual intercourse apply.

The father is also the possessor of the body of the children in the second social relationship, the familial. Children have hereditary (minimum) rights and the father cannot sell the landed property without regard to the future of the children (1980, 415ff.). The relationship child–parent is also based on a strong instinct (Veblen's parental belt). As long as the parents feed the children they have the right to use the powers of the children, i.e. they can let them work (1980, 422). Slavery is against nature, manorial law is not.

A state or a people are the association of many families. The function of the state is to secure the happiness of the individuals, the protection of their property, and the increase in the means of consumption (1980, 451, 457).[5] The ruler has to obey the natural laws (1980, 455). After a certain quasi-utilitarian emphasis, he reemphasizes the importance of truth and love and the superiority of the spiritual-religious aspects of man (1980, 459–460). Very general remarks on the distribution of the three powers (1980, 462ff.) and the action spheres of the ruler who has e.g. no right to enforce a particular religious creed (1980, 478), and different forms of government (democracy, monarchy, oligarchy, without a personal preference, see 1980, 488ff.) follow.

His proposals on the finance of the state exhibit a liberal-physiocratic spirit. He argues that the yearly income of the state should depend on the taxes of the people and not on regalia or domains because only taxes guarantee that the ruler has the (material) well-being of the population in mind (with a lower income they have a lower ability to pay). Another argument especially against regalia is that they restrain the natural right for private property (1980, 481). Taxes should only be levied on the pure surplus or gift given by nature which does not reduce the earned income or wealth of the citizens. In so far, this physiocratic landed single tax does

[5] "Daher besteht das wahre gemeine Beste eines Staats in der vollkommensten Versicherung des gesamten Personal- und RealEigenthums eines jeden Gliedes, und des beglückendsten Genusses desselben, oder in der vollkommensten Versicherung des PrivatBesten eines jeden, und aller" (1980, 449).

not interfere with the property rights of the citizens.[6] In these lines we see the ardent supporter of physiocracy who combines its value theory with cameralist-liberal ideas.

Schlettwein's Political Economy

Schlettwein's book on the state and political economy (1971/1779) focuses almost exclusively on the increase of material production as a precondition of happiness and the main target of the policy of the state (Schlettwein 1971, 2–3). Therefore, he will highlight the immutable laws of economy and society (1971, 12, in the text no pagination, preface). Happiness consists in consumption of: housing, clothing, and food. Government is to increase these means as much as possible.[7] The first part reiterates the basic tenet of physiocracy right away: the earth, the soil is the sole source of all materials whose possessions make humans happy (woods, flowers, vineyards, minerals, metals, 1971, 6ff.). Mining is only second best because it produces only intermediate products which cannot immediately be consumed. It does not increase the means of subsistence (1971, 220–223).

They can only be found on plots of land whose property is therefore very important (1971, 14). Schlettwein is a growth economist: The more land is cultivated the better for the welfare of human society (1971, 20; 1978, I, 5–7). He does not see any limit or exception to this.[8] Despite his materialist-ecological approach we find no limits to growth arguments at all in his writings, not even when he discusses nonrenewable resources. We only mention this point of view here but he comes back to it again and again. Human work cannot create all these endowments. It can only transform them (1971, 10). For Schlettwein it obviously follows that nature is the only source of wealth and surplus. He does not consider the possible emergence of a service economy with a certain decoupling of welfare and material throughput. It could also be argued that the one cannot do without the other, i.e. that untransformed nature has no value for us or that the natural endowments are abundant and therefore without value at all. In any case, he introduces the main thrust on an intuitive and plausibility basis.

[6]"... dem Personal- und RealEigenthumsRechte der Menschen, und dessen bestmöglichen Benutzung nicht den geringsten Ertrag thun. Daher sind die Abgaben, welche von dem wirklichen Gewinn, den die Natur den Menschen für die Verarbeitung und Benutzung ihrer Kräfte schenket, die einzige Art, die der Ordnung der MenschenRechte gemäs ist. Der reine Gewinn, den die Natur schenkt, ist kein Theil des Vermögens, welches der Mensch schon hat, sondern ein Geschenk, das ihm die Natur zu seinem Vermögen noch hinzusetzt. Wenn also alle Auflagen des Staats auf diesen reinen Gewinn gelegt werden, so wird durch keine das wirkliche Haben, oder Eigenthum der Menschen vermindert, und durch keine die Personfähigkeit des Menschen eingeschränkt. Jeder Mensch behält sein ganzes Eigenthum unverkürzt" (1980, 482–483).

[7]"So besteht dann die ganze Kunst, die Menschen in dieser Welt glücklich zu machen, darinne, dass man die Menge unaufhörlich vergrössere" (1971, 4).

[8]"Nirgends muß ein Stück der Erde, das nicht seiner Natur nach unbrauchbar ist, öde, oder unbenutzt liegen bleiben" (1971, 14–15).

Industry and trade are obviously important but he argues that all of these activities involve resources as a precondition: No trade without goods which consist of material throughput. So the material exploitation of the natural resources is the basis of the productive superstructure. It should be mentioned that we find no discussion of possible technological improvements or the use of knowledge to increase output with less throughput. But he discusses the necessity to cultivate the land in an optimal way (e.g. what the distance of the plants to each other is concerned). He does not consider technological improvements, he only mentions agricultural implements for cultivation and focuses on the necessary manure, the timely plowing, feeding of the cattle in barns, and an intensification of land use by abandoning fallow land. His understanding of cultivation is ecologically sound and sustainable and does not coincide with the modern system of agribusiness, i.e. the use of machines, fertilizers etc.

He deduces straight away that private landownership is absolutely necessary because only completely unlimited or nonattenuated property rights – when the owner reaps all benefits – guarantee the best cultivation (1971, 25). This argument – which includes the assumption that the owner is also the producer or at least the organizer – follows closely the Demsetz thesis in the Property Rights literature.[9] In the tradition of the housefather literature, he describes empirically what the landowner has to take care of. His examples also show that Schlettwein knew very well the production conditions of his time and was not an abstract philosopher of physiocracy, he had a lot of empirical knowledge and practical expertise (see also 1978, I, 159ff.). Those who do not possess land have to work for the landowners and get money or food in exchange for their services (1971, 71). He takes this distribution (owners and nonowners) as given. But he mentions that it contradicts external rights to expropriate the owners (1971, 70–71). He does not discuss what should be done in the case of a class of unproductive landowners; according to his nonviolability theorem vis-à-vis property, we can assume that an expropriation would not be allowed and that educational measures would be proposed by Schlettwein.

As a classical physiocrat he makes clear that what counts for human welfare (immediate consumption or the means for further melioration of the land) is the disposable net surplus (*reiner Ertrag*, 1971, 40), i.e. the value of production minus the material costs of production including the expenses for the landowner.[10] He does not offer a *Tableau Économique* but he describes empirically the interdependence of the different parts of the economy in a society with a moderate division of labor. But the landowner is the key, the main element in the chain of production, the originator because manufacturing can only transform the materials and the increase of a productive population depends on the stock of consumables which originate in the primary land agricultural sector. This fact precludes a policy which is detrimental to the landowners (1971, 88).

[9] "Wer wird sichs aber zum Anliegen machen, die Grundstücke des Erdbodens durch die vollkommenste Bearbeitung zu ihrer höchsten Fruchtbarkeit zu bringen, wenn er nicht das völlige Eigenthumsrecht über dieselbige hat?" (1971, 25).

[10] "Der reine Ertrag des Erdbodens ist das einzige Vermögen, welches zur Bequemlichkeit und zum Vergnügen der Menschen disponibel ist" (1971, 49).

He continues with a strong plea for what he calls free competition. Without any instruments of the toolbox of modern microeconomics he delineates clearly the welfare enhancing effects of free competition (prices measure scarcity, self-interest leads to productive activities which reduce the most pressing scarcities) and the mechanisms of supply and demand (the more suppliers the lower the price, the more demand the higher the price, 1971, 94ff.). Competition always leads to the fullest possible equilibrium between buyers and sellers ("das vollkommenste Gleichgewicht," 1971, 105). Implicitly, he shares the view of the spontaneous market order and a dynamic Austrian analysis of the market process. He rejects all allegations of possible negative consequences of a competitive system and castigates monopolies, and guilds (1971, 109ff.). If we compare A. Smith with Schlettwein, Smith with his 20 reasons for state interference in the price mechanism is an interventionist (Viner 1958).

But in his *Grundveste der Staaten* (1779) we find an important exception of the desirability of free exchange: Land should not be traded like movable objects. In principle, it should not be traded at all. The special quality of land consists in the fact that land offers a never ending yield. If land is included in an exchange process it is only acceptable if the land will/can be bought back. Krebs (1909, 81ff. with Schlettwein's references) explains this contrasting view to Quesnay with his roots in the Germanic law tradition in contrast to the Roman law tradition (Quesnay). Krebs also mentions that Schlettwein comes close to ideas of the land reform movement in Germany which wanted to tax profits originating from landownership (e.g. Damaschke) but which only neglected or criticized him (Krebs 1909, 82–83).

But in the next paragraph he talks about the perfection of the cultural order. He evaluates the production of the land and argues that it is only optimal, when (if?) it is dedicated for the increase of food, clothing, and housing; the production of luxuries e.g. food for dogs or tobacco is wrong for two reasons: It is detrimental to bodily or spiritual health and/or it reduces land to feed and cloth and house more humans or to feed and house and cloth them in a better way (1971, 125ff.; he comes back to this questions several times, see e.g. 1971, 272–286). He leaves open the priority question: Is it more important to increase the population or should much be invested in the increase of land productivity or in the (although limited) affluence per capita? It is clear that he does not share the increase of population as a major aim as in the older cameralists. The wealth of nations consists in abundance of the products of nature.

Implicitly he proposes to focus on all three aspects mentioned above. But in any case here we find a twist in his free enterprise philosophy because he negates the consumer and producer freedom and sovereignty in a certain sense. The book does not give an answer how to deal with this, he at least does not make proposals how the state could guide the production processes in the right directions. In a long part of the book he delineates the best practice of the landowner (what to produce, how to plan, accounting etc., 1971, 145ff.). His many recommendations need not be repeated here. They make clear that he has a rational planning landowner in mind.

He also criticizes the bad habit to cut into pieces the plots of the landowners beyond the acceptable and efficient minimum (by hereditary customs etc.) with the consequence that more and more free small peasant families have to give up. Schlettwein does not have big agricultural estates in mind as the optimal agricultural structure but plots of 12 *Morgen* of land as a minimum.[11] His policy is typical: He rejects a direct policy intervention even in this important respect because it contradicts the holiness of property and would be a violent interference. An elucidated education (*hinlänglicher lichtvoller Unterricht*, 1971, 103) should take place with the eventual result that the citizens will refrain from splitting up the land and will deliberately and by conviction ask for a respective law (1971, 202–205). This attitude demonstrates the surprising liberal and democratic stance of Schlettwein's thinking.

What the value theory is concerned, he vividly defended the physiocratic point of view: Only nature is productive in the sense of generating usable matter and surplus. Human labor (manufacturing) can only transform matter but it cannot add any net value to it.[12] Labor cannot change the value of a natural product. The question is if a logical link exists between the fact that obviously matter cannot be produced by labor and the allegation that the transformation of matter does not add value to a product. For Schlettwein, one follows from the other. He argues further that in the processes of working, processing, and treatment of matter, other natural products (means of production and transformation) are used up.

The total sum of natural products is reduced in the melioration process. The value of manufactured goods includes the necessary food and other necessities for the workers (1978, I, 110). The increase in value by the transformation of the form of the natural products is equivalent to the value of the additional material which is used up in the process of transformation. The total final value has not increased by the addition of labor in the process of transformation but it is simply the addition of the values of the material products which have been combined in the working process.[13] Tribe mentions, one of "the standard criticisms [was]: that to make a distinction between productive and sterile labor was invalid and impracticable" (Tribe 1988, 127). This was also the main point in an anonymous critique of Schlettwein (reprinted in Schlettwein 1772, 5–62): Without work (e.g. the extraction of) natural products have no value for us, without the plow the harvest would be much less so

[11] A *Morgen* is a unit of measurement comprising between 2.500 and 3.400 square meters (Langenscheidts Handwörterbuch Englisch. Part II. Berlin: Langenscheidt, 2001, 1329).

[12] It is clear "daß die Menschenkraft nicht ein Gran von Materie machen kann, und daß sie sonst nichts vermag, als die Figuren, Zusammensetzungen und Mischungen, welche die Natur ihren Producten gegeben hat, zu verändern, und durch neue Trennungen und Verbindungen andere Gestallten herzustellen" (1971, 228–229).

[13] "Soviel kostet also diese Form, oder soviel ist sie werth, als die ganze im Fasoniren, und während des Fasonirens verzehrte, und verbrauchte Materiemasse beträgt. Es wird demnach durch die Kunstindustrie kein Werth hervorgebracht, der nicht vorher schon ganz da war. Es wird nur der Werth aller der Producte, welche der Künstler und Fabrikant während seiner Arbeit verbraucht, zusammengerechnet, und auf den durch all diesen Aufwand hergestellten Effect, auf die Form, oder Facon des Fabrikats, geschlagen. Der Werth … war vorher in den Materien da, welche der Fabrikant durchs Fasoniren, oder während des Fasonirens wirklich verbraucht" (1971, 233–234).

that the manufacturing (plow producing) sector is also value enhancing. The author asks why the value contribution of the peasant does not consist in an increase in value determined by the necessary food etc. he needs for his productive activities. This would lead to a general theory of labor value including the work of peasants which would have no superiority in comparison with labor in manufacturing.

Schlettwein holds an objective theory of value. The value of a product is the sum of primary goods necessary for its production, including labor inputs. He does not ask in how far the mere material of products and the valuational aspect of the form transformation must include use value aspects which are missing in his analysis. He puts in one the view of the first (matter is indestructible) and the second law of thermodynamics (the quality of matter matters for us). He also holds a certain equilibrium theory of the different compartments of production: If the industrial superstructure becomes dominant, too much primary products are used up for the process of transformation and the prices rise. But he has no consistent theory of prices and distribution in this respect (1978, I, 122–123). This is not to say that he holds that the activities of the sterile class is unnecessary, it only says that the sterile class does not produce surplus (1978, I, 231).

He shared the typical physiocratic class distinction, a class of landowners, a class of tenants, and a sterile class (1978/1772, I, 207). It coincides exactly with Quesnays *classe des propriétaires, classe productive,* and *classe sterile*. The sterile class includes the merchants, the artisans, traders, storekeepers, craftsmen, manufacturer, and artists. He sometimes mentions the other parts of the transforming classes ("aller übrigen Glieder der zehrenden Classe", 1978, I, 249).

But he was fully aware of the German special constellation in which the first two classes were not distinguished in reality (1978, I, 207). It can be asked if the nondifferentiation of the two classes matter or not. According to his single tax proposal production and consumption is not reduced because the landowner does not spend some part of his rent which would stay idle and which could be a danger for a thriving economy (a leakage or circulation effect; he calls it *Hinterhaltsfond*, 1978, I, 227). If the tax is paid by the peasant/landowner: Does this mean that the invested amount in the following year will be reduced, does the small peasant also have a saving motive? If not, does this affect the single tax approach?

If the separation exists, three reasons are in favor of the single tax. First, all users of natural products have to pay according to the amount they consume. Second, it will not reduce the needed necessary infrastructure investments by the landowners (if the tax is not too high), and third, it does not reduce the property of anybody because only the donations of nature are taxed. Schlettwein also puts forward a practical reason: cheating is almost impossible when immovable land and production thereupon is taxed. It cannot be hidden, reduces the enforcement costs, and does not require distrust of the government against the citizens.[14]

[14] "Es sind also bey dieser Auflage ihrer Natur nach nicht leicht Hintergehungen und Betrügereyen von Seiten der Unterthanen möglich, und die Regierung bedarf keiner Maaßreglen, die ein Mißtrauen gegen die Bürger zu erkennen geben" (1978, I, 258).

Practically, a land register should be developed in which different forms of land (wood, vineyards, farmland, meadows etc.) should be distinguished and be classified in three quality categories (good, medium, low quality). The tax therefore depends on the form of land, its quality, and the square meters (1978, I, 156–258). All 6–9 years a new quality classification should take place considering the upgrading of the quality due to melioration activities. He does not discuss the potential discouragement effect when a plot of land is taxed higher as a result of melioration and he leaves open what happens if no cultivation takes place. According to his individual property and individual rights approach the state should not force the owners what to do with their land. But his single tax would have the effect of a taxation of the substance if the land is not cultivated as usual. This conflicts with his idea of liberty and potentially with his interdiction of the sale of land.

But it can be asked if a value added tax does not also fulfill the main functions. Schlettwein argues that it does not because it would necessarily increase the final price (and hurt the consumers) or the prices for the peasants would be reduced (1978, I, 259ff.). His neutrality assumption only holds when the landowners are not able to increase the lease to keep their normal rate of rent. This may be a plausible assumption under certain conditions (abundance of land) but his discussion of the small plots of land and the poverty in Baden among the rural population does not coincide with this assumption. But taken that the landowners cannot shift the tax on other groups or classes: In how can he argue that the burden of the taxes is distributed equally among all producers and consumers if they do not share the burden in the form of price increases?

With regard to the net surplus (rent) this makes no difference for him. The functional role of the landowners remains to improve and meliorate the infrastructure (drainage etc.) and pursue the administration (1978, I, 208). It was Quesnay's hunch that only larger estates will generate a net surplus. In Schlettwein's opinion this would already be possible if the plot of land would suffice to give the tenant and his family enough work all over the year. His practical proposals for the peasants demonstrate that he did not have huge capital investments in mind; instead he proposed for example the cultivation of clover instead of tobacco etc. In our view it is not evident, as has often been remarked in the secondary literature (Gerteis 1989, 106), that Schlettwein wrongly and mechanically applied the physiocratic system which was at best adequate for the French economy to the very different German system. His practical proposals (see below) were not prima facie incompatible with the more modest development of agriculture and a different class structure.

The question pops up how profits in manufacturing can emerge at all. Here, Schlettwein makes a mistake in the sense of a fallacy of misplaced concreteness because he links the question on the level of a value theory with a simple supply and demand argument: Profit depends on the number of demanders and the respective demand prices which may be higher than the production prices (1971, 238).

But how is the real value determined in contrast to the potentially diverging market prices? In a later chapter he deals with this intricate problem. The "true internal price" (*der wahre innere Preiß*, 1971, 300; Quesnays *prix naturel*) is determined by the plot of land which is necessary to produce the natural product. The value of cattle for example depends on the corn which is necessary to produce and feed the cattle, measured in square meters of land. He does not discuss the question of technical progress: If by an invention the necessary space of land is reduced, will, as a consequence, the value (of e.g. cattle) be reduced too?[15] He further argues that the inner real price of a commodity and the market price (Quesnay's *prix courant*) may deviate (even strongly) depending on the supply and demand situation.[16]

He has neither a time period analysis (short vs. long period) nor does he consider the (Marxian) transformation problem, i.e. how the values of prices interact and equal out in the total system. In contrast to Quesnay and most other physiocrats, who put a major emphasis on the use value, he does also not really consider the relationship between value in use and value in exchange.

In this vain, he also supports a liberal foreign exchange policy. It makes no sense to produce commodities in the confines of the state and suppress imports when they have an absolute cost advantage due to the better respective local production advantages (Heckscher-Ohlin), especially with regard to a better resource base (1971, 252–257). He also rejects export restrictions (1971, 262–263). The basis for free exchange and trade is the affluence of goods which are directed towards the consumer who will experience the greatest pleasure if the exchange is not enforced but is based on mutual interest and advantage. Unhampered exchange is therefore a necessary precondition for the greatest happiness (1971, 290–292). The same holds for unrestricted credits (and drafts) with spur growth and the fixing of the interest rate by the creditor (1971, 354–355). In contrast, A. Smith (and with a different argument Quesnay) proposed to fix the interest rate at 5% for reasons of adverse selection.

The tenth chapter deals with money in the form of gold, silver, and other metals (1971, 327ff.). They have an intrinsic value and practical properties to serve as money and he defines the essence of money in modern functional terms. The amount of money or precious metals is no indicator of substantial richness (contra certain mercantilist allegations) because it cannot be consumed. Like trade it is a secondary phenomenon (1971, 331–333). A money maximization policy by the state is obvious nonsense to him. He is fully aware of the need of an increase of the money supply in a growing economy. He makes a distinction between price increases due to real commodity scarcities and a general increase due to the increase in the supply of money (1971, 347–348). This shows that he knows the basic relationships formulated in the quantity equation of money. He even mentions the effects of the velocity of circulation. To keep the economy liquid with money gold and silver should only be used as money (1971, 353).

---

[15] "Alles also, was ein Gegenstand des Handels werden kann, erfordert zu seiner Werdung immer nur einen bestimmten District Landes, auf welchem es wächst, oder welcher den Aufwand giebt, der auf die Hervorbringung gemacht werden muß. Diese Größe des Erdstriches, der auf die Entstehung, oder Wirklichwerdung einer Waare gebraucht wird, bestimmt den wahren inneren Werth, oder den sogenannten kostenden Preiß der Waare" (1971, 301).

[16] It is evident, "daß der VerkaufsPreiß einer Waare von ihrem innern Werthe oder kostenden Preiße sehr abweichen kann und muß, je nachdem sich die Nachfrage nach derselbigen vermehrt, oder vermindert, und die Menge der Waaren zu- oder abnimmt" (1971, 304).

After the exposition of the major economic phenomena he switches to the customary and moral code (1971, 383ff.). Three virtues are essential for a happy human life: Justice (interestingly only defined as not to take away the private property of others!), benevolence (to use our own property only in those ways that also help to increase the property of others or to make their use of property more optimal), and thirdly wisdom (insight into the working order of the productive forces, 1971, 385–386). He also sometimes mentions the Kantian imperative as a general behavioral device (1987, II, 85). These virtues, today often described as social capital, are also essential for the practical function of a system of liberty. A long criticism of ostentation and conspicuous consumption and display (a dishonesty based on cheating by impression management) which undermines our potential to work and feel naturally follows (1971, 389). He calls goods which are aimed at impression management imagined goods. Instead of investing in these positional goods, consumption goods should be produced to support the life amenities of people.[17]

Schlettwein is an ardent supporter of free trade and the maximization of production but only with regard to primary production and immediate basic and elementary consumption goods in a rural environment. He rejects luxury (e.g. gold and silver décor, 1971, 406) and relational goods. Luxury tries to irritate, confuse, and deceive our senses and in so far contradicts the search for truth and honesty. His ideal society has a modest consumption level and should prefer the support of the primary life processes and the increase of a well fed and housed population. He does not discuss the problem what should be done if the production of luxury goods would generate the highest profit. As a child of the enlightenment he beliefs in and proposes a good education and contact with nature which should prevent wrong orientations (1971, 415ff.). Dancing (!), theater, and card playing should be prevented, religion should be supported (1971, 427) because our soul needs an idea to prevent vanity and the lust of the senses.

But in Schlettwein (1978, II, 221ff.), the rejection of luxury is much more nuanced. The basic scepticism against the motivational forces behind luxury remains the same but he nevertheless considers luxury in eating and drinking as benevolent because it at least improves the income of the peasants. Also luxury in clothing (and housing) is not bad because the workers' income is partially spent on agricultural products. But these forms of luxury should not include gold and silver because this would reduce the money supply. He criticizes the luxury with horses and other animals which must be fed with agricultural products and necessarily reduce the space for the cultivation of products for human consumption. His arguments show that he had a very moderate and not strict attitude against luxury.

The next chapter deals with the political order and the needs and deeds of the government and the authorities (*Obrigkeit*, 1971, 435). A government is necessary because most of today's people exhibit vanity and lust and a lack of moral orientation,

[17]"Der Werth, den eine blose Sinneslust kostet, und der, welchen die Eitelkeit zu ihrer Befriedigung erfordert, konnten ein Menschenleben von seinem Untergange retten, oder noch für ein Menschenleben Materialien zubereiten" (1971, 398).

the function of the authorities is to correct these tendencies. Schlettwein does not ask in how far this is possible, i.e. where the superior moral qualities of the rulers come from. He firmly states that their only function is to increase the real human happiness, no separate reason exists for its existence (1971, 438). As in his earlier text he differentiates between the judicative, the executive, and the protective powers. Later, he also mentions independent judges and due process of law (1971, 548ff.). Interestingly no analysis of the different forms of government (democracy, monarchy etc.) and a delineation of the best governmental system takes place. But, we know from other writings of Schlettwein that he was in favor of a monarchy (Gerteis 1983, 190–194).

The idea of a balance of power does not exist in the narrower sense. The protection of property is a major function. The true laws are universal and not dependent on time and location of the state (1971, 448). His detailed proposals like enough space for fresh air notwithstanding (but concrete legal-institutional proposals are mostly missing): He describes a state which delivers (basic) education for all, the delivering of infrastructure (also in the health sector), the protection of property, a judicial system, and (the control of) precautionary measures against fire etc. (1971, 537–538; 1978, I, 238).

In contrast, e.g. to the French physiocrats he puts a strong emphasis on the support of the poor. Schlettwein had open eyes to the concerns for the fourth estate. Those who could not work should be recorded in a register of the poor so that the means of support could be planned in the public budget. The poor should be dealt with according to the idea of help for work (1971, 511–513), this includes financial aid and the distribution even of cattle among the financially distressed small peasants.[18] He also envisages a public sector where poor people who cannot find work are employed (mainly natural melioration activities like digging dykes, 1971, 513).[19] Finally, those who cannot work should be supported (not with money but) with elementary goods like food (1971, 516). We have presented longer citations in the footnotes because they show that Schlettwein was not a simple marketer but an early ardent supporter of a state with strong social commitments. Without showing this in detail most of the assessments of the secondary literature

[18] "Man muß ihnen Klee und andere Sämereyen, welche sie zur Bestellung ihrer Felder nöthig haben, vorschießen; man muß ihnen das Vieh verschaffen, welches sie zur Düngung brauchen und von welchem sie zur Haußhaltung verschiedene Nutzungen gewinnen können" (Grundveste 1779, cited in Krebs 1909, 98).

[19] "... so lange muß die Regierung selbst große Pläne und Operationen veranstalten, bey deren Ausführung sie die Hände der Armen anwenden, und ihnen ihren Unterhalt rechlich verschaffen kann, Straßen machen lassen, weitläuffigste morastige Distrikte austrocknen lassen, große öde Erdstriche umreuten, und zu fruchtbaren Feldern machen lassen, den großen Flüssen womöglich ihre schädliche Gänge nehmen und bessere Wege anweisen lassen, Uferbefestigungen und Dämme an großen reißenden Strömen anlegen lassen, Uferbefestigungen und Dämme an großen reißenden Strömen anlegen lassen, Flüsse schiffbar machen, und Canäle graben lassen, öffentliche nützliche Gebäude aufführen lassen. Dies sind Werke, der Staatsverwaltung und großen Landespolizey, durch welche viele tausend Arme, die sonst ohne Brod und in Elend leben müssen, beschäftigt und ernähret werden können" (Grundveste 1779, cited in Krebs 1909, 98).

do not get the spirit of his thinking and interpret his oeuvre wrongly as a simple repetition of the French physiocratic system. Quesnay for example only supported aid in the form of guaranteeing the bare minimum level of subsistence. As mentioned, Schlettwein always argued in favor of the lower classes. Even in his last publication (Wider Aufruhr und Empörung, 1791) he asks for a balance between the classes and castigates a situation in which the rich consume luxuries and the bulk of the population lives in misery.[20] His approach was closer to the German social policy approach than to a Manchester liberal attitude.

Finally, he discusses the revenues of the state (1971, 576ff.). Again an obvious fundamental rule exists which implies that only those taxes should be levied in which the interest of the ruler to increase the wealth of the population prevails. Prima facie it is not easy to say which tax conforms to this (his explanation on page 593 is not convincing). The state should not get revenue or income by owning and using public property (lakes, land, and other domains) because then this property cannot be owned privately by citizens (1971, 583ff.). Also regalia are not allowed because the authorities takes away a part of formerly private property (1971, 591), it contradicts the unlimited disposal of private property. According to his physiocratic approach wherever the taxes may be levied, finally the landowner has to pay the tax because he is the possessor of land/nature, he is the only creator of net wealth and surplus (1971, 594).

His first argument of a direct taxation, i.e. a taxation of the landowner is that the enforcement costs are lower (his arguments are again not really convincing, 1971, 615–616). Indirect taxation, i.e. taxes on consumption or a tax for the agricultural producers, the peasants, leads to higher prices and will reduce their disposal of goods and their happiness. In so far via the direct method the tax only refers to a part of the net surplus. Schlettwein who has no value theory of distribution cannot answer the question why in this case the prices of the agricultural products will not rise. He mentions that the tax should be too high because otherwise the landowner would have less incentive to improve the use of the land (*Lust zu Culturverbesserungen*, 1971, 619). The lower the tax (he discusses 20 or 25%, see 971, 619), the higher the net surplus and the higher the income of the people *and* the ruler (1971, 619–620). We have here some Laffer curve argument.

But the more important seems to be that this contradicts the thesis of the superiority of a single tax on the landowners and their receipt of the net surplus because, however the tax is levied: In either case no neutrality or impediment condition holds. He can only argue that if the tax on the surplus is not high the same expenses of melioration on the side of the landowner will take place. But this is only an (empirical?) assumption. It can also be said that a landowner who gets the net surplus by nature owns this surplus because it originates from his land and may be partially due to

[20] "Wo dieses arme nothleydende unruhige Volk bey seinen nagenden Sorgen immer noch mehr gedrückt wird, und dagegen sieht, wie unter den Großen des Landes lauter Herrlichkeit und Freuden untereinander abwechseln, und dort die Früchte des Schweißes der Armen in Wollust und Üppigkeit und eitler Pracht unsinnig verschwendet werden, so empört sich schon im Herzen des Volkes ein Unwille wider diesen Zustand der Dinge, in welchen die Waage der gesellschaftlichen Verhältnisse gar zu tief zu seinem Nachtheil niedersinkt" (cited in Krebs 1909, 102).

his melioration activities. In so far it is also theft and an appropriation of private property by the state. We see here that Schlettwein never elaborated a deeper version of a physiocratic theory of value and that he consequently never could derive a well-reasoned theory of just and efficient taxation. In so far, it is not surprising that critics asked if not "the notion of a single tax on a net product would result in increased burdens for the peasant and a general increase in prices" (Tribe 1988, 125–131, here 127).

In Schlettwein (1978), we find another argument for the single tax (Quesnay's *impôt unique*): It divides the burden of the tax equally on the different classes.[21] Since there is no transformation of products and no consumption without material agricultural products, nobody can evade the tax. In our view this is a very different argument compared with the reasoning presented above because there it was implied that the single tax only reduces some net surplus (the rent) of the landlord which has no real function for the production process in society and which is a profit donated by nature which does not reduce anybody's else's property or income. It should be mentioned in addition with Krebs (1909, 94–95) that Schlettwein modified his ideas on taxation in his last writing(s), where he proposed to levy a kind of general income and/ or general property tax (a fifth or tenth of the yearly income).[22] The tax should be moderate and the tax payer must be able to pay it without problems. He leaves open what the same standard means in taxation. This shows that he did not think through his alternative taxation principles very deeply at the end of his life. He does not discuss if this was a late temporary different emphasis or if he was convinced that the physiocratic single tax was a mistake.

The Three Villages Experiment in Baden

The experiment took place in the years 1772 and 1773. Only very few well informed accounts exist (see e.g. Emminghaus 1872; and Krebs 1909, 106ff. who also makes full use of the hitherto completely neglected two articles by Schlettwein in his journal *Neues Archiv für den Menschen und Bürger* in 1786 and 1788).

---

[21] "Es trifft aber diese Auflage, welche unmittelbar von dem reinen Ertrage des Landes erhoben wird, alle Classen der Einwohner des Staates ohne Unterschied ihres Geschlechtes, ihres Alters, ihrer Lebensart, und ihrer Bestimmungen. Nicht der Landmann allein ist es, der diesen Imposten bezahlt: nein! die ganze bürgerliche Gesellschaft entrichtet diese Auflage" (1978, I, 249).

[22] The public authority "erhebt die nöthigen Staatseinkünfte von den jährlichen wahren Einkünften der Unterthanen nach einem gleichen Maaßstabe, so daß durchgehends der 5. oder 10. oder ein anderer beliebiger Theil dieses jährlichen wahren Einkommens, von Einem wie von dem Andern Theilhaber desselbigen entrichtet werden muß, und daß also die jährlichen Einkünfte des Staats nur nach dem Maße anwachsen, als jener proportionierte Theil des Einkommens größer wird … wenn sie keinem ihrer Unthertanen eine Last auflegt, der nicht Kraft hat, diese Last zu tragen und nicht überzeugt ist, daß dieselbige um seines Wohlstandes willen nöthig ist, und wenn sie die Staatsbeyträge unter allen ihren Unthertanen in dem gerechtesten Verhältnis zu ihrem Vermögen nach dem vollkommenen gleichen Maaßstabe vertheilt" (Wider Aufruhr und Empörung, 1791, cited in Krebs 1909, 94).

Schlettwein and the Margrave converted to physiocracy circa in 1768. In these years many people left Baden for the new world, especially Pennsylvania. Also many people of Dietlingen near Pforzheim who fell into poverty and asked the prince in the system of serfdom for permission to leave. This was rejected but an investigation was set up by the government to investigate the reasons for the impoverishment of the 1,000 inhabitants. Schlettwein who was in close contact with the prince at that time was asked what should be done. He proposed to make a historical-statistical visitation and investigate the land, people, the cultivation methods, and extend this analysis to the past to get an historical overview. He was asked to execute the investigation by the Margrave.

Using the available data the yield from 1733–1768 was analyzed. The exact data for corn, wine, rye, barley, oats etc. can be found in Schlettwein's article. After this collection of data Schlettwein started personal investigations of the inhabitants of Dietlingen with a catalog of 25 questions. The questions included: marriage, the number of children, the profession, the number of cattle, the type of land and agricultural product, the available manure, the need and expenses for the clothing of the family, the division of labor, the debts, the need for firewood, etc. The investigation had shown that the village was in a lamentable situation: high debts, low yields, and no possibility to change this circumstance.

He continued to ask the superiors of the village certain questions: How can the high debts be explained? The answer was that the soil had by nature a very low quality and the people did not use enough manure and because they have not practiced to cultivate, e.g. clover, they had to pay a lot for fodder for the animals. The second question refers to the young age of marriages and the early birth of children which makes the self-provisioning of the young families difficult. Another question asked for the state of mind of the people, if they often were careless and sluggish. The answer was that this mentality aspects were not so common, but more important was ignorance and ineptitude. The question if the interest rate was still too high was rejected.

Next, Schlettwein made an inspection of the territory and the land. He found out that the cultivated land was often located in a hilly environment and that the soil was washed away during rainfall. The fields were lacking manure because the cattle were on the pasture all over the summer. The population had increased tremendously. The taxes and other duties were high, many different institutions asked for tributes. They had often to deliver statue labor whenever the rulers wanted it. Most were not able even to pay their annual interest payments.

Schlettwein saw that a lot of different problems intermingled and that the inhabitants could not solve them alone. His action plan which was accepted by the Margrave included the following aspects: The number of cattle had to be increased; clover should be cultivated; the fallow land should be abolished; melioration of the meadows; the abolition of many diverse taxes and the introduction of a general tax on the yield; abolition of soccage services in kind by a soccage in the form of money payments; unlimited freedom of exchange and commerce for the village; and he recommended the planting of chestnut trees (for the vineyards) and a plantation of trees. Finally, the very small holdings should be abolished.

In 1769 Schlettwein started the plan to increase the cattle in the village. Therefore, he collected together with three women private money for the project. They bought twelve young cattle and gave it to some inhabitants who were not allowed to sell it and who had to introduce some of the other proposals mentioned above. He also wrote an appeal to the public of Karlsruhe to support the project. He also payed money to those who helped to clear some stony districts in Dietlingen to make the cultivation of potatoes possible. In addition, he tried to establish a regular relief fund to loan out money with a low interest rate but only to those who improve their methods of cultivation.

The experiment shows that Schlettwein was not unpractical and dogmatic, and at first all started well. But a lot of negative propaganda was uttered by the many enemies of Schlettwein at the court. Nevertheless, when he left the Margrave, the experiment was well under way and it was even extended for three more years in 1774. When Schlettwein left, the Margrave himself became the organizer of the project. But it did not develop as expected. He asked for help but Mirabeau only had very abstract remarks to offer and Schlettwein's successor became Charles de Butré, a man with leanings to mysticism. Especially in the villages Bahlingen and Theningen where the experiment started later in 1771 a lot of resistance emerged so that they finished it in 1776 accompanied by rather negative expert's opinion of Schlettwein's enemy Schlosser.

In Dietlingen, envy and malevolence popped up and a group which was against the reforms came at the head of the local council. In 1790 a petition of the rural commune asked vividly to abandon what they called the Schlettwein system. It should be mentioned that at this time not only did the Margrave had lost his faith in the physiocratic creed but that Schlettwein himself had changed his opinion on the single tax and would have changed the single tax idea but not the other reasonable proposals which had no competent proponent and organizer any more after Schlettwein's demission.

The physiocratic single tax was indeed the main problem of the plan. The Margrave was fully aware of this point what his repeated questions to Mirabeau confirm: Is it reasonable to tax exclusively the yield of small peasants (the other question was if a law could forbid the division of the land in the process of inheritance). In fact the land was divided into different uses (fields, vineyards etc.) and qualities. This was done by one person despite the high information and time costs of the development of a (n in fact very imprecise) land register. But the main problem was that the total amount of the single tax was equivalent to the tax income before the single tax was introduced, i.e. it was relatively high. A second point was that it had to be paid in money whereas some quasi-taxes in the past could be paid in kind or in the form of work. A third problem was that the tax had to be paid annually at a time and not in rates. Because of the still existing late feudal social and political structure and the relatively underdeveloped infrastructure, the freedom of commerce did not change much. Although the taxes on beverages did not exist anymore the prices for beer were the same (for a detailed analysis see Emminghaus 1872, 37ff.). So the Margraves doubts concerning the introduction of a single tax in a relatively undeveloped rural economy at the advent of a monetarization of exchanges were justified (see also the comment by Oncken1902, 410ff.). Emminghaus (1872, 62) raised the interesting question if the experiment would have succeeded with a less strict application while retaining the basic idea (a more moderate taxation, partly in kind, at more than one date, a more accurate land register etc.). After the reintroduction of the old system indirect taxes, value added taxes, tolls and fees were introduced and a substantially reduced tax on the yield of land continued to exist.

Conclusions

Our discussion of two main contributions of Schlettwein (and few additions from other works) has shown that the rather negative comments on him by his contemporaries, Schumpeter, and also by Roscher (1874; whose relatively uniformed comments in have been omitted here) may not be justified in their severity. Schlettwein was not read by most of his critics (including Roscher).

He shared some points with most other physiocrats (single tax, free competition etc.); he also set very specific emphases, e.g. with respect to social policy and the education of the lower strata of society. He also practically tried to influence economic policy. He supported a system of laissez-faire but with major reservations and extensions. He never thought that most problems will be solved after the establishment of a general system of natural liberty and exchange. He also demonstrates that a natural rights approach need not be indifferent to social concerns. Unfortunately, no discussion of his value theory takes place in any of these comments (this also holds for Krebs (1909) the best work on Schlettwein). Before we resume his particular physiocratic approach some general remarks on physiocracy in general may be warranted.

Maybe one of the most surprising aspects of physiocracy is the intermingling of the old and the new, the feudal heritage and agricultural supremacy and ascendant capitalism, a liberal exchange economy and a natural rights philosophy with inalienable personal rights. He has an interesting intermediate position because he for example criticizes feudal statute labor and services in kind because the subjects have no motivation to work efficiently and are compelled to work when the work on their own fields is needed most, but he does not castigate comparable taxes in money (1978, II, 11–38).

As we have seen, we also find these ambiguities in Schlettwein who never put into question the feudal structures of his time. As Marx pointed out the physiocrats never questioned the division of classes, especially the division between the landlords and the tenants. They interpreted their historical specificities as transhistorical configurations which operated according to general or universal laws of economy and society.

Marx correctly points out their ambiguity: It directly legitimizes an agrarian based feudalism but at the same time undermines it by introducing the logic of equivalent and market exchanges (Marx 1974/1862–1863, 23). In the original version, the emergence of surplus was in a certain sense based on observation: The tenant received an income, a subsistence wage, the production of nature (the growing of crops etc.) was free and the landlord received as a rent the difference between the subsistence wage of the tenant and the value of the total product of the land.

In Schlettwein, we found neither a subsistence wage (the iron law) nor a (Malthusian) law of population increase which usually was combined in the literature. This may be due to the "underdeveloped" situation in the German countries at his time which were characterized by small peasant farms in which both laws did not hold. But Schlettwein followed the typical classification scheme of the physiocrats, i.e. the classes of the landowners, the productive tenants, and the transforming class (the *classe stérile*). But, he was fully aware that in Germany the first two classes were not separated.

This may also be a reason why Schlettwein's value theory is very deficient in many respects. When he argues that the value of a product is due to the necessary space of land it may be asked in how far, for example: (more or less dispersed) minerals in the ground can be measured accordingly. Another problem occurs when the exchange value is unilaterally determined by the increase of matter (Marx 1974, 33). How to deal with technological, gardening, and planning activities which increase the productivity of the ground? The value problem emerged but was not resolved. Schlettwein's analysis is much less theoretical than e.g. Quesnay's, it is more descriptive although he presents a well-rounded description of the input and output relationships of the different classes (1978, I, 214ff.). But he cannot be called a vulgar economist because he also accepted – and this is the great theoretical achievement of the physiocratic school – that the economy (and the value problem) have to be understood from the background of production (instead of the sphere of circulation) leaving aside accidental political, cultural, or historical accidents. But they could not precisely show that their law of the emergence of surplus was correct in its strictness.

As Quesnay already argued a net product will only occur when a certain minimum productivity is achieved, otherwise the agricultural product would at best cover the subsistence wage. Schlettwein gives hundreds of pages rules on how to cultivate the land in order to increase the surplus. Cultivation, planned labor, and knowledge therefore play a major role. The landowner would by itself get no agricultural product without the work (planning, energy and effort, knowledge) of the tenant. In so far it is admitted that labor in a certain sense "produces" value.

It is an open question in how far the liberal laissez-faire attitude is necessarily connected with the value theory of the physiocrats. Marx argues that because manufacturing only changes the forms it may be left undirected but this argument is not convincing in our view (Marx 1974, 23).

Schlettwein's laissez-faire attitude was deeply embedded into his Christian creed. The laws of nature were given by god. He combined it with the belief in enlightened reason. He supported a religion based on reason. Society could not exist without a major idea for our soul which also would be a strong basis for the necessary social capital. The maximization of the satisfaction of endless material needs was not the final aim of the economy but a well balanced interplay of moderate affluence and an increase in population in a growing economy with an increase in the elementary need dimensions (food, housing etc.).

But, he did not see any limits or reasons for limits of growth in general; the natural growth processes he had in mind were mainly focused on renewable resources with the exception of e.g. minerals. Although the manufacturing sector only plays a transforming role, Schlettwein – in distinction to many other physiocrats – accepted the important role of industry in the overall growth process. His anthropology is balanced: We have animalistic drives and instincts but also the capacity to reason and plan and control our ambitions. The drives should be and can be controlled by reason as an expression of moral liberty. Self-love and the drive to survive are normal but moral egotism is not.

According to Schlettwein the human soul is disoriented by (too much) sensual impressions. Therefore, luxury production should be prevented and the average standard of consumption should be focused on the necessities to prevent vanity and emulation. But he is not against any consumption beyond the minimum. The final aim is to cultivate the personality which includes the concern for the fate of others.

Obviously, Schlettwein's reference to the natural law tradition did not aim at a critique of a religious anchoring of social theory (as in Locke). But like most defenders of an *ordre naturel* he believed in its universal validity. The natural rights focus on the negative rights of freedom the individual has a very strong position with regard to the rights and duties of the authorities. Surprisingly, he does not forcefully castigate the feudal political dependencies. But any ruler can only act in a narrow margin of discretion because his natural rights approach does not know a collective interest or a conception of the common good beyond the happiness of the individual. The prohibition to expropriate private property and the strict limits to tax show that the ruler has the role of a public servant and not the authority to pursue his own aims and goals (wars, population policy, commodity exchange controls, the accumulation of species etc.).

Schlettwein supports a minimal state in a feudal and monarchical environment. But he was not at all a minimalist what social policy is concerned. In contrast to Quesnay and to a naïve invisible hand assumption of the benevolent working of the market mechanism, he advocated a nuanced three tier social policy to prevent poverty and misery (for those who could not work, those who could work in public institutions and those who need financial support). Realistically, he did not believe in an overall lifting all boats development. This aspect is missing in Gerteis' (1983, 174–178) description of Schlettwein's economic liberal conception which deviates from modern neoliberal concepts.

From a modern ecological viewpoint, the basic view of the physiocrats is very advanced because they see the economy as a process of material throughput that matters. There is no doubt that the natural process of photosynthesis is the basis for all life and human reproduction, the laws of thermodynamics cannot be discussed away (Daly and Farley 2004). The care for the land and a sustainable form of cultivation are the survival questions of this century, modern manufacturing is not a sterile activity but maybe endangering (for the present catastrophic state of our planet earth see Fischer and Wiegandt (2005)). Some argue that the survival of the human species is only possible in small peasant communities (Bahro 1987).

The physiocrats at least propose to change the emphasis and have a major concern for land, i.e. the environment. The physiocrats did not see the ecological constraints but they had a simpler life in mind and they castigated luxury fevers. The last essence of value for them is the land necessary for producing things.

Today, we discuss the ecological footprint (see Wackernagel et al. 2005) which is a parallel unit to measure human activities in units of square meters of land. It is based on physical units only. It measures our consumption of the natural resources. The ecological footprint could also be used for a deep ecological tax reform in the sense of a single tax. An activity or consumption good would be only taxed according to its footprint. Practical proposals for a sustainable Germany have therefore an implicit affinity with a physiocratic worldview.

References

Bahro R (1987) Logik der Rettung. Weitbrecht, Stuttgart

Blaich F (1983) Der Beitrag der deutschen Physiokraten für die Entwicklung der Wirtschaftswissenschaft von der Kameralistik zur Nationalökonomie. In: Scherf H (ed) Studien zur Entwicklung der ökonomischen Theorie. Duncker and Humblot, Berlin, pp 9–36

Borel A (1923) Die deutschen Physiokraten. Freiburg

Braunreuther K (1955) Über die Bedeutung der physiokratischen Bewegung in Deutschland in der zweiten Hälfte des 18. Jahrhunderts. Wissenschaftliche Zeitschrift der Humboldt Universität zu Berlin. Gesellschafts- und sprachwissenschaftliche Reihe, V,1. Berlin

Daly HE, Farley J (2004) Ecological economics. Island Press, Washington

Emminghaus A (1872) Carl Friedrichs von Baden physiokratische Verbindungen, Bestrebungen und Versuche, ein Beitrag zur Geschichte des Physiokratismus. Jahrbücher für Nationalökonomie und Statistik 19:1–63

Fischer EP, Wiegandt K (eds) (2005) Die Zukunft der Erde: Was verträgt unser Planert noch? Fischer, Frankfurt

Foucault M (2004) Geschichte der Gouvernementalität, vol 2. Suhrkamp, Frankfurt

Freyseng E (1925) Die Physiokratie in Deutschland. Halle-Saale

Gerteis K (1989) Johann August Schlettwein (1731–1802). Aufklärung, 4, 105ff

Gerteis K (1983) Bürgerliche Absolutismuskritik im Südwesten des alten reiches vor der Französischen Revolution. Trierer Historische Forschungen, Trier

Gömmel R, Klump R (1994) Merkantilisten und Physiokraten in Frankreich. Wissenschaftliche Buchgesellschaft, Darmstadt

Klippel D (1994) Johann August Schlettwein and the economic faculty at the University of Gießen. Hist Polit Thought 15:203–227

Krebs AJA (1909) Schlettwein, der "deutsche Hauptphysiokrat." Fugmann, Leipzig

Liebel HP (1965) Enlightened bureaucracy versus enlightened despotism in Baden 1750–1792. Transactions of the American Philosophical Society, 55, Part 5, 49ff

Marx K (1974) Theorien über den Mehrwert, vol 26, 1 (1862–1863). Dietz. Marx-Engels-Werke, Berlin

Meek RL (1962) The interpretation of physiocracy. Duckworth, London

Muhlack U (1982) Physiokratie und Absolutismus in Frankreich und Deutschland. Zeitschrift für historische Forschung, 9, 15ff. und 42ff

Oncken A (1902) Geschichte der Nationalökonomie, vol 1. Hirschfeld, Leipzig

Parsons T (1937) The structure of social action. Free Press, New York

Peukert H (2005) Justi's moral economics and his system of taxation (1766). In: Backhaus JG (ed) Essays on fiscal sociology. Lang, Frankfurt, pp 211–237

Priddat BP (1998) Produktive Kraft, sittliche Ordnung und geistige Macht. Metropolis, Marburg
Roscher W (1874) Geschichte der National-Ökonomik in Deutschland. Oldenbourg, Munich
Schlettwein JA (1980) Die Rechte der Menschheit oder der einzige wahre Grund aller Gesetze, Ordnungen und Verfassungen. Meisenhain, Scriptor, (11784)
Schlettwein JA (1971) Grundfeste der Staaten oder die politische Ökonomie. Athenäum, Frankfurt, (11779)
Schlettwein JA (1978) Die wichtigste Angelegenheit für das ganze Publikum: Oder die natürliche Ordnung in der Politik überhaupt, vol 2. Topos, Vaduz, (11772/73)
Schlettwein JA (1772) Erläuterung und Verteidigung der natürlichen Ordnung in der Politik. Michael Macklot, Karlsruhe
Schlettwein JA (1981) Johann August Schlettwein: Ein deutscher Physiokrat – Verzeichnis seiner Schriften. Schlettwein, Basel
Schumpeter JA (1965) Geschichte der ökonomischen Analyse, vol 1. Vandenhoeck and Ruprecht, Göttingen (11955)
Specht AH (1929) Das Leben und die volkswirtschaftlichen Theorien Johann August Schlettweins. Heß, Braunschweig
Tribe K (1988) Governing economy: the reformation of German economic discourse 1750–1840. Cambridge University Press, Cambridge
Viner J (1958) Adam Smith and Laissez Faire. The long view and the short. Free Press, Glencoe, pp 213–245
Wackernagel M et al (2005) National footprint biocapacity accounts 2005. http://www.footprintnetwork.org/gnf_sub.php?content=download. Accessed May 2005
Zimmermann C (1983) Reformen in der bäuerlichen Gesellschaft: Studien zum aufgeklärten Absolutismus in der Markgrafschaft Baden 1750–1790. Scripta-Mercaturae, Ostfildern

Chapter 6
Cameralism and Physiocracy as the Two Sides of a Coin: Example of the Economic Policy of Johann Friedrich von Pfeiffer

Hans Frambach

About the Person and His Writings

Johann Friedrich v. Pfeiffer, born in 1718 in Berlin, was the son of an official of the royal administration of state property [Domänenverwaltung]. His honorary title is controversial. Pfeiffer first served as a soldier and then took on different positions within the Prussian cameralistic administration. He rose to the position of a privy councilor [geheimer Rat]. From 1747 to 1750 he organized the settlement of small-holders and the construction of 150 villages in the Kurmark, also founding an iron factory there. He quit his Prussian position and lived in different German territories, temporarily working for different electors [Kurfürsten] and also traveling to Switzerland, Austria, and England. In 1768 he worked as a director of a company which carbonized coal in Austria but the enterprise failed just like a second attempt in 1776. In 1778 he founded a starch manufactory in Hanau with a similar result. In 1781 he fled to Offenbach because of alleged difficulties with a mistress. Nevertheless, the University of Mainz offered him a professorship for cameralistic sciences in spite of his advanced age of 64 years and despite him being of Protestant confession. The dissolution of three monasteries or convents and the assignment of their possessions to the University then allowed introduction of the study of cameralism which had already been in the making for 20 years. Pfeiffer was the founding professor [Gründungsprofessor], at first without any relationship to the traditional faculties, and from 1784 on being the first and only professor of the independent faculty of cameralistic sciences. Pfeiffer died in Mainz at the age of 69 on March 5th, 1787 (Napp-Zinn 1955, 19–22; Wilhelm 1995, 225).

H. Frambach (✉)
Department of Economics, University of Wuppertal, Gaußstraße 20,
42119 Wuppertal, Germany
e-mail: frambach@wiwi.uni-wuppertal.de

J.G. Backhaus (ed.), *Physiocracy, Antiphysiocracy and Pfeiffer*, The European Heritage in Economics and the Social Sciences 10, DOI 10.1007/978-1-4419-7497-6_6,

Pfeiffer's complete writings were published during the last 15 years of his life (except his paper about sericulture, 1748, and the first volume of the "Lehrbegriff," 1764). His writings can be divided into four groups (Dreitzel 1998, 151–152; Napp-Zinn 1955, XIII–XV; Wilhelm 1995, 226–227):

1. *Business-economic treatises on technological issues.* For example, on sericulture, peat-harvesting, coal utilization, and manufactories.
2. *Textbooks of the cameralistic sciences.* The first volume of the "Lehrbegriff sämtlicher Oeconomischer und Cameralwissenschaften" was published in 1764, a fundamentally expanded edition in 1772, and a second volume in 1773, two further volumes appeared 1777–1779; "Polizeiwissenschaft" in 1779, "Grundriß der Finanzwissenschaft" in 1781, and "Grundriß der Forstwissenschaft" in 1781. Finally, "Grundsätze der Universal-Cameral-Wissenschaft" of 1783 and the "Staatswirtschaft" from his unpublished works of 1787.
3. *Documents on political theory and discussions with contemporary positions.* Part of it are the "Grundriß der wahren und falschen Staatskunst," 1778–1779, "Der Antiphysiokrat," 1780, "Berichtigungen berühmter Staats-, Finanz-, Polizei-, Cameral-, Commerz- und ökonomischer Schriften dieses Jahrhunderts" in six volumes, 1781–1784, and "Grundriß der Staatswirtschaft zur Belehrung und Warnung angehender Staatswirthe" of 1782.
4. *Documents discussing the situation of Germany.* For example, "Die Manufakturen und Fabriken Deutschlands, nach ihrer heutigen Lage betrachtet," a document about the manufactories and factories, 1780, and "Prüfung der beträchtlichsten Verbesserungsvorschläge zu Vermehrung der Glückseligkeit und Macht Deutschlands," 1786.

His theoretical documents often contain identical text passages which he reorganized again and again and did not change significantly. Pfeiffer was strongly influenced by the works of the famous cameralist Johann Heinrich Gottlob v. Justi. Pfeiffer even simply copied whole paragraphs from v. Justi's "Grundriß" (Wilhelm 1995, 232–233). Pfeiffer not only studied the works of the cameralists Jakob Friedrich Freiherr v. Bielfeld, Veit Ludwig v. Seckendorff, and Josef v. Sonnenfels, but he also took a close look at the writings of Johann August Schlettwein (1731–1802) – who can reasonably be called his arch-enemy – and he had read other physiocrats like Guillaume Francois Les Trosne, Victor Riquetti Marquis de Mirabeau, and Jacob Mauvillon. Pfeiffer was familiar with the works and ideas of thinkers like the mercantilist Antonio Genovesi, the classical national economist Adam Smith, and the philosopher John Locke. For example, he borrowed elements from Genovesi's price theory, the thoughts about work as the most important production factor and its productivity from Smith, and the idea that the ownership of man as one's own person can be found as a natural right in Locke's writings (Dreitzel 1998, 156; Wilhelm 1995, 227).

Following his own statement, Pfeiffer directed all of his efforts into systematizing the experiences and the knowledge he had gained over many decades of organizing the state and its administration, checking this understanding, transforming it into general principles, and reporting it in such an order and clarity that his work could be used by different nations (Pfeiffer 1778, 5). Therefore, his method can clearly be characterized as inductive.

Mercantilism and Physiocracy: Why Becoming an Antiphysiocrat?

What made Pfeiffer become a real antiphysiocrat at a time when mercantilism had already gone down and cameralism was regarded as outdated in theory yet still flourishing in the German offices and administrations? Among the English mercantilists still alive were the priest Josiah Tucker (he died in 1799), and the advocate James D. Steuart (died 1780), the last becoming well known through his book "Inquiry into the principles of political economy," 1767; it is regarded as one of the best works in mercantilistic literature. The only Italian mercantilist still alive was Giammaria Ortes (died 1790) whose known work "Della economica nazionale" was published in 1778. Among the German cameralistic authors, we can find Justus Möser (1720–1794), the chancellor of the diocese Osnabrück and a predecessor of the historical school of law, who suggested in his "Patriotische Phantasien," published 1774–1786, the possibility for citizens to acquire land property by subscribing for "shares of the state" [Staatsaktien]. Furthermore, there was the professor in Vienna, a systematizer of sciences, Josef v. Sonnenfels (1732–1817), whose "Grundsätze der Polizei, Handlung und Finanzwissenschaft" already appearing in 1763–1767. The titan of German cameralism, v. Justi, had already died back in 1771, yet his influence on the further development of the German practice of administration, and particularly on Pfeiffer's thoughts, was a lasting one.

We now have to briefly survey what we are talking about when we refer to mercantilism. It is immediately obvious from the advantages and disadvantages of mercantilism, why physiocracy replaced mercantilism. This in turn immediately leads to the decisive question why a man like Pfeiffer defended the old cameralistic system against the new edifice of physiocratic theory. Supposing Pfeiffer was a rational actor – and this can safely be assumed – we ought to find reasons against physiocracy. Therefore, after a brief explanation of the advantages of physiocracy, let us examine its disadvantages. Then, we turn in detail to Pfeiffer's criticism of the physiocratic system and his arguments why this theoretical approach was not acceptable from his point of view. This will shed some light on how Pfeiffer ought to be judged from today's perspective, and this, in turn, will elucidate the similarities and differences of cameralism and physiocracy; we will see that Pfeiffer may not simply be dismissed as anachronistic.

Mercantilism was replaced by physiocracy, the precursor of liberalism, because of the criticism of its weak spots. The advantages of mercantilism are undoubtedly its contribution to have improved and facilitated the money economy between the principalities and nations, and to have supported the development of a variety of economic activities between European countries. Furthermore, mercantilism has created the foundation for a well organized financial system – after all, mercantilism and cameralism are the starting points of the theory and practice of public finance. Although mercantilism had not established a really comprehensive theoretical edifice of economics, it had, however, led to important singular insights:

1. The theory of money was developed and the important role of money in the economy was recognized.
2. Mercantilism had a theory of production and of productive strengths (the Irishman Cantillon, for example, described land as a source of wealth but recognized work as a factor of equal importance to land for the production of wealth).
3. Mercantilism founded the theory of international exchange of goods. The knowledge about the nature and the meaning of the balance of trade can be traced back to mercantilism.

The disadvantages of the mercantilistic system:

1. The one-sided emphasis of national aspects of the economy harms other nations and misguides investments in the own country.
2. The mercantilists misjudged the difference of the balance of trade and the balance of payments; they strived for an export surplus of goods and an inflow of capital without realizing the negative effects arising from the resulting disequilibrium.
3. Direction and control of the economy by the State has an ever more depressing effect as the economy develops further; in fact, this is the starting point for the strong criticism by physiocracy.
4. The one-sided preferential treatment of trade and industry compared to farming. It has to be taken into account, though, that trade and industry were weakly developed and required support.
5. Finally, mercantilist theory tended to overestimate the significance of money.

The opposing approach of physiocracy, represented by such prominent authors like Francois Quesnay, Victor Marquis de Mirabeau, Anne Robert Jaques de Turgot, Marie Jean Antoine Nicolas de Caritat Marquis de Condorcet, the Markgraf Friedrich von Baden, and Johann August Schlettwein, made important contributions to national economics.

1. To start with, they recognized the circulation of money as an essential process of the economy and logically removed the "veil of money" from the economic process.
2. Secondly, they established the first comprehensive system of the national economy and made political economy an independent science.
3. Thirdly, they introduced the deductive method to political economy by starting out from a basic concept and inferring connections that had not been seen before.

On the other hand, in physiocracy the one-sided opinion of the idea of productivity is somewhat problematic, because:

1. The value-creating activities of industry and trade were completely misjudged. This, in effect, is a relapse even to pre-mercantilist insights. The physiocrats made the mistake of confusing the quantity and the value of material.
2. Secondly, the physiocrats overestimated farming, which again was correctly understood as a setback compared to the policy of mercantilism.
3. Thirdly, the physiocrats' demand for a single unit tax is theoretically untenable, at the latest when the productivity of trade and industry is undoubtedly accepted – Pfeiffer particularly commented on this point of criticism in great detail. Furthermore, the unit tax proved to be completely unpractical during the French revolution.
4. The fourth point of criticism is directed against the theory of social classes suggested by the physiocrats. The physiocrats based their explanations uncritically on the existing French social order. Consequently, the results they derived were caused historically and applicable only for a special period of time and a very restricted area. Above all, the largest portion of people is missing in the physiocrats' division of social classes: the people without property.

Pfeiffer's Criticism of Physiocracy

Pfeiffer is completely within the tradition of mercantilism. This is discernible by his consideration of the meaning of the state in any action of each individual (Pfeiffer 1781, 453), meaning that every individual action should be directed to the welfare of the state. It is this view already that makes Pfeiffer both a real cameralist and an "anti-liberalist." Pfeiffer asks how the central category of the physiocrats has to be understood, the often quoted nature and the natural liberty derived from it (Pfeiffer 1780, 9). In agreement with the physiocrats, Pfeiffer appreciates, of course, that man is a product of nature, both as a physical and social being; that man naturally has the right for freedom, the limits of which are reached when the rights of others are infringed or threatened to elicit negative sanctions (first and general law of nature). According to Pfeiffer (1780, 10–11), mankind recognizes this right as a "consciousness of the moral instinct" and not, however, as a result from reason. Pfeiffer agrees with the physiocrats this far. In contrast to the statements of some physiocrats, Pfeiffer then claims (1780, 12) that individuals are far more occupied with their own well-being than that of others and, therefore, the only motives of human actions consist of self-love, self-interest, and passions. Self-interest is the key to the human heart, the most powerful lever of human strengths (Pfeiffer 1786, 11). He who imagines people working and, even more, working with pleasure without considering their own benefit, he knows neither himself nor his fellow citizens (Pfeiffer 1780, 107). According to Pfeiffer, promoting welfare of a country requires the connection of all private interests (1786, 12, 69), and a wise system of administration of the state must logically start exactly here: with the individual and its interests.

Holding such an opinion, however, Pfeiffer cannot be regarded as a representative of liberalism. Modern economic theory, for instance, regards individuals as agents who maximize their utility by pursuing their own selfish interests and matters. In contrast to this modern view, Pfeiffer is convinced that the focus on one's own selfish interests just as likely may lead to the opposite effect, meaning that the pursuit of one's own interests can actually reduce one's own utility. His reasoning is that when people concentrate on their own utility, they are blind to see the equally natural and justified desire of others to work for the benefits of their own. Being unaware of this drive in one's neighbor, people fall back on cunning and force to achieve their goals (Pfeiffer 1780, 12), leading of course to counteraction and resistance and, finally, in people not succeeding in maximizing their utility. Pfeiffer does not regard the nature of man as being corrupted, nor as vain or malicious. What he regards as aberrant is the ignorance about the true and natural forces that drive man's actions, their incompetence to see the advantages of such a view, one of which is a real understanding of why vices are harmful. Most people simply do not know these connections and therefore they are incapable at all to understand natural liberty and to live accordingly. The physiocratic claim to produce a state of natural liberty must therefore be absurd (Pfeiffer 1780, 13–14). As soon as people join together in a society to promote their common welfare and bliss, a republic comes into being, whereas the state of natural unlimited liberty, as demanded by the physiocrats, has already ceased to exist (Pfeiffer 1780, 14).

In order to increase its welfare, the individual – tacitly or explicitly – gives up parts of its legal rights – understood as a non-appealable personal property – of liberty, disposal over his body, religion and thinking, rights to property, and choice of goals in life. In this way a political body arises whose aim is to connect the welfare of all members of society as a whole with the welfare of every single individual and thereby to promote the welfare of each and everyone. This is where the conception of a state begins[1]:

> I imagine to be allowed to regard the state as a large family and the ruler as a wise housefather whose first and most important obligation is to secure the inevitable needs of his family, next to this to provide it with decent comfort, and finally to help it finding all joys and innocent pleasures of life. (Pfeiffer 1780, 129–130).
>
> The ultimate aim of healthy statecraft is directed to finding the most skilful means which make a state frightening from the outside and happy from the inside. (Pfeiffer 1778, 3).

However, since the state, like every other power, also has the tendency to expand boundlessly, Pfeiffer regards mixed monarchy as the best form of organization,

---

[1] "Ich bilde mir ein, den Staat als eine große Familie und den Regenten als einen weisen Hausvater betrachten zu dürfen, dessen erste und angelegentlichste Pflicht es ist, sich der unumgänglichen Bedürfnisse seiner Familie zu versichern, ihre diesemnächst anständige Bequemlichkeiten zu verschaffen, und ihr endlich zu allen Freuden und unschuldigen Vergnügungen dieses Lebens behilflich zu sein" (Pfeiffer 1780, 129–130).

"Der ganze Endzweck einer gesunden Staatskunst dahin gerichtet ist, die geschicktesten Mittel zu erfinden, welche einen Staat von aussen furchtbar, und von innen glücklich machen" (Pfeiffer 1778, 3).

marked by a good balance of powers including a representative legislature created through the choice of its citizens. Absolute monarchy, in his view, requires at least its link to an established basic law, independence of jurisdiction as well as the determination of a robust plan of government. The constitutional "legislative basic power" ["verfassungsgebende Grundgewalt"], however, has always to remain in possession of the people, just like the right of resistance against tyrants and despots who break the positive or general constitution of the state (Dreitzel 1998, 153–154; Pfeiffer 1783, 25–33).

Why does Pfeiffer strive just for monarchy, however? One has to realize that Pfeiffer finds the greatest problem of Germany in the large number of its clergy and princes of the Reichsstände, the immediate rulers and in the fragmentation of the German state body into the territorial system – "that way the majesty of the Reich is cancelled out" (Pfeiffer 1786, 46). This is where he sees the causes of disorder and low welfare; the particular nobility [partikularer Adel] being too much orientated in its own interests like the extension of splendor, armies etc., this also being a strong influence that inhibits trade, an important factor of the economy, and contributing to the emergence of anticommercial monopolies (Pfeiffer 1780, 326–327). Pfeiffer, at his time, only considers monarchy as being able to get rid of this mess (Pfeiffer 1786, 24). The tough criticism against the nobility culminates in claims to lift the nobility's privileges completely (Pfeiffer 1786, 72). Against this background of experience and analysis, Pfeiffer has to reject the physiocrats' ideas of state and government, which are based on principles of ideal liberty, because they are idealistic and unrealistic.

For Pfeiffer, the question of the type of state is always guided by the economy. He is completely focussed on the economy, often paraphrasing it as "nourishing state" [Nahrungsstand] (e.g., Pfeiffer 1780, 125, 333, 343). Actually, whenever Pfeiffer speaks of happiness and satisfaction of needs, he always means the economy. In this respect, the structures of society and state are also dependent on the structural requirements of the economy. The following factors are decisive for the structure of the economy and society:

- Individual interest in one's own benefit and profit as the most important motive of action.
- Liberty in the choice of means.
- Independent property and its free disposability, protection against interventions.
- Industriousness and education of the labor force.
- Chances for profit and improvement.
- Absence of force and compulsion to the greatest possible extent.
- For society a balanced development of the different economical sectors in their mutual dependence (increasing circulation of money, capital formation, development and application of more productive technologies).
- Development of the population as a factor of work and consumption.

Pfeiffer does not believe, however, that a political body could arise from such a kind of natural order alone and according to a process of self-control; a political body, furthermore, on the one hand capable to steer the economic powers, and on the other hand capable to combine individual interests with the interests of all individuals as a whole, resulting in a state of harmony which proceeds without disturbance (see, the modern idea of general equilibrium). That such a general situation could develop completely independently, in Pfeiffer's opinion contradicts all historical experience. He demonstrates this by referring to the example of the success of the English and Prussian policy of the cloth trade and the prohibition of the free exportation of wood in the Styrian iron industry. Intervention and "direction" by the state (Pfeiffer 1779, 85–94; 1780, 111–116), obliged to the *bonum publikum*, are necessary to take people, who are misguided by striving for their own individual interests, by means of law and order to act in the common interest (Pfeiffer 1779, 110–117; 1780,126). What is missing in Pfeiffer's considerations, from the modern point of view, is the idea of the market as an instrument of control, although he definitely treats its elements (price, demand and supply, production and consumption).

Pfeiffer essentially criticizes physiocracy for two of its principles (Pfeiffer 1780, 323; 1781, 439; 1786, 35):

1. The absolute freedom of trade.
2. The collection of a single tax (unit tax) based on the production factor ground – in the opinion of the physiocrats the only factor creating value.

The physiocrats demanded the absolute freedom of trade as the first incontrovertible principle and as the most important criterion to establish a state of bliss in the whole world. This not only satisfies the natural right of man for liberty but also creates the prerequisite to lastingly increase the wealth of a nation. From Pfeiffer's point of view, the causes of most problems lie in the different nature of the countries, their different distributions of property, rules of classes and ways of thinking, forms of government etc. These causes are not accessible with general analyses and suggestions. The physiocrats always take a look at their own country only and generate systems "which can be read immensely well, and are guarantor for the philanthropic character of their originators, but at the same time, however, they have the indelible fault of being impracticable." Free trade fails the reality because many nations retain their customs (Pfeiffer 1786, 44). The "beautiful often inimitable drafts" from England, Italy, France, and Germany are in glaring contrast to the misery of the people, the bad condition of agriculture, the property being in only a few hands, general abuse, the unmarried state of many people in some classes etc. (Pfeiffer 1786, 7). The most impractical suggestions would come from the physiocratic system, like the claim to impose a single tax on crop yields, the unit tax, because in physiocratic opinion only ground can produce values (Pfeiffer 1786, 34).

Pfeiffer sharply opposes the physiocratic idea of ground being the sole factor to add value. For Pfeiffer, all production factors are productive; agriculture, industry, and trade being the general sources of wealth: agriculture yielding the products of the soil, industry and trade increasing their use and extending their value. Consequently, taxes ought to be imposed on all kinds of revenues (Pfeiffer 1780, 23, 288; 1786, 4, 38–39, 52, 56). Nobody doubts, Pfeiffer (1780, 18) remarks, the statement that the earth is the source of all human requirements and comforts and, in the end, also the source to extend the wealth of nations. However, there are also examples of states that are wealthy despite not having any natural riches, such as Switzerland, its wealth resulting from the further processing of products and trade. Further examples are cities like Hamburg and Frankfurt, having gained wealth through trade. Towns richly equipped with natural economic resources such as good soil, like Nuremberg, become impoverished because its manufactories are no longer able to survive (Pfeiffer 1780, 19–23).

Imposing the unit tax as demanded by the physiocrats does not mean to start from completely wrong prerequisites, namely the exclusive production of value by the factor ground. Even more, it does not consider the consequences in terms of deficits in revenues due to lost customs and "Accisen,"[2] and in terms of what this means for the economic situation of a country (Pfeiffer 1781, 443–446). The unit tax can never be sufficient as a source for public taxes and charges (Pfeiffer 1780, 209–211, 226–227, 323). The state must raise a variety of taxes and charges to finance itself. Without sufficient income, the state could not pay his officials etc. and as a consequence, the entire economic and social system would suffer. The wealthier a state is, for example, the more it is in danger of being attacked by jealous foreign countries, and the greater, therefore, is the need for a strong army. To be acknowledged and feared within the country, the government needs great authority which requires a large machinery of state with many public employees (Pfeiffer 1786, 78–81). Therefore, the claim of the physiocrats for a unit tax forbids itself, and the same is true for the relinquishment of other kinds of income which free trade or the absolute freedom of trade would bring, for example earnings from customs and Accisen (Pfeiffer 1781, 442–443).

However, imposing various taxations also must allow exceptions. For example, the physiocrats proposed to assess the properties of clergymen, knights, and the aristocracy according to quantity and size of land property – which at that time mostly was free from taxation (see e.g., Schlettwein's claim to impose taxes on all properties; Pfeiffer 1781, 423). In contrast to this physiocratic claim, Pfeiffer demanded to leave this group of people exempted from property taxes (Pfeiffer 1781, 418–419) because he regarded it as unjust to pay taxes on these properties when taxes were already paid on incomes and yields. If, however, no yields could be drawn from the property, a taxation according to the quantity or size of land property would merely substantially harm the landowners and, in the last step, force them to leave their country, rendering the property insecure, and trampling on justice, as Pfeiffer says (Pfeiffer 1781, 416, 420, 423, 431). Now, this is something entirely different than a general tax exemption for the clergy and noblemen, which Pfeiffer definitely did not intend. He meant to apply these exceptions to taxes only to property which was subject to sovereign right or had other sovereign privileges and immunities. However, he definitely examined the properties of those clergy and noblemen who had no sovereignty and therefore were committed to pay taxes (Pfeiffer 1778, 294).

[2] Accise = Akzise meant in former times a kind of custom, for example the charge at the gate to gain admission into the town.

Measures of Economic Policy for the Improvement in Welfare

All and about, the era when Pfeiffer lived was characterized by the transformation from a cooperatively, feudally, and grandly organized society into one of economically free citizens. Pfeiffer treated all problems arising from this transformation critically but he also made practical suggestions for the improvement of welfare in Germany, equating his suggestions with the tasks and measures of good policy for the public sector (e.g., Pfeiffer 1783, 219; 1786, 84):

1. The core of Pfeiffer's "reform suggestions" for Germany consisted in the abolition of the fragmented nobility and a reorganization of the various princely territorial states which he described as "Reichs-Landeigenthum of the higher nobility." The heads of the German state body should be brought back to life by one spirit. Germany should form an economic unit through a customs union. Pfeiffer emphasized an accompanying idea again and again: by means of companies, Germany, i.e. Prussia or Austria, should make use of the international reaction against the maritime "universal monarchy" of England in the war of independence in North America in order to establish direct commercial relations to the former colonies and also to the other non-European countries, thus earning "Germany a surplus in the general balance of trade." He even demanded a common policy of the Reichsstände to liberate North America and the Antilles. In their effort for economic independence he pledged for all nations to catch up the lead of England and France.
2. Land reform

   - Pfeiffer demanded, just like the physiocrats, the restriction of the fief classes [Lehenstände], the abolition of bondage of the fief workers to their landlords as well as excessive and hard compulsory labor [Frondienste], and he stood up for clear regulations. He demanded lowering the burdens on independent farms. He agreed to Schlettwein's suggestion on transforming compulsory labor into a compulsory monetary contribution [Frongeld], but pleaded for exceptions, like maintaining services during harvesting or otherwise some large estates could not survive. The Frongeld could also be paid as grain but it should always be assessed at market rates and not at uniform prices (Pfeiffer 1780, 194–195, 201–206; 1786, 63).
   - Improvement in utilization of land and development of farming along scientific criteria included several steps: modernization of the organization of farms; optimal partitioning of fields, meadows and vineyards and the abolition of fallow or resting fields [Brach- und Ruhefelder]; right fertilization; the cultivation of nourishing food herbs like clover; improvements in livestock breeding; introduction of stable feeding; lowering of charges on fattened cattle; free trade of certain animals; and an improved education of the farm's employees (Pfeiffer 1780, 120, 332–333; 1786, 11, 62–63, 85). Pfeiffer complained about the bad management of the big estates, particularly those of the nobility and the church. He fought against the ignorance, laziness, and inability of some landowners and called on them to employ persons having the appropriate qualifications for the administration of estates – preferably,

of course, managers having received cameralistic training).[3] Pfeiffer connected his claims with a moral appeal to the nobility (Pfeiffer 1778, 297, 307–308; 1786, 65).

- Restructuring of properties. Pfeiffer (1778, 125; 1780, 332–333) at first wants to carry out a survey of all properties; the reason why some properties would be taxed while others not, could be found here. One fault that he criticizes is the predominant practice to give smallholders properties that are too large so that they cannot cultivate them adequately because they usually do not have the necessary resources. Another burden on the farmers is taxes that are too high, especially for farmers whose properties are taxed on size and number. Large farms should be divided into small ones, e.g. by handing them over to the children (Pfeiffer 1778, 126). The partitioning of the properties often is too much torn apart to be cultivated efficiently and thus cannot produce a worthwhile result. An interest in a common solution does not exist since every ruler and every property owner considers only his own individual interests and not the interests of the whole state. Pfeiffer regards it as possible that at least the most powerful Reichsstände could move with united strengths and formulate a plan without having any change in the relation of ownership. Pfeiffer was convinced that a centralized [arrondierter] state needs a smaller number of employees and thus could impose fewer burdens on his subjects (Pfeiffer 1786, 58). As the most important and most comprehensive instrument of national policy, Pfeiffer assesses the common organization of the great and small nobility, including the properties of private individuals (Pfeiffer 1786, 85).

[3] How does one cameralist have to be trained? The cameralistic science covers the complete area of national economics, public finance included (Pfeiffer 1778, 4). The subject matter also includes lessons in farming and agriculture, forestry, geography, history, mechanics, physical science, architecture and shipbuilding engineering, nature of trade and manufactories, mathematics, natural right and international law, rhetoric, and statesmanship. The duration of the education depends on the learning success of the single person. The best ones shall be able to finish their education already after 4 years. The timetable of a cameralist being in education approximately corresponds to the following sample (Pfeiffer 1778, 23–25):

To dress and undress	1 h
To pray	1 h
Public lessons	8 h
To repeat	3 h
Time of delight [Ergötzungen]	2 h
To eat	2 h
To sleep	7 h
Sum	24 h

Manifold are the fields of application that open up to the cameralist in the administration of the economy. Only the cameralist is capable to give an exact status report of the economy and thereupon to take sensible measures of its control, all these by the exact calculation of the data of the economic sectors, the observation of the money in circulation, and the detailed control of the foreign trade (Pfeiffer 1781, 449–450). Therefore, a cameralist is an administrator, not of an estate but of a principality, a province or a country.

3. The treatment of the guilds and the introduction of the freedom of trade and the simultaneous reorganization of the educational system of economics. Like the physiocrats, Pfeiffer criticizes the nature of the guilds, seeing no sense in fixing the years for an apprenticeship for crafts of simple skills to 4–6 years, impeding skilled workers from becoming masters, or restricting the number of the masters etc. Guilds are a sickness which should never have been allowed to develop but because they exist, Pfeiffer advises sensible treatment (Pfeiffer 1780, 124–125, 149–151). In order for the economy to work optimally, those people who follow-up flawed and imaginary interests have to be managed, and part of this is the intervention in the trades. Guilds therefore are nothing other than instruments of the government to preserve the political body and the community (Pfeiffer 1780, 125–127). Among the different reasons given by Pfeiffer against unrestricted freedom of trade, the most plausible seems to be that farmers should work in farming and tradesman in trade, meaning that not everybody should be allowed to work anywhere (Pfeiffer 1780, 332–333).
4. Improvement of the tax system. The distribution of burdens on the subjects should be comprehensible and uniform (Pfeiffer 1786, 85). The burdens must not restrict the efficiency of the economic subjects, but have to be so high that the state can perform its tasks towards the members of society.
5. Manufactories and factories should be centralized at certain places, not the least due to the fact that too many workers could be withdrawn from farming (Pfeiffer 1778, 568).
6. Renewal of the municipal constitution by citizen participation and citizen representation (Pfeiffer 1783, 320–322; 425–427).
7. Reforms of schools and universities to adapt to the needs of the economy (Pfeiffer 1783, 139–149; 276–286; 499–504).
8. A strong population is described by Pfeiffer as the most important pillar of true power and the strength and the wealth of states; everything is possible for a state having a population that is large and strong enough (Pfeiffer 1780, 330–334). Germany should therefore have so many people that they can be employed and be fed well. To improve the conditions for the population, a means of control by the state is to enable people to get married and provide for a family (Pfeiffer 1786, 33). However, Pfeiffer does not comment very much on this point, stating, after all, that it falls within the responsibilities of politics when the number of married persons is smaller than the number of those who are unmarried (Pfeiffer 1786, 33). In terms of population policy, Pfeiffer argues quite similarly when he demands a division of classes for every branch of production. The classes act within their own realm of responsibility and grow as long as they are economically successful and have enough to feed on. Here, the statesman has "to do nothing else but putting those into work who must live from it, and keeping their numbers in the right proportion to the sales of their work" (Pfeiffer 1786, 68).[4]

[4] Der Staatsmann habe hier – "(…) nichts anderes zu tun, als diejenigen so davon leben müssen in Beschäftigung zu setzen, und ihre Anzahl in der rechten Proportion zum Absatz ihrer Arbeit zu erhalten" (Pfeiffer 1786, 68).

9. Trade and freedom of trade

   - Monopolies should be allowed only as exceptions due to their anticommercial effects (Pfeiffer 1780, 288, 336–342; 1786, 63, 85).
   - Trade, industry, and manufactories shall be promoted; this also is of benefit to agriculture (Pfeiffer 1786, 25–26).
   - Pfeiffer (1780, 43, 54, 336–342; 1786, 65) stands up vehemently for trade and its support; this explicitly includes foreign trade (Pfeiffer 1780, 101). "In my eyes, rich and active merchants who are led by well considered principles, great experience and checked honesty are benefactors of the nation. They stimulate the industry, increase wealth and bring it into circulation; prejudices against nationalities and religions cease in face of commercial interests; from an economic point of view Jews, Roman Catholics, Lutherans, Reformed, Baptists are empty names, because all of us are of the same origin and we all bow to the interest by which all people are connected" (Pfeiffer 1780, 65).[5]

One could have the impression that the "really sensible physiocrats" are the cameralists. This, however, is not the case. According to Pfeiffer, freedom of trade is nothing else but the free circulation of goods which may not be held back as long as the "true advantage of the state necessitates change" (Pfeiffer 1780, 55). The export of goods which yet could be reprocessed within the country destroys jobs at home; the import of goods which could also be produced at home damages domestic trade; unlimited trade strengthens the trading power of a few merchants and undermines fertile trade. For example, whereas Schlettwein welcomes the unrestricted exportation of wood in Styria [Steiermark] (saying it had to be interesting enough to the owners of the forests to run the wood business; Pfeiffer 1780, 111–112), Pfeiffer considers it a big fault in case of a shortage of wood in the country, which will be followed by an increase in wood prices and prices for the goods of those industries which use wood as a production factor (melting plants, hammer mills etc.) (Pfeiffer 1780, 116). In this case, private trade interests definitely go against state interests, according to Pfeiffer (1780, 61–67; 1786, 71). The state therefore is asked to intervene. Above all, the central principle of trade politics is to keep the money supply within the country, and to produce first and foremost for the domestic demand, i.e. an export surplus (Pfeiffer 1780, 45–54, 67–68; 1786, 27–29).

- The most important instrument to reach an export surplus is to set customs carefully (e.g. Pfeiffer 1780, 249–256, 373–374). In this context Pfeiffer opposes Schlettweins claim to abolish all transit duties (Pfeiffer 1780, 260–262). The state has high expenditures simply to build streets and waterways and keep them

[5]"In meinen Augen sind reiche und unternehmende Kaufleute, die von wohl überlegten Grundsätzen, großer Erfahrung und geprüften Redlichkeit geleitet werden, Wohltäter des Vaterlandes. Sie beleben die Industrie, vermehren die Reichtümer, und bringen sie in Umlauf; die Vorurteile gegen Nationalitäten und Religionen verstummen vor dem Kommerz; Türken Juden, Katholiken, Lutheraner, Reformierte, Baptisten sind in Betrachtung des wirtschaftenden Publikums leere Benennungen, weil wir alle eines Ursprungs sind, und uns alle vor dem Interesse beugen, welches die Menschen verbindet" (Pfeiffer 1780, 65).

in good condition. Those who use the ways should pay for it; but the amount of the gateway customs should be moderate.

- Foreign trade also requires governments to allow trade with each other, to overcome "bureaucratic obstacles" and guarantee protection (Pfeiffer 1780, 60). The main purpose of customs and tolls is to guarantee safety to travelers, allowing them to move within the country (Pfeiffer 1780, 262–264).
- The facts of different qualities of goods, their measures, weights etc. between the countries are in contrast to the absolute freedom of trade. The most successful trading nations would take great care on exactly these facts, and on the observation of the corresponding laws and regulations; thus preserving the quality standard of production and supporting the principle of good faith (Pfeiffer 1780, 63).
- All in all Pfeiffer approves trade, yet never absolutely. Pfeiffer gives examples where regulations by the state have contributed to the promotion of the wealth of the nation: England has the best wool manufactories because an imposed export ban of wool from England has forced Dutch companies to come to England and to build new manufactories; extra pays from the government have encouraged farmers to produce sheep with improved wool. France's sericulture was created by rewards; its progress in the production of color can be traced back to Colbert's commitment to a bonus equipment of the French Academy of Sciences to carry out experiments etc. (Pfeiffer 1780, 43–44).

Assessment of Pfeiffer

Pfeiffer was primarily a practitioner and less a theorist, a cameralist who was educated and trained excellently, who probably understood much more of agriculture, livestock breeding, and trade as most of the physiocrats and classical national economists. As a scientist, he was a thoroughly practical person, observing the smallest details, as seen in his description of the right use of a plow (Pfeiffer 1778, 21–24). He was a theoretical practitioner, no visionary; in his economic thought he always tried to vividly remember reality. He built principles only within the prevailing conditions of the economic system in Germany. He was an active and hard-working man, an honest character with pragmatic insights. In the last paragraph of the article "Die letzten Blätter des Testaments eines den öffentlichen Geschäften entsagten alten Cameralisten," from "Vermischte Verbeßrungsvorschläge," the reader can gain an impression. It is a letter to his son who wanted to enter the civil service. Against the background of his long-standing professional practice, Pfeiffer entertains doubts and argues critically, whether this profession is the right choice for his son. He explains that policy often depends on fortuities and atmospheres of the rulers. Sometimes, the smallest things would cause the greatest revolutions or are responsible for the advancement and decline of kingdoms. A couple of stylish gloves, for example, which the duchess of Marlborough denied to the queen, and a cup of coffee which a finery lady of the queen poured over her dress, are reported to have prevented the dissections of the French provinces and given peace to all of Europe.

The death of a bird, a dog and the farewell of a popular singer, and similar examples can put a ruler in a bad mood and prevent the best plan (Pfeiffer 1777, 14). Yet, to the decent person "the secret testimony of the conscience is much more valuable (...) than an ambiguous great name" (Pfeiffer 1777, 17).

Pfeiffer designed his ideas on the basis of a consistent sensualistic empiricism, which strictly declined reason as an independent source of ethical norms and independent principles of knowledge, only knowing instrumental and practical reasons – which are more restricted. The only remains of disdained metaphysics were a residual natural theology, which guaranteed the sense of (autonomous) "nature." Basic to this ethics was the feeling of goodwill, the moral instinct which usefully completes individual interest because man, in his striving for preservation and happiness, also depends on social interaction. The difference of people and their often inadequate insight into the true – specifically, sustainable – opportunities to satisfy their interests, makes it inevitable to coordinate and manage society by the highest force. A monarchy legitimized and controlled by the people seems the best solution to Pfeiffer. It honors Pfeiffer to have integrated principles of the Schlettweinsche "natural science" [Naturlehre] just like the principle of greatest possible liberty into his national liberalism. Pfeiffer indeed had the opinion that a nation could never reach its real significance if liberty, property, safety, reasonable taxes, and industry were not provided for (Pfeiffer 1783, 38–47).

Pfeiffer's economic theory lingers in the technological and business-economic practice which uses images and pictorial categories like circulation, proportion, drive spring, machine etc. which also echoes the limits of his reception of ideas. (Dreitzel 1998, 156, fn. 10; Pfeiffer 1782, 6–18).

It has to be taken into account that Pfeiffer developed his pragmatic theory in an economic situation in which a collapse of the elementary supply of material goods and a population catastrophe still represent real and ubiquitous dangers. Therefore, it is obvious for him to propose influencing the market through direct intervention by the state, for example, to cushion the free trade of grain by introducing a policy of decentralized state magazines (e.g., Pfeiffer 1786, 72). Nations were not yet highly internationalized so that there was a permanent risk of getting caught in an underdevelopment due to the superiority of other European economies. And, of course, Pfeiffer and his contemporaries were surrounded with an agrarian economy of small-scale companies (Dreitzel 1998, 156).

It was beyond Pfeiffer's understanding, of course, to completely comprehend the allocating forces of the market as they were shown by the liberalists and their predecessors, the physiocrats. It would, however, be wrong to assume that Pfeiffer was surpassed by the events and theoretical developments of his time; he just tried to take into account the feasibility of political and economic means. His opinions are not rejected easily, because even nowadays the state intervenes in many fields: one may think of the state supervision in the bank and insurance sector, the price control in the energy sector, and the stipulated qualification in many professions, such as the license to practice as a doctor, the admittance for pharmacists, nonmedical practitioners, midwives, notaries, tax consultants, accountants etc. (the example of the healing professions is in fact mentioned by Pfeiffer (1780), 128–129). Pfeiffer thinks exactly along these lines when he refuses unrestricted liberty of trade. Sure, many of his examples are not chosen entirely luckily. Thus, he actually justifies the ban for carpenters not to produce any shoes by arguing that there wasn't the slightest reason to assume that a carpenter might want to produce shoes (Pfeiffer 1780, 128).

The article shall be concluded with a quotation from Pfeiffer's "Antiphysiocrat": The most essential parts of happiness in Germany consist

> Of a true and sensible liberty, which is – for both the ordering and obeying – subjected to compulsion of wise and just laws; Of a large quantity of healthy, well-bred, diligent, skilful people; Of an excellent culture of the surface of the ground, and numerous well chosen and sufficiently fed livestock herds; Of the finding and sensible use of the products from the underground; Of the most proper flourishing manufactories and factories; Of well established domestic action and foreign trade; Of a good connection of the whole national economy; Of cheap and fair distributed burdens from taxes on the properties, mines, well established customs duties, trade and capitation taxes; Of an external safety against all hostile attacks; Of an inward safety against disturbances, fraud, contempt, compulsion of conscience and other oppressions.
>
> (Pfeiffer 1780, 343–344).[6]

References

Dreitzel H (1998) Universal-Kameral-Wissenschaft als politische Theorie: Johann Friedrich von Pfeiffer (1718–1787). In: Grunert F und Vollhardt F (eds) Aufklärung als praktische Philosophie. De Gruyter, Tübingen, pp 149–171

Napp-Zinn AF (1955) Johann-Friedrich von Pfeiffer und die Kameralwissenschaften an der Universität Mainz (entstanden 1921), Beiträge zur Geschichte der Universität Mainz 1. Franz Steiner Verlag, Wiesbaden

von Pfeiffer JF (1777) Vermischte Verbeßrungsvorschläge und freie Gedanken über verschiedene, den Narungszustand, die Bevölkerung und Staatswirtschaft der Deutschen betreffende Gegenstände. Eßlingerische Buchhandlung, Frankfurt am Main

von Pfeiffer JF (1778) Lehrbegrif sämtlicher oeconomischer und Cameralwissenschaften. T.F. Schwan, Mannheim

von Pfeiffer JF (1779) Natürliche aus dem Endzweck der Gesellschaft entstehende Allgemeine Policeiwissenschaft. Eßlingersche Buchhandlung, Frankfurt

[6] Die wesentlichsten Stücke der Glückseligkeit Deutschlands liegen – "in einer wahren und vernünftigen Freiheit, die sowohl für die befehlenden, als für die gehorchenden, dem Zwange weiser und gerechter Gesetze unterworfen ist; In einer großen Menge gesunder, wohlerzogener, fleißiger, geschikter Menschen; In einer fürtreflichen Cultur der Oberfläche des Erdbodens, und zahlreichen wohlgewählten und gehörig ernährten Viehherden: Im Aufsuchen und vernünftigen Benutzen der unterirdischen Produkte; In der schicklichsten blühenden Manufakturen und Fabriken; In wohl eingerichteten inländischen Handlung und auswärtigen Commercien; In einem guten Zusammenhang des ganzen Nahrungsstandes; In billigen mit gleichen Schultern getragnen, aus den Steuern auf die Grundstücke, aus den Bergwerken, aus wohl eingerichteten Zöllen, aus Gewerb- und Kopfsteuern gezogenen Auflagen; In äußerliche Sicherheit, wider alle feindlichen Anfälle; In innerlicher Sicherheit wider Unruhen, Betrug, Verachtung Gewissenszwang, und andere Bedrükungen, bestehen" (Pfeiffer 1780, 343–344).

von Pfeiffer JF (1780) Der Antiphysiocrat oder umständliche Untersuchung des sogenannten Physiocratischen Systems vermöge welchem eine allgemeine Freiheit, und einzige Auflage, auf den reinen Ertrag der Grundstücke, die Glückseligkeit aller Staaten ausmachen soll. Verlag der Eßlingerschen Buchhandlung, Frankfurt am Main

von Pfeiffer JF (1781) Grundriß der Finanzwissenschaft nebst einem Anhang über die Unausführbarkeit des physiokratischen Systems. Verlag der Eßlingerschen Buchhandlung, Frankfurt am Mayn

von Pfeiffer JF (1782) Grundriß der Staatswirtschaft zur Belehrung und Warnung angehender Staatswirte. Varrentrapp Sohn und Wenner, Frankfurt am Mayn

von Pfeiffer JF (1783) Grundsätze der Universal-Cameral-Wissenschaft oder deren vier wichtigsten Schulen nämlich der Staats-Regierungskunst, der Policey-Wissenschaft, der allgemeinen Staats-Oekonomie, und der Finanzwissenschaft, vol 1. Eßlingersche Buchhandlung, Frankfurt am Mayn

von Pfeiffer JF (1786) Prüfung der beträchtlichen Verbesserungsvorschläge zu Vermehrung der Glückseligkeit und Macht Deutschland, worinn die Unzulänglichkeit dieser Vorschläge bemerket und zugleich ein wahrscheinlich sicherer Weg zu Erreichung dieses großen Endzweks vorgeleget wird. Varrentrapp Sohn und Wenner, Frankfurt und Mainz

Wilhelm U (1995) Der deutsche Frühliberalismus. Von den Anfängen bis 1789. Peter Lang, Frankfurt am Main

Chapter 7
Physiocrats and Laws of Population

Gerhard Scheuerer

Introduction

This essay deals not with the whole theory of Physiocrats. In the following, it only referred to the special aspect, which contribution physiocratic theory has brought forth to study rules and patterns of population and to what extend Physiocrats contributed to the development of population theory.

In the first part, the status of demography in the eighteenth century will be described and shown that science of demography started at that time. In this context, a view is taken on the science of statistics, which also started at that time. In the second part, the role will be analyzed, that population plays in the law of nature in Schlettwein's physiocratic theory. At the end of this essay, to what extent Physiocrats have given input to the laws of population, which was formulated by the classical political economist Thomas Robert Malthus in "Essay of the principle of population" in 1798, will be discovered.

Demography and Statistics in the Eighteenth Century

The German cameralism of the seventeenth/eighteenth century looked upon population as an important production factor. At that time, it was common sense that prosperity of a nation depends on the highest possible number of subjects which is coordinated with the achievable food. Besides others, the national production should be increased to raise the revenues of the state. People were required as workers to increase the production and, on the other hand to intensify the demand.

G. Scheuerer (✉)
Krupp Chair in Public Finance and Fiscal Sociology, Leitender Ministerialrat,
University of Erfurt, Nordhäuser Str. 63, 99089 Erfurt, Germany
e-mail: gerhard.scheuerer@t-online.de

J.G. Backhaus (ed.), *Physiocracy, Antiphysiocracy and Pfeiffer*, The European Heritage in Economics and the Social Sciences 10, DOI 10.1007/978-1-4419-7497-6_7,

Cameralists postulated therefore to settle people in areas which were depopulated during the Thirty Years War from 1618 to 1648 (Peuplierung). An active population policy was made by immigration policy, which was combined with religious considerations sometimes. The treatment of questions about population was more practical and less scientific during that time. The aim was only to increase the population.

The population of Europe rose only with very small ratios up to the year 1750. Since the mid of the eighteenth century, the population started to increase more and more constantly and dramatically in Europe. In the period from 1740 to 1800, the European population increased between 35 and 50% in 60 years (on the average 1.2–1.7% per year).[1] Most of the territorial states in Europe and the German Reichsstädte suffered from famine from time to time and were economically underdeveloped compared with Great Britain, the Netherlands, and partly France. The number of urban proletarians grew rapidly. The consequence had been a very terrible situation of the urban population with widespread famine and epidemics. Whenever the industrialization started – in the mid of the eighteenth century as dedicated by some writers, others say the industrial revolution started in 1780 – the industrial revolution started earlier in Great Britain than in Germany. Therefore, it is no surprise that Malthus, who lived in Great Britain, researched in detail on laws of population, or as he said on principles of population. The European model of demographic transformation[2] explains as main reasons for the population development at this stage a decreasing mortality provoked by improvement of farming,[3] and an improvement of supply with food, an improvement of medical care (for example medicines against the plague, typhoid, smallpox, spotted fever). At that time, the birth rate remained at the former level. In the context we deal with these means, the Physiocrats watched population growing in their countries, but the population of Germany grew less during that time than the population of Great Britain did.

During the eighteenth century, the curiosity for scientific demography awoke, but at the beginning of this development statistical data was not available to the necessary extent. So the scientific interest was focused on empirical data at first. In the Middle Ages, occasional empirical data of population consisted in small territories. The German Johann Peter Süßmilch, an army priest and statistician, can be named the founder of scientific population statistics based on empirical data. Furthermore, he can be named as precursor of econometrics. He and others could use empirical data about population and tried to find out the reasons of natural

[1] Armengaud, André (1971), p 129.

[2] This model was introduced by Notestein (1945), which analyzed crude birth rates and crude death rates from the middle age to the mid of the twentieth century. It is a descriptive model and does not fulfill claims of scientific theory (see for example: Hummel (2000)).

[3] Justus von Liebig (1803–1873) is considered to be the founder of agricultural chemistry. He was a professor at the Ludwigs University of Gießen from 1824 to 1852, which later was named Justus Liebig University. Johann August Schlettwein (the leading German Physiocrat) was a professor at the Ludwigs University of Gießen from 1777 to 1785 (Justus von Liebig was not a good pupil and records indicate that his teacher said to his parents: 'Your son will become nothing (in Hessian language: "aus dem Bub werd nix")).

population development (birth and death; migration is not of special interest in his research, because data of immigration and emigration were not available to the scientifically necessary extent at that time; sampling theory did not exist, only probability calculations were known). Süßmilch describes in his main publication[4] patterns and laws of human life. He analyses birth, death, and reproduction of mankind on the basis of the Divine order and tries to find out rules and laws of population. The Physiocrats themselves derived the nature rights also from the Divine order. For example, Süßmilch deduces from the empirically realized fact that the number of born babies and the number of dead persons are at regular intervals that the Lord wants to avoid overpopulation. Furthermore, he deduces from the also empirically realized fact of sexual proportion of 100 born girls to 106 born boys and balanced proportion of women and men in the age when they get married, that the Lord appoints monogamy.[5] Among other things, Süßmilch proposed for example to abolish bans of marriage and to support immigration.

The scientific German university (academic) statistics was founded by Hermann Conring[6] and purely descriptive orientated. It had been a verbal description of states at that time. For example constitution, administration, finance, and army have been examined; figures did not play a role. The more population and economic situation grew in importance, it was necessary to use statistical data and to present them in tables. Gottfried Achenwall[7] continued the scientific German university (academic) statistics in the eighteenth century. He argued sharply against tables: How can the faith in the Lord, self-confidence, diligence and personality of people be shown? His criticism was surely right concerning qualitative data. Nevertheless tables got their way, because of their advantages describing quantitative marks. Scientific statistics developed especially in Great Britain, the Netherlands, France, and Belgium during the second half of the seventeenth century. This science was named political arithmetic. Aim of political arithmetic was to find out patterns and rules of social and economic life, which can be used to political problems. Political arithmetic arose from mathematical questions of insurance and tried first to inform about correlations with death. John Graunt[8] examined registers of births and deaths in London to find out patterns and rules of natural population development. He is precursor of scientific population statistics. The above named German Johann Peter Süßmilch[9] was pioneer for the development of scientific demographic statistics. He summarized the whole methodical and materialistic knowledge at due course and added it with many details.

---

[4] Süßmilch (1741/Faksimile 2001).

[5] Süßmilch (1741/Faksimile 2001), §64.

[6] Conring (1606–1681) was a professor of nature philosophy and besides other an academic for policy in Helmstedt (1650). He wrote in his book *Thesaurus totius orbis quadripartibus* (1675): "Pertinet ad cognitionem hominum ut sciamus eorum numerus civium sit magnus vel parvus," quoted from Mols (1971), p 18.

[7] Achenwall (1719–1772) was historian, lawyer, and professor at the University of Göttingen (Lower Saxonia).

[8] Graunt (1620–1674) was a business man in London.

[9] Süßmilch (1707–1767).

The physiocratic economic theory supported a liberal economy, which is free of production monopolies and protecting customs duties as realized by cameralistic governed states. Physiocrats tried to show the grievance caused by mercantilistic interference in economic course. Therefore, physiocratic theory is criticism of mercantilism. The absolute preference of agriculture was an obvious rejection of mercantilistic economics founding nationalized factories and of guilds of handicrafts.

Physiocrats at the second half of the eighteenth century knew existing empirical data as well as patterns and rules of population, which were formulated and published by Süßmilch in the year 1741. Early Physiocrats did not know the principles of population justified by Malthus, which he published in the year 1798. Malthus[10] argues as a classical political economist against opinions up to that time, that growth of population is a sure sign of prosperity of nation.[11] The theoretical way of thinking of Malthus overlaps with the thinking of David Ricardo,[12] who also is a representative of classical political economy. Therefore, the theory is often named the Mathusian–Ricardian idea. Later Physiocrats[13] knew the laws of population and theories of Adam Smith,[14] which spread English liberalism and were published in his main publication in the year 1776.[15] It took for about 20 years until the German translation was available.

Significance of Population in Schlettwein's Physiocratic Theory

Founder of physiocratic way of thinking is Francois Quesnay.[16] Starting point of his physiocratic theory is the power of nature, which means the law of nature and the natural laws of the economic process. Physiocrats distinguish generally between complete (natural) order (*ordre naturel*), as well as temporary and caused by time order (*ordre positif*). The last one should be approached by laws as far as possible to the law of nature. Representatives of physiocratism developed and changed details of Quesnay's theory in course of time.

The central idea of Quesnay was that only agriculture produces value, because it increases the goods. Handicrafts and factories only change existing raw materials.

---

[10] Malthus (1766–1834) was a professor of history and political economy since 1805.

[11] Malthus (1798).

[12] Ricardo (1772–1823).

[13] A relatively unknown representative is Joseph Lang, born in Germany and Professor in Charkow (Russia). He published in 1811 a book "Grundlinien der politischen Arithmetik."

[14] Smith (1723–1790) met considerable physiocrats on a trip through France and Switzerland in the years 1764–1766.

[15] An Inquiry into the Nature and Causes of the Wealth of Nations.

[16] Quesnay (1694–1774), French physician and economist, was a private physician of Ludwig XV. and of Madame de Pompadour.

Therefore, agriculture has to be promoted. He drew up a three sector model: *Classe productive* is the agriculture, which consists of farmers and tenant farmers. Only this class produces net value or surplus value. *Classe de propriétaires*, also named *classe distributive* comprises the king as well as ecclesiastical and secular land owners. Task of this class is to distribute and to use the rent by buying agricultural or commercial goods. *Classe stéril* consists of commercial economy like handicrafts and traders. This class adds no value, but increases the value of their production of goods only by costs of capital and wages they spent for it. Permanent contribution to the scientific methods of economics is Quesnay's idea of circulation in total economy, the so-called tableau economique (1758). The *tableau economique* shows the mutual dependencies of the three sectors resulting from development and use of income. It is the first closed macroeconomic system of streams of money and goods in an economy.[17] He can be seen as pioneer of national accounts as well as input–output-analysis. Physiocratism persisted only a short period and was followed by classical political economy founded by Adam Smith. Opposite to the Physiocrats, Smith looked very similar upon human work and division of work as the source of prosperity as cameralism did. Cameralism considered money as wealth just like Smith did in his main publication.

Johann August Schlettwein[18] is the leading German Physiocrat. The first right of people is the duty to keep living in good condition.[19] His main paper is published in 1779.[20] Schlettwein postulates happy life for people and distinguishes between animal and mental urge of people. The animal urge of people needs material objects like food, house, and bed.[21] The mental urge is combined with the duty to be religious and to fulfill the Commandments of the Lord.[22] Schlettwein argues that Law of nature is deduced from Divine order, very similar to the German cameralist Süßmilch, who also deduced laws of population from Divine order. Schlettwein distinguishes the three societies[23] (1) nuptial society, (2) parents society, and (3) principal society, which reflects the spirit and the absolutistic distribution of power in Europe at that time. Reproduction of mankind is the sole essential main purpose of cohabitation.[24] It is completely against the nature, when one woman lives together with many men (Vielmännerei) just as when a community of men lives together. The latter criticizes the catholic monasteries and is an influence of Lutheranism.[25] This is no surprise, because Schlettwein was professor at the

---

[17] Uebe (1992).

[18] Schlettwein (1731–1802) was a professor at the University of Basel in 1776 and professor of policy, science of cameralistics and science of finances at the University of Gießen from 1777 to 1785.

[19] Schlettwein (1784/1980) § 69.

[20] Schlettwein (1779).

[21] Schlettwein (1784/1980) §§ 74, 75.

[22] Schlettwein (1784/1980) §§ 86.

[23] Schlettwein (1784/1980) § 224.

[24] Schlettwein (1784/1980) § 225.

[25] See 18th Heilbronn Symposium, 16–18, 2005.

University of Gießen, when he published his fundamental book in the year 1784. Gießen is located in the state of Hessen-Darmstadt, a state where reformed Lutheran Church prevailed.

As said before, Süßmilch deduced from the balanced number of men and women in the age when they get married that the Divine order allows only monogamy. Opposite to this, Schlettwein deduces solely from sexual proportion of 100 born girls and 106 born boys that polygamy (Vielweiberei) corresponds with the Law of nature and therefore with the Divine order.[26] He argues without statistical data that there is no proof that monogamy has a general preference of polygamy.[27] Already in the year 1780, the cameralist and Antiphysiocrat von Pfeiffer pointed out that complete statistical knowledge of population registers and censuses is necessary to assess the real situation and the facts.[28] Von Pfeiffer continues the method which Süßmilch had collected from other authors and further developed by his own. Schlettwein ignored statistical data, which have been generally known already in due time. So Schlettwein's physiocratism is a more theoretical theory, which is hardly based on empirical data known at that time.

Schlettwein supports and recommends child labor. Parents have the right to use the animal urge of their children for the own advantage of the parents as long as they feed and educate them.[29] Children are co-owners of the possessions of their parents immediately when they are born,[30] but children do not have to take care of their parents when they are old. This corresponds with the spirit in due course when life expectancy came around to 35–40 years. So Schlettwein argues that the property right, which the father alone has during his lifetime, goes over to the mother immediately when the father dies. The husband has the right of possession of his wife and her body[31] during marriage. The mother gets back her human rights when the father dies.[32]

As said before, Physiocrats think that growth of population is source of the national prosperity. Therefore on the physiocratic basis of Law of nature, a state has to guaranty completely for each citizen the personal rights and the rights on possessions in reality. Furthermore, a state also has to guaranty blessed enjoyment and benefit of the rights of each citizen.[33] The true natural order requires that people train their possibilities by dealing with religion and the Lord. The sovereign is never entitled to force his citizen to be a member of a certain religion.[34] Schlettwein describes very detailed cohabitation and in which way it affects the duties and

[26] Schlettwein (1784/1980) § 223, rightly counted 232.

[27] Schlettwein (1784/1980) § 234.

[28] von Pfeiffer (1780), pp 98/99.

[29] Schlettwein (1784/1980) § 246.

[30] Schlettwein (1784/1980) § 241.

[31] Schlettwein (1784/1980) § 236.

[32] Schlettwein (1784/1980) § 240.

[33] Schlettwein (1784/1980) §§ 261, 262.

[34] Schlettwein (1784/1980) §§ 268, 280.

natural rights of men and woman, if a woman is a virgin and the man is not married, the woman is a widow and the man is not married and so on.[35] His argumentations follow clearly Christian ethical values.

The Antiphysiocrat von Pfeiffer agrees with Schlettwein that production of food is most important to give a population the opportunity to build up a family and to feed the family. Therefore farming is very important. Opposite to Schlettwein, he argues that not only farming but also factories and manufacturing produce value and wealth,[36] and refers to the wealth of Frankford, Cologne, and Hamburg at that time.[37] Von Pfeiffer recognizes that extreme shortage of food can arise despite all intelligent precautions and that caused from this rising prices can emerge or that there is widespread famine.[38] Schlettwein is convinced that a sovereign and a state will have no famine, when they follow the Law of nature. He is optimistic that there are no epidemics on a big scale, when the population has enough to eat. The classical political economist Malthus is pessimistic on this subject. He formulates principles of population that population growths are faster than the production of food.[39] This is coherent on the basis of his experiences of the misery of the population at that time. Among others, we see similar reasons looking today on the misery of the population of many developing countries.

Physiocrat's Input to Laws of Population

The "rearguard"[40] of Physiocrats saw no basic difference between physiocratism and classical political economics. Physiocrats believed in the possibility to educate people to sensible natural existence. Aim of human life is happiness and wealth in a society of many healthy, happy, and agriculturally educated intelligent mankind. Concerning population development, Physiocrats take over cameralistic ideas. The methodological difference in this coherence consists in the following: Cameralism takes the aim of the sovereign to increase the number of people as basis for example to develop a theory of correlation between offer and realizable income. Physiocratism develops theory of market prices and formulates recommendations for immigration policy. Physiocrats make no contributions to the laws of population in the sense that they described rules and patterns of population development like the cameralist Süßmilch did. As we know today, there exist no laws of population, there only exist regularities of population development depending on territory and time.

---

[35] Schlettwein (1784/1980) §§ 225.

[36] von Pfeiffer (1780), pp 23/24.

[37] von Pfeiffer (1780), pp 22.

[38] von Pfeiffer (1780), p 100.

[39] Malthus (1798).

[40] Blaich (1983), p 35.

References

Armengaud A (1971) Die Bevölkerung Europas von 1700–1914. In: Cipolla CM, Borchardt K (Hg) Bevölkerungsgeschichte Europas. Mittelalter bis Neuzeit. Aus dem englischen übersetzt von Anjuta Dünnwald. Drei Aufsätze aus: The Fontana Economic History of Europe. R. Piper, München, pp 123–180

Blaich F (1983) Der Beitrag der deutschen Physiokraten für die Entwicklung der Wirtschaftswissenschaft von der Kameralistik zur Nationalökonomie. In: Scherf H (Hrsg) Studien zur Entwicklung der ökonomischen Theorie III; Schriften des Vereins für Socialpolitik, Gesellschaft für Wirtschafts- und Sozialwissenschaften, Neue Folge Band 115/III. Ducker & Humblodt, Berlin, pp 9–38

Hummel D (2000) Der Bevölkerungsdiskurs. Demographisches Wissen und politische Macht. Leske+Budrich, Opladen, p 224

Malthus TR (1798) An essay on the principle of population, as it affects the future of society. Murray, London

Mols, Roger (1971) Die Bevölkerung Europas 1500–1700. In: Cipolla CM (Hrsg) deutsche Ausgabe herausgegeben von K. Borchardt: Europäische Wirtschafts-geschichte. The Fontana Economic History in 5 Bänden; Band 2: Sechzehntes und siebzehntes Jahrhundert. R. Piper, München

Notestein FW (1945) Population – the long view. In: Schulz T (ed) Food for the world. University of Chicago Press, Chicago, pp 36–57

Schlettwein JA (1980) Die Rechte der Menschen oder der einzige wahre Grund aller Gesetze, Ordnungen und Verfassungen, bey Justus Friedrich Kriegen, Gießen 1784; Faksimiledruck, Scriptor

Schlettwein JA (1779) Grundfeste der Staaten oder die politische Ökonomie. bey Justus Friedrich Kriegen, Gießen

Süßmilch JP (2001) Die göttliche Ordnung in den Veränderungen des menschlichen Geschlechts, aus der Geburt, dem Tod und der Fortpflanzung desselben erwiesen; Berlin 1741, Faksimile-Ausgabe, Verlag Wirtschaft und Finanzen, Düsseldorf

Uebe G (1992) The model of lang – national income accounts in 1807; computers mathematical application, vol 24, no. 8/9. Press Ltd, UK, pp 167–179

von Pfeiffer J (1780) Der Antiphysiocrat oder die umständliche Untersuchung des sogenannten physiokratischen Systems vermöge welchem eine allgemeine Freiheit, und einzige Auflage, auf den reinen Ertrag der Grundstücke, die Glückseligkeit aller Staaten ausmachen soll; im Verlag der Eßlingerischen Buchandlung, Frankfurt am Main

Chapter 8
On the Reception of Quesnay's Economic Thought in German History of Economics

Günther Chaloupek

Introduction

In his history of economics in Germany, Wilhelm Roscher notes that, compared to other European countries, it was only in Germany where the Physiocratic doctrines found a significant number of followers.[1] As long as this interest prevailed, it was concentrated mainly on practical applications of essential policy prescriptions of Physiocracy, particularly as regards the promotion of agriculture as a means to increase the economic potential of the *Staatswirtschaft* of the territories, and also with respect to tax policy. If, according to Roscher,[2] Theodor Schmalz[3] with the textbook *Staatswirtschaftslehre in Briefen* (published 1818) was the last representative of Physiocracy in Germany, then the doctrine ceased to exert any direct impact on economic policy soon after the turn of the century.

Thereafter, Physiocracy survived as a subject of the history of economic doctrines which was, however, not a subject of its own in German economic science in the first half of the nineteenth century. Most of the learned textbooks of economics, such as those by Rau,[4] Hillebrand,[5] and Knies,[6] include introductory sections on the history of economics which, however, account only for minor parts of the whole tracts.[7]

---

[1] Roscher (1874, p. 484).

[2] Ibid, pp. 449 f.

[3] Theodor Schmalz (1760–1831) was a professor at the universities of Königsberg and Halle before he was appointed to the position of the first rector of the University of Berlin in 1810.

[4] *Grundsätze der Volkswirtschaftslehre*, published 1826.

[5] *Die Nationalökonomie der Gegenwart und Zukunft*, published 1848.

[6] *Die politische Oekonomie vom Standpunkte der geschichtlichen Methode*, published 1853.

[7] See Howey (1982).

G. Chaloupek (✉)
Chamber of Labour, Prinz-Eugen-Straße 20-22, A-1041 Vienna, Austria
e-mail: Guenther.CHALOUPEK@akwien.at

J.G. Backhaus (ed.), *Physiocracy, Antiphysiocracy and Pfeiffer*, The European Heritage in Economics and the Social Sciences 10, DOI 10.1007/978-1-4419-7497-6_8,

It appears to be true that it was Karl Marx who rediscovered Quesnay's *Tableau économique* (1965), certainly the most important treatise of Physiocracy from the viewpoint of theory, in the middle of the century.[8] But the author who deserves praise for being the first to give a comprehensive account of the Physiocratic doctrine was an "Austrian" – or, rather a Hungarian economist who is largely unknown today although, according to Richard Howey's *Bibliography of General Histories of Economics,* his history of economic theory is "a longer, and more studious, survey of the literature than that found in any previous history"[9]: Julius (Gyula) Kautz.

Julius Kautz on Physiocracy

In his presentation of the principles of the Physiocratic system (pp. 338 ff), Kautz identifies the doctrine of labor applied to land being the sole productive activity as the central element of Physiocratic economic thinking. This doctrine has to be seen as a consequence of the more general idea of the preponderance of nature in which all Physiocratic social thought is based.

Julius – in Hungarian: Gyula – Kautz was born in Györ (or Raab, western Hungary) in 1829. As a member of the national guards, he was an active participant in the Hungarian insurrection of 1848. After having completed his studies at the universities of Pest, Berlin and Heidelberg, he could obtain a teaching position at the Pressburg (now: Bratislava) law academy in 1851. When he published the first volume of his *Theorie und Geschichte der National-Oekonomik,* under the title *Die National-Oekonomik als Wissenschaft,* in 1858, he was a professor at the law academy of Großwardein in Transylvania (now: Oradea in Romania), from where he was promoted as a professor to the University of Pest. He wrote the book in German, a Hungarian translation was published only in 2004.

As a student of Wilhelm Roscher, Kautz was strongly influenced by the German Historical School. Kautz explicitly objected to J.B. Say's verdict that there was no benefit to be expected from discussing obsolete and discarded old opinions. By contrast, he emphasized the relevance of history and of the history of economic thinking in particular in order to understand in depth the fundamental socio-economic problems of his age, as well as the significance of the teachings of economics as it has become a fully developed branch of social science. In his general approach, Kautz cannot be considered a follower of the Historical School. His interest in abstract analytical concepts enables

[8] Blaug (1968, p. 27); similarly Schumpeter (1954, p. 232).

[9] Howey (1982, p. 40).

him to be among the few economists who took note of J.H. Gossen's *Gesetze des menschlichen Verkehrs* (1854).

Kautz was elected to the Hungarian Diet in 1863. In 1883 he was appointed vice governor of the Austro-Hungarian Bank (the central bank of the Austro-Hungarian empire), of which he became *Generalgouverneur* in 1892 (until 1900). Kautz died in Budapest in 1909.

As an advocate of political liberalism, Kautz was more interested in those aspects of the teachings of the Physiocrats, which are important for the further evolution of liberal economic and political thinking. Therefore, he emphasized the Physiocrats' engagement for freedom of exchange and freedom of property in order to improve economic and social well-being, once they are freed of the impediments imposed by the mercantilist system. Kautz also mentions the Physiocrats' high praise of consumption, and their rejection of the monetary theory of the mercantilist economists. He devotes a special section to Quesnay as the founder of the Physiocratic system (pp. 345 ff) who is given credit for having reduced "the economic organism of society to its simple basic essential elements" (p. 348). At the same time, Kautz objects to Quesnay's narrow productivity which degrades industrial producers to a *classe sterile,* and also to the proposal derived thereof, the *impot unique.* Kautz rather briefly refers to Quesnay's *Tableau économique*, which he criticizes for its "barren, abstract, and boring" form of presentation.[10] Kautz points to the *Tableau's* relevance for the emergence of the concept of circular flow when he remarks that it deserves recognition for "foreshadowing the truth that, who wants to sell, must at the same time be a buyer,"[11] but he does not really appreciate this line of development of economic theory.

In his survey of other representatives of Physiocracy in France, Kautz mentions – among others – Gournay and Condillac who maintained that not only agriculture but also industry should be considered productive. Turgot gets the praise for his concise and clear presentation of the Physiocratic system, but it was also Turgot who "came to destroy it" through "exposing its one-sidedness, its errors and its deficiencies by implementing it in practice" (p. 359).

In the final section on the subject (p. 364 ff), Kautz gives a comprehensive evaluation of Physiocracy. He re-emphasizes the doctrine that the products of land are the only sources of economic wealth constitutes a fundamental error in Physiocratic economic thinking. In a more general sense, Kautz considers the view that only labor which produces material results is productive, and that therefore all other

[10] He asserts that the *Tableau* ("das, beiläufig erwähnt, wegen seiner trockenen, abstrakten, nicht recht genießbaren Form am wenigsten günstig aufgenommen wurde," p. 349) was therefore the least well-received part of Quesnay's writings.

[11] "Seine richtige Ahnung der Wahrheit, daß wer verkaufen will, auch zugleich Käufer sein müsse" (p. 350).

kinds of economic activity – not only industry but also trade and transport – are "sterile," as fundamentally erroneous (p. 369). Hence, the single tax-proposal that is derived from the theory of productivity is equally mistaken. These errors, however, seem to be outweighed by the merits of the Physiocratic doctrine, which are both economic and political. If economic thinking that preceded the Physiocratic system, and mercantilist economics, in particular, appeared only as a "loosely connected aggregate" of ideas, without being formed into an organic whole of a scientific system, Physiocratic doctrine made significant progress in the evolution of economic thought toward such a "unified organism of scientific ideas and insights" (p. 364). According to Kautz, the Physiocrats, and Quesnay in particular, first discovered certain laws of evolution on which material social order, economic progress, and the wealth of nations are based, and in this context Quesnay was the first to point out the *soziale Frage* ("social question," p. 365). Fundamental concepts of French enlightenment such as *droit naturel* and *ordre naturel* enable the Physiocrats to liberate economic thinking from the mercantilist ideals of an absolutist state with its feudal prerogatives, its politically granted privileges and monopolies, and establish instead of them the principles of freedom of property and of economic activity, of *laissez faire*, and also of universality and cosmopolitism instead of national egotism. These principles also constitute important ethical elements which in Kautz's view are essential also for economic thinking (p. 366). In this respect, he follows the ethical approach of the Historical School.

For Kautz (1860), the liberal political thinker, the essential merit of Physiocratic thought was that it incorporated the ideas of enlightenment in economic thinking. It can, however, not claim "absolute scientific value for itself." The "greatest achievement of the eighteenth century" was the replacement of Physiocracy by "the system of free industry, Smithianism" (p. 371).

Friedrich Engels and Karl Marx on Quesnay

In his *Theories of Surplus Value*, Marx gives the utmost possible praise to Quesnay where he writes that Quesnay's "attempt to portray the whole production process of capital as a process of reproduction, with circulation merely as the form of this reproductive process … was an extremely brilliant conception, incontestably the most brilliant for which political economy had up to then been responsible" (vol. 1, p. 334[12]). Indeed, by providing essential analytical instruments for the understanding of the economic process as a whole, Physiocratic writers and Quesnay in particular were an indispensable source of knowledge for Marx from the very beginnings of his life-long effort to develop a theory of political economy of capitalism. When in 1846 Marx asked the publisher for postponement of publication of his book on the critique of political economy, the main reason he mentions was the necessity to give

[12] Indications of page numbers to Volume 1 of Theories of Surplus Value and to Volume II of Capital refer to the English translations (see References).

appropriate consideration to the Physiocrats.[13] His estimate that his studies of their writings would take another 3 months turned out to be overoptimistic. There are hardly any references to the essential doctrines of the Physiocrats in Marx's writings published before his death. The book which shows the highest indebtedness to Quesnay is the second volume of *Das Kapital*, published posthumously by Engels in 1885. To be sure, *Das Kapital* cannot be considered a work of *Dogmengeschichte*. Yet, as a treatise on political economy, it has extensive sections on the development of the relevant economic theories, and – as has often been noticed – Marx preferred old and old-fashioned theories to those of his contemporaries. The *Theories of Surplus Value* where special sections are devoted to Physiocratic economics was first published by Karl Kautsky between 1905 and 1910, although the manuscripts had been written in the early 1860s. As in many other instances, Marx was unable to produce a final version of his very detailed account of Physiocratic economics. Hence, it was left to Friedrich Engels to publish the first comment in a classic book of socialism on Quesnay – in his *Anti-Dühring*.[14]

Engels on Quesnay's Tableau

The aim of Engels' discussion of Quesnay's *Tableau* is a rather limited one. He wants to defend Quesnay against the critique by Eugen Dühring who had charged Quesnay for confusion, vagueness, and mysticism. According to Engels, Dühring had criticized Quesnay for the – alleged – inconsistency that he was unable to trace the net product which is appropriated by the landlords in the form of rent in the circular flow of the economic process. As a consequence, the *Tableau* produces only "confusion and arbitrariness resulting in mysticism" (Dühring quoted by Engels 1894, p. 262).

To counter Dühring's charge, Engels in a first step gives a stylized account of Quesnay's *Tableau* which for its abstract clearness can be called an early example of modern economic analytical thinking. Engels demonstrates that in Quesnay's *Tableau* everything that is produced either by the tenant class or the industrial class ("*classe sterile*") also has its final use either in the form of nonproductive or productive consumption, and that it is correct to identify the two billion that landlords receive from tenants as "net product," although the landlords spend only half of it for consumption of products of the tenants, and the other half on products of the industrial class. If Dühring had also pointed to Quesnay's frequent switching between exchange in real terms and in money terms as a possible source of confusion, Engels invalidates the argument by making Quesnay's tacit assumption of constant

[13] Letter to the publisher Leske, dated 1 August 1846 (MEW vol. 27, 1977, p. 49 f). At that time Marx had started to work on his first major economic treatise, which was published only in 1859 under the title "*Zur Kritik der politischen Ökonomie*."

[14] The section which is referred to here is generally attributed to Marx.

prices explicit. What Quesnay calls "interest" is in fact only the reproduction of the part of the fixed capital that is used up for production in 1 year. Therefore, it is correct not to include this "interest" in the net product.

Engels' brilliant account of Quesnay's *Tableau* is essentially identical with the one which Shigeto Tsuru gives in the appendix to Paul Sweezy's *Theory of capitalist development* (1970), where he does, however, not mention Engels' achievement of 1878. As we know from their exchange of letters,[15] for his admirable presentation of the essence of Quesnay's *Tableau* Engels could build on intensive studies of Marx with which the latter had begun a few years after publication of the Communist Manifesto. Similar to many other writings of Marx, these studies existed in the form of excerpts in copy books or of manuscripts, which Marx himself never finalized for publication.

Marx

In the second volume of *Das Kapital*, it becomes clear that Quesnay's analytical approach in the *Tableau* served Marx as a model for his theory of labor value which he presented in the context of the circular flow of commodities and money. If Quesnay distinguishes between two forms of advances by tenants, the *avances annuelles*, which are recovered within on production period, and the *avances primitives*, of which only a fraction (1/10) is recovered each year, he treats them as different forms of the same type of capital, i.e., productive capital, which is used in the production process. In Quesnay's view, surplus value which he called net product can only originate from this phase of the circular flow. In Marx's terminology: The *avances primitives* are identical with the fixed part of "constant capital," while one part of the *avances annuelles*, namely current inputs of commodities used up in production, forms the liquid part of constant capital, and "wages" for the labor employed in production as the other part are identical with what Marx calls "variable capital." Marx gives credit to Adam Smith for one single advancement in economic theory: If for Quesnay, only capital and labor (constant and variable capital) employed in combination with land is "productive" (i.e., has the capacity to generate surplus value), the step forward made by Smith was "to generalize these categories. In his work, they no longer relate to one special form of capital, farmer's capital, but to every form of productive capital" (p. 269) But at the same time, Smith "falls far behind Quesnay" when he includes in his concept of constant and variable capital not only advances made on behalf of production of commodities (agricultural or industrial) but also of mere commerce: Smith held that capital "may be employed in raising, manufacturing, or purchasing goods, and selling them again with profit"[16] (p. 270).

---

[15] In his letter to Engels on July 6, 1863, Marx gives a detailed summary and discussion of Quesnay's *Tableau*. See Marx and Engels, *Briefwechsel*, vol. 3, 1983, pp. 148 ff.

[16] Wealth of Nations, quoted in Marx, *Capital*, vol. 2, p. 191. Marx criticizes Smith for committing a partial confusion of "circulating capital" (in the sphere of circulation, i.e., trade and commerce) with "constant capital." For the sake of brevity I must avoid here going into the details of terminology and their consequences.

For Marx, the reason why the Physiocrats failed to identify labor in itself as the source of surplus production, and as criterion for an activity to be termed "productive," lies in the fact that in their concept of *avances annuelles* they lump together means of subsistence for agricultural labor with inputs of agricultural raw materials needed for production of current output of land. By contrast, Marx in this respect draws a sharp distinction between "variable capital" – the advances for wage payments to workers – and "constant capital" of which the other current material inputs form a part (together with "fixed capital"). Therefore, according to the Physiocrats' view, "the portion of value which labor adds to the product (like the portion of value added by raw materials, instruments of labor, etc. – in short by the material components of constant capital) is equal only to the value of the means of subsistence paid to the workers" (p. 289 f). What they did not see is that the part of the *avances annuelles* spent on wages was the source of command over "labor power," which is capable of adding more value to the product than what is necessary for its reproduction. "The very doctrine of the Physiocrats prohibited them from discovering the distinction between constant capital and variable capital. If it is labor that produces surplus value ..., then it produces it in industry as well as in agriculture. But since in the Physiocratic system labor produces surplus value in only one branch of production, agriculture, surplus-value was not seen as arising from labor, but rather from the special activity (collaboration) of nature in this branch" (p. 290). Marx thought that only the restriction that labor is "productive" (in the sense of Quesnay and Marx) only in combination with land constituted an a priori-assumption, and that the lifting of this restriction would make the "true" insight possible. He never realized that it might be equally legitimate to consider the doctrine that only labor as such is productive – an a priori-assumption of the same kind (Schumpeter 1954, p. 238). Or, if he realized it, he never admitted it.

In his evaluation of Physiocratic economic doctrines, Marx argued that the Physiocrats had – unknowingly or not – taken an outdated perspective for their social categories on which they had based their economic system. If Quesnay and his immediate disciples believed in the feudal garb of their principal agents landlord, tenant, and industrial workman, "in point of fact, their system is the first systematic conception of capitalist production" (Marx 1978, p. 436). In this "bourgeois reproduction of the feudal system" the productive agent, i.e., the farmer, is not the owner of the means of production, whereas Quesnay presents "the landowner as the true capitalist, that is, the appropriator of surplus labor. Feudalism is thus explained and portrayed from the viewpoint of bourgeois production" (*Theories of Surplus Value*, p. 49 f). At the surface, the Physiocratic doctrine amounts to a glorification of feudal land ownership, in effect "becomes transformed into the economic negation of it" (ibid, p. 52). During the French Revolution, land owners were partly expropriated, partly their rent was taxed away. The liberal postulate of laissez faire, intended by the Physiocrats to benefit land owners and tenants, eventually conformed to the interests of the industrial class.

If bourgeois writers later denied any interrelationship between Quesnay's theory of circular flow and net product on one side and the doctrine of laissez faire on the other side, they failed to realize that the Physiocratic system in its essence amounts to "proclaim(ing) the rise of the bourgeois system of production on the ruins of the feudal" (p. 53).

In a footnote to chapter 17 on the circulation of surplus value of *Das Kapital*, vol. II, Marx makes another reference to Quesnay in the context of his distinction between the "circuit of money" (essentially the flow of income) and the "circulation of money." "The circuit of money – i.e., the return of the money to the starting-point – in as much this forms a moment of the turnover of capital, is a phenomenon completely different from and even opposed to the circulation of money, which expresses its constant removal from its starting point through a series of hands" (p. 416). At this point, Marx makes a reference to Quesnay: "If the Physiocrats still lumped the two phenomena together, they were at least the first to have stressed the return of money to its point of departure as an essential form of the circulation of capital, as a form of the circulation that mediates reproduction" (ibid).

In his *Theories of Surplus Value*, Marx elaborates in great detail a several concrete forms in which the transactions between the three principal agents could take place. I mention only two examples. If Quesnay assumes that the landlord's (L) purchase of commodities from the manufacturer (S) valued 1,000 milliards is effectuated *uno actu*, it could also be imagined that "L bought from S in installments and similarly received his rent from F (the farmer) in installments, the 1 milliard of manufactured commodities could be bought say with 100 millions ... The whole circulation would then have been carried out with 100 million" (p. 319). Or, if mutual deliveries on credit terms are assumed between farmers and manufacturers, less money is needed, or, in the case that the final payment of rent to the landlord of 2,000 milliards must be made in a single payment, the velocity of money is smaller (ibid, p. 329 ff). If it is difficult to follow Marx's painstaking exercises, it seems not clear what he intended to demonstrate with them beyond the effect on velocity.

August Oncken

August Oncken,[17] 1844–1911, economist and historian of economic theory, was a professor at the universities of Aachen in Germany and finally in Bern, Switzerland. The first volume of his *Geschichte der Nationalöklonomie* was published in 1902. It covers the period before Adam Smith. A second volume which the author had intended to cover the evolution of economic theory since Adam Smith was announced in the preface of the book but has never appeared. The first volume ends with an extensive section on the Physiocrats whose system, according to the title of this section, marks the beginning of economics as a science.

Oncken's comprehensive presentation of the Physiocratic system centers on Quesnay's writings. In the detailed discussion, which covers the philosophical foundations together with Quesnay's political and economic teachings, equal weight is given to all of Quesnay's writings among which the contributions to Diderot's

[17] For a short *vita* of Oncken, see Herz and Weiberger (2006, p. 377). August Oncken must not be confused with the historian Hermann Oncken, who is more widely known for his biography of *Ferdinand Lassalle* (1920) and other books.

Encyclopédie (several of them, however, were withdrawn and remained unpublished) and the *Théorie de l'Impot* (1760, jointly with the elder Mirabeau) offer a more detailed treatment of economic policy issues than the short text of the *questions* and *maximes* appended to the *Tableau.*

In comparison with Kautz, Oncken's discussion of the Physiocratic doctrine as forerunner and pathbreaker for Adam Smith's economic liberalism is free of the enthusiasm of Kautz who emphasized the political aspect of "progress" in economics. In respect of economic policy, a synthesis between Colbert's propensity toward excessive experimenting and Turgot's exaggerated doctrinarism is Adam Smith's highest achievement in Oncken's view (p. 481).

In sharp contrast to Schumpeter's judgment (Schumpeter 1954, 243 ff), Oncken puts all the blame of doctrinaire delusion on Turgot. Turgot's failure as a politician, who during his brief tenure as *Controleur Général des Finances* liberalized grain trade and abolished craft guilds with politically disastrous consequences, is ascribed by Oncken to Turgot's incorrect interpretation and application of Quesnay's teachings.[18] On the other hand, Oncken defends Quesnay against the charges of utopianism and idealism. If Quesnay envisages a "perfect ideal condition" which is contrasted with imperfect factual realities, he does not understand this concept as an "absolute blueprint which is to be forced upon human society in order to achieve the greatest possible happiness" (p. 399). With respect to "idealism," Oncken argues that it was inappropriate for Roscher and the Historical School to come up with such a criticism when, at the same time, they emphasize the "ethical component" in economics (ibid).

It appears quite obvious that with the term "idealism" Roscher et al. had in mind that Quesnay's system rested fundamentally on Cartesian rationalism. From this philosophy, Quesnay deduced his conviction that those laws can claim the highest degree of evidence which can be expressed in mathematical terms.[19] If Oncken – in accordance with Marx and in contradiction to Schumpeter[20] – rightly emphasizes the unity of the Quesnaysian system,[21] he acknowledges its fundamentally rationalist approach. It is not at all convincing to attribute the difficulties which Turgot, Mirabeau, and elsewhere Schlettwein encountered in their attempts to implement some of the core prescriptions of Physiocratic economic policy to lack of pragmatism on the part of the actors, as Oncken argued, and not to the fundamental character of Quesnay's system.

---

[18] "Turgot verdient in Wahrheit nicht den Platz, den ihm eine wohlwollende Geschichtsschreibung bisher eingeräumt hat" (p. 469).

[19] On this point, see Pribram (1992, vol. 1, p. 206).

[20] "The over-all description of a stationary economic process which Quesnay embodied in his tableau is not, as his pupils and practically all critics believed, the centerpiece of that structure but an addition to it that is separable from the rest" (Schumpeter 1954, p. 239).

[21] "Die ganze bisherige Besprechung des Tableau économique dürfte außer Zweifel gestellt haben, dass die 'Formule arithmétique', die 'Questions' und die 'Maximes' ein zusammenhängendes Dreigestirn bilden, wobei jedes Glied den Schlüssel zum vollen Verständnis der beiden anderen darstellt" (p. 401).

With respect to the *formule arithmétique* of the *Tableau*, Oncken criticizes Engels' treatment in the *Anti-Dühring*. According to Oncken, Engels did not succeed in his attempt to clarify the meaning of Quesnay's *zic-zac* when he defends it against Dühring's charges. However, Oncken's discussion of the *Tableau* itself to which he devotes only a few pages falls far behind Engels' penetrating understanding of the subject, and thereby confirms the judgment that, for a long time, only Marx and Engels really understood its mathematical content. Needless to say, that Oncken did not touch upon the aspect emphasized by Marx that the Physiocratic doctrine had presented the capitalist system in the sociological categories of feudalism.

Physiocratic Elements in Werner Sombart's Late Economic Thinking

In one of the sections on the history of economics in his magnum opus *Der moderne Kapitalismus*, Werner Sombart categorized Quesnay together with Smith, Ricardo, Marx, and Roscher as representative of "static-mechanic theory of exchange" (*statisch-mechanistische Tauschlehre*) which he contrasted with the "social economics" (*Sozialökonomik*) of List, Dühring, and Carey (Sombart 1916, vol. II/2, p. 920). Although Sombart in his late economic thinking increasingly distanced himself from pure exchange-type economics, he nonetheless turned to the model of Quesnay *Tableau* as an analytical device. Sombart argued that disproportions between products of land (foodstuffs and raw materials) were partially responsible for the weakening dynamics of the economy in the period of *Späkapitalismus*. For remedies, Sombart proposed "re-agrarianization" and the restriction of production of luxuries – both proposals are in the spirit of Quesnay.[22] The development of the world economy since 1930 invalidates such an explanation, at least with regard to the twentieth century. But the success of books like "Limits to Growth" and recent debates about impending shortages of food and energy suggest that the issues raised by Quesnay will remain topical in the future.

References

Blaug M (1968) Economic theory in retrospect. Richard D. Irwin, Homewood

Engels F (1894) Herrn Eugen Dührings Umwälzung der Wissenschaft. Verlag J. H. W. Dietz Nachf., Stuttgart

Gossen JH (1854) Entwickelung der Gesetze des menschlichen Verkehrs, und der daraus fliessenden Regeln für menschliches Handeln. Vieweg Braunschweig

Herz D, Weinberger V (eds) (2006) Lexikon ökonomischer Werke. Wissenschaftliche Buchgesellschaft, Darmastadt

[22] For a discussion of this aspect of Sombart's last works see Priddat (1996, pp. 279 ff).

Howey RS (1982) A bibliography of general histories of economics, 1692–1975. The Regent Press of Kansas, Lawrence

Kautz J (1860) Die geschichtliche Entwicklung der National-Oekonomik und ihrer Literatur. Second part of Theorie und Geschichte der National-Oekonomik. Verlag Carl Gerold's Sohn, Vienna

Marx K Theories of surplus value, Part I. Foreign Languages Publishing House, Moscow, s.a

Marx K, Engels F (1977) Briefe Februar 1842-Dezember 1851, MEW Vol. 27, Berlin

Marx K, Engels F (1983) Der Briefwechsel, 4 vol, dtv München

Marx K (1978) Capital, vol. II. Penguin Books, London

Pribram K (1992) Geschichte des ökonomischen Denkens, Zwei Bände. Suhrkamp, Frankfurt a. M

Priddat B (1996) Werner Sombart's late economic thinking: back to Physiocracy? In: Backhaus J (ed) Werner Sombart (1863–1941) social scientist, vol 1. Metropolis, Marburg, pp 271–296

Quesnay F (1965) Tableau économique. Akademie, Berlin

Roscher W (1874) Geschichte der National-Oekonomik in Deutschland. Verlag R. Oldenburg, München

Schumpeter JA (1954) History of economic analysis. Allen & Unwin, London 1982

Sombart W (1916/1927) Der moderne Kapitalismus, 3 vols. Duncker & Humblot, München-Berlin

Sweezy PM (1970) Theorie der kapitalistischen Entwicklung. Suhrkamp, Frankfurt

Chapter 9
Mature Cameralism According to Pfeiffer

Marcel van Meerhaeghe

Il avait du bon sens; le reste vient ensuite.[1]

Jean de La Fontaine (1621–1695)

eine zeitgenössische Kameralistik tut uns bitter not[2]

Werner Sombart (1863–1941)

This paper deals with cameralism, and examines in particular Johann Friedrich von Pfeiffer's (1721–1786) main views and places him in historical context. First, I sketch the characteristics of mercantilism and cameralism. Then, I consider the most important points of view of Pfeiffer on the policy issues of that time and finally, some concluding comments on cameralism follow. Throughout the text 'von Pfeiffer' and 'Pfeiffer' are used as synonyms.

Mercantilism and Cameralism

Oxford Dictionary defines "mercantilism" as "the economic theory that trade generates wealth and is stimulated by the accumulation of bullion, which a government should encourage by means of protectionism" (although mercantilism is no theory at all), but it ignores "cameralism" (2001, p. 810). The German *Brockhaus* gives a better but still unsatisfactory definition of mercantilism: "The state measures shaped by interventionism influencing the economic process; also: certain loose conceptions

---

[1]The translation proves again *traduttore traditore*: "Well stock'd with sense, all else upon demand Would come of course, and did, we understand" (de La Fontaine 1975, p. 188).

[2]*A contemporary cameralism is very necessary (Sombart* 1929, *p. 331).*

M. van Meerhaeghe (✉)
University of Ghent, Kriekenbergdreef 21, B-9831 Deurle, Belgium
e-mail: hvm@klaproos.be

J.G. Backhaus (ed.), *Physiocracy, Antiphysiocracy and Pfeiffer*, The European Heritage in Economics and the Social Sciences 10, DOI 10.1007/978-1-4419-7497-6_9,

related to economic theory and policy"[3] (*Brockhaus* 2000, vol. 3, p. 3008). "Interventionism" is too strong, especially for the later mercantilists. In fact, mercantilism is the "entire body of measures designed to make the state as powerful and as rich as possible" in the sixteenth, seventeenth, and eighteenth centuries (van Meerhaeghe 1986, p. 86).

Cameralism is "a practical doctrine" of the seventeenth and eighteenth centuries relating to all aspects of public administration taking especially into account the treasury of the local ruler and referring particularly to the German-speaking countries. It also "designates the German form of mercantilism"[4] (*Brockhaus* 2000, vol. 3, p. 2279). This is questioned in the comments below.

The setting-up of nation states and the discovery of America (1492) had profound economic repercussions. The rationalist spirit gained more and more ground; profit-seeking assumed unusually large proportions. The formation of national armies made vast monetary demands on the sovereign rulers. The influence of the state increased at the expense of the authority of the Church.

The principal means employed to fulfill the mercantilist aim were acquisition of a maximum amount of precious metals and the pursuance of an active population policy. Mercantilism embodied the precept that states possessing gold and silver (e.g., Spain) should endeavor to keep such metals, their export being prohibited. Other countries exerted every effort to obtain gold and silver; if they had no mines to develop, they had to stimulate imports of precious metals. This could be done if there was a favorable trade balance.

The accumulation of precious metals was influenced by the observation that an increase of the quantity of money led to a decrease of the rate of interest while the availability of credit rose. The major mercantilist (and cameralist) policies are: (a) furtherance of an active trade balance, (b) an active population policy; (c) the furtherance of crafts and industries (e.g., Colbertism).

In England mercantilist policies were effective in creating a skilled industrial population and a large shipping industry. Through a series of Navigation Acts, England finally destroyed the commerce of Holland, its chief rival. Henry VIII, Elizabeth I, and Cromwell conformed their policies to mercantilism. British trade with the Baltics and with India required the acquisition of gold and silver.

Civil servants in the numerous German small principalities attempted to find enough money for the *camera* (treasure chamber) of the head of state: the science of the *camera* (Kameralwissenschaft) got its first chairs only in 1727.[5] Machiavelli

---

[3]Bez. für die zw. dem 16. und 18 Jh. durch Interventionismus und Dirigismus geprägten Eingriffe des Staates in den Wirtschaftsprozess sowie für bestimmte, in sich nicht geschlossene wirtschafts-theoret. und –polit. Konzeptionen (*Brockhaus* 2000, vol. 3, p. 3008).

[4]… alle Bereiche der öffentl. Verwaltung umfassende prak. Lehre des 17. und 18. Jh. unter besonderer Berücksichtigung des landesfürstl. Haushalts. … auch als dt. Ausprägung des Merkantilismus bezeichnet, …(*Brockhaus* 2000, vol. 3, p. 2279).

[5]In Halle (Saale) and Frankfurt (Oder).

advised rulers about expedient political policies, the cameralists did the same by advising them about economic policies. Adam Smith even used the improved economic analysis, especially on the trade balance, of the later cameralists.

Veit Ludwig von Seckendorf[6] (1626–1692), Johann Joachim Becher (1635–1682), and Phillip W. von Hörnigk (1638–1712) were among the earliest cameralists. One of the later, best-known cameralists is Johann Heinrich Gottlob von Justi (1717–1771), whose book *Die Grundfeste zu der Macht und Glückseligkeit der Staaten oder ausfürliche Vorstellung der gesamten Polizeiwissenschaft,* published in 1760–1761, in two volumes (the groundwork of the power and welfare of states or comprehensive presentation of the science of public policy) gives a complete and essential view of cameralist ideas.

The government is responsible for the economic and social conditions of his citizens, in other words for their employment and their livelihood, which corresponds to the current present view. Freedom and security are essential to industry and commerce, but the cameralists were not opposed to government regulation, when particular purposes and particular circumstances justified it. Justi is in favor of free imports, but is not against small import duties.

There was little dissent before the 1750s from the core of Cameralist doctrine by writers on economic matters, but it left room for extensive debate within the adherents of the doctrine. Some cameralist authors, for example, were adherents of the "store of wealth" function of the precious metals in their role of money, others insisted on their "circulation" function.

Johann Friedrich von Pfeiffer (1718–1787) is another author of the later Cameralist period. His best-known books are the *Grundsätze der Universal-Kameral-Wissenschaft*[7] (Principles of the Universal Cameralist Science), published in 1783 in two volumes (abbreviated *Grundsätze*). He is a man of his time and writes his books for the "prince." A prince is by definition "wise," but Pfeiffer knows that it is rather the exception and he knows also his vices and passions. But he avoids anxiously – at least in this publication – to make any proposal in respect of a better form of government. And he does not forget to stress the exemplary role of Joseph II in Austria (von Pfeiffer 1783, p. 54).

In the next paragraphs, I consider Pfeiffer's position with respect to population increase and furtherance of crafts and industries on the one hand, and trade policy on the other. Pfeiffer is an author who belongs to what could be called the mature period of cameralism. The advantage of dealing with such authors is that their publications are normally of a higher quality (see infra) than those who belong to earlier periods.

[6]See Chaloupek (2005).

[7]Subtitle: Oder deren vier wichtigsten Säulen, nämlich der Staats-Regierungskunst, der Polizeiwissenschaft, der allgemeinen Staatsökonomie und der Finanzwissenschaft: or its four main pillars, the art of state government, the "police" science, the state economy science, the finance science.

Population Increase

First the causes of depopulation should be opposed. This means checking the origins of diseases, care for foundlings, childbirth, and schools, interdiction of recruitment for foreign countries, the diminution of reveling, and the contempt of nonmarried people being entitled to marry. In respect of population policy, agriculture is essential; hence, the fields at the disposal of the farmer must warrant a decent livelihood (not too small, not to extensive): a general survey should provide the answer; serfdom is to be prohibited and compulsory enrolment as well, common cultivation is not permitted. Artisans and farmers should not do each other's jobs. As in other sectors for other risks an insurance against fire, cattle mortality and crop failure has to be organized.

Matrimony must be promoted, but concubinage permitted, although subject to some rules. Dowries must be legally protected. All taxes on copulation and baptism are prohibited. The state is responsible for all children's education. The father exercises the paternal authority that "is his due by nature" ("die ihm von Natur zukommende häusliche Regierung": p. 197). In order to finance the cost of the measures just enumerated the wise prince will start to prune his expenses.

It is essential to dispose of good population statistics (e.g., register of deaths). In Chapter 5 of Volume II, Pfeiffer returns to the population problem. He enumerates again possible causes of the population decline: shortage of competent midwives, doctors, especially in the rural areas, the use of inefficient medicine, plague; venereal diseases, the always increasing number of inhabitants of the cities causing "enormous stoppages, malign moistness, which hinder the blood circulation in the political body,"[8] neglected children education, depraved morals, the privileges of the first-born, and large armies.

The following chapter examines the hospitals. A general Health, Medical, and Surgical College should be in charge of the entire medical organization. It issues the rules and controls its application. Similar colleges would work in every province. Special care should go to the quality of water. Chapter 7 is devoted to the educational institutions. The religious instruction should distinguish the essential from the less important. For children from 6 to 12, three kinds of schools are necessary, according to Pfeiffer: one for the nobility, one for the other classes, and one for the farmers. The last one would provide a simpler program, limited mainly to religion, the German language, reading, writing, elementary arithmetic, and civil virtues.

Finally, Chapter 13 deals once again with the principles of population policy.

Pfeiffer would allow all soldiers to marry and he would facilitate immigration. The last proposal is, of course, easier at a time that immigrants were not of different races. When the marriage remains childless after 6 years Pfeiffer envisages the possibility of a marriage annulment. He thinks that the authorities are not bound by religious prescriptions, when, for example, a man has two wives or a wife has two men. Nor is he opposed to morganatic marriages. Only the supreme objective is important!

[8]… vergrösserte Hauptstädte verursachen gewaltige Verstopfungen, erzeugen böse Feuchtigkeiten, die den Umlauf des Bluts im politischen Körper verhindern (von Pfeiffer 1783, p. 266).

Crafts and Industries

In Chapter 20 of Volume I, Pfeiffer examines how the working of the urban handicrafts can be improved. But an increasing population does not mean necessarily that all enterprises are thriving. This is only the case when many goods are in supply and there is a good connection between all enterprises.[9] The following measures or/and actions are required:

(a) The growth of the city must further its final purpose. The more all enterprises contribute to this aim, the greater will be their mutual connection
(b) Facilitate the sales of the most important enterprise of the town. Pfeiffer does not like free ports, but they should be allowed when all neighboring countries have one (pp. 424–425)
(c) A competent administration of the city that has to render an account of its activity. Pfeiffer is right in criticizing the heritable principle (for the city!). It is absurd to believe that an accidental competence will be inherited from father on son for centuries (p. 426)
(d) The citizens must have their say
(e) Among the facilities a town is in charge of, the supply of water is the most important one
(f) Transport by land to the city is not the competence of the local officials, but still essential to this city. The use of roads is often hindered by "exaggerated contributions" (übermässige Contributionen) and "important amounts" (beträchtlichem Geldbeitrag: p. 430). It is the care of the regional police that the fares of the rural road transport for persons and goods are cheap, and the coachmen are responsible for the transported goods
(g) Essential are postal services and road haulage. Since the postal services are there for the public, the postmen have to be "modest, polite, cheerful, orderly, punctual, concerned about the security of the letters, money, and goods entrusted to the post." This is possible only in countries which care more for the public facilities than for the increase of the public revenue. Pfeiffer quotes Austria as the country where this is the case (p. 431)
(h) The security of the citizens requires good lighting. Pfeiffer criticizes the fact that some cities are only lighted during the winter months, but not when there is moonlight! The police must control whether the lamps are cleaned and supplied with oil every morning
(i) Cleanness is again essential and requires control by the police (for example that no liquids are thrown out the windows)
(j) Building prescriptions should contribute to avoid useless, superfluous construction parts. Pfeiffer does not say how possible conflicts will be resolved

Such an enumeration is, of course, fastidious, but it illustrates the thoroughness of cameralist measures. The next chapter deals with manufactures and factories.

[9] von Pfeiffer (1783, p. 423): So gewiss der blühende Zustand aller Gewerbe ganz vorzüglich auf einen grossen Zusammenfluss aller Güter, und auf einen guten Zusammenhang aller Arten von Gewerben ankommt, ….

The first refer to the initial form of capitalist industrialism, organized by important merchants and buyers, often financed by rulers of the many principalities. The numerous guild rules did not hinder them. Specialization and division of labor were the rules of the manufactures, but few machines were used. More mechanization and higher division of labor changed them progressively into factories.

According to cameralist rules they should use mainly the materials (from agriculture and mining) produced in the country. Essential is "a high concentration of people, provisions, materials."[10] To diminish labor costs, machines can be bought abroad, if necessary. Entrepreneurs should be treated with respect (titles, prerogatives). In the mining sector, Pfeiffer regrets incompetent civil servants, indifferent governments, and faulty regulation (p. 442).

In Chapter 22, Pfeiffer examines the guilds and explains soon his position: some guilds can be abolished immediately without any difficulties (p. 443), others must be freed from the damage they inflict and from their public abuse. He enumerates the many disadvantages, which are partially those of monopolies (pp. 445–446). As from the eighteenth century, the freedom in the sectors concerned was introduced in France in 1791, in Prussia in 1810–1811, and in Austria only in 1859.

In Volume 2, Pfeiffer devotes many chapters to the establishment and operation of numerous industries. I do not dwell on these rather long and technical matters, but mention them in order to give an idea of a course on public policy of that time.

Trade Policy

Pfeiffer is clear and he repeats it several times: trade requires liberty, without restriction. He states the principle in respect to corn-trade ("corn-trade has to be free: soll der Getreidehandel ganz[11] frei sein": p. 195) and repeats further

> … as other branches of commerce, corn-trade must promote the welfare of the state and be free, even be stimulated by export subsidies as long as it respects this condition. As soon as any branch of commerce and consequently the corn-trade obliges the state to handle urgent shortages, freedom has to be curtailed to the extent the circumstances require.[12]

[10] …einen grossen Zusammenfluss von Menschen, von Lebensmitteln, von Materialien (von Pfeiffer 1783, p. 439).

[11] Of course, "ganz" is useless; it is typical of Pfeiffer's prolix style.

[12] … der Kornhandel mit allen anderen Handelszweigen dies gemein habe; dass er die Wohlfart des Staats befördern müsse, und ganz frei sein, ja noch durch Prämien auf die Ausfuhr aufgemuntert werden soll, so lange er diese Bedingung erfüllt; dass aber auch, sobald ein oder der andere Handelszweig, folglich auch der Getreidehandel, das Gegenteil bewirkt, und den Staat in seinen dringendsten Bedürfnissen dem Mangel aussetzt, die Freiheit in den Umständen angemessenen Grenzen eingeschlossen werden müsse (von Pfeiffer 1783, p. 415–416).

As soon as the price in the corn market exceeds by 50% the average normal price, "free exports are pernicious, and must be limited or abolished according to circumstances that may be different from country to country."[13]

The main principle of trade policy is to keep in the country the disposable money and to do its utmost to attract foreign money (p. 461). To combine the advantages of private persons with the interest of the state requires a great intelligence and an ardent patriotism (p. 464). Free trade needs freedom and protection. Freedom is not a chimerical, unlimited power of merchants. There are restrictions that stimulate and make trade efficient. Freedom must respect a number of rules. It means free circulation, unrestricted, undirected, not interrupted. When the true interest of the state necessitates changes, often even small physical and moral obstacles can cause commerce much harm. The welfare of the prince must not be confused with that of the state (p. 465).

Those who make an effort to increase their exports should be rewarded. Only exceptional circumstances related to the welfare of the community justify restrictions to free trade. Price control, tariffs, and rough treatment of traders are to be avoided. Pfeiffer formulates rules in respect of foreign trade:

(a) Hinder the rise of the needs of foreign goods
(b) Exports of surpluses of natural and produced goods should surpass imports
(c) Export, when possible, the most profitable goods
(d) Prefer the export of manufactures and factories
(e) Produce more than you need, in order to increase the possibility of exports
(f) Import only the raw materials you need, not the products themselves (cotton, not the cotton textiles)
(g) Do not import foreign goods competing with own goods
(h) Foreign goods can be classified as necessary (imports free), luxury (high tariffs), or harmful (in principle, no imports, although the interests of other states have to be taken into account)
(i) Imports that are to be reexported with own ships or by other means may be very profitable and should be promoted, provided they do not hurt national trade
(j) The ownership of many ships produces a certain income, provided it does not cause a lack of labor in agriculture
(k) The competitive position will be improved (and government action can be important in this respect) by low taxes, a sufficient supply of food, cheap transport facilities, a kind reception abroad
(l) Trade is not an aim in itself, its increase neither. Nations, whose wages are too high, cannot meet competition abroad

Pfeiffer also examines how trade can be assisted and promoted: first of all by trade treaties, if necessary by soldiers. He deals with credit, bills of exchange and insists

[13]… ist die Freiheit der Ausfuhr verderblich, und muss nach Beschaffenheit der Umstände, die in den verschiedenen Staaten auch verschieden sind, eingeschränkt, oder aufgehoben werden (von Pfeiffer 1783, I, p. 411).

on the desirability of commercial courts (pp. 476–403). Further, he wonders why all Europeans entrust intermediate trade (e.g., with India) to exclusive companies, although everybody is in favor of free trade (p. 494–495). If Germany considers such a trade, it should establish a big, but not an exclusive company (p. 496). It should convince foreigners that it does not aim at conquests of territory, nor people, but at a mutual beneficial trade.

Finally, Pfeiffer insists once again on the harmfulness of monopolies, in particular on hawking (Chapter 28).

Concluding Remarks

1. Pfeiffer is avaricious with references. Some authors deserve one mention (e.g., Hume, Genovesi, Montesquieu, Cataneo, Sonnenfels, Rolley), Locke even five, but Justi and his books are privileged; they are mentioned many times in both volumes, although never quoted. But many other chapters where he is not mentioned are clearly inspired by him. This is, for example, the case in Chapter 19 where Pfeiffer also stresses how essential the choice of intelligent ambassadors can be.

   Compared with Justi, Pfeiffer does not expose many new points of view, but he was one of the first to deal with forestry (see the chapters 1 and 10 by J. Backhaus, this volume). While Justi raises, for example, questions relating to innovation (and not using, of course, a word that did not exist at that time).

   > The sciences, that brighten the intelligence of a whole people, bring it the "genie," the capabilities and skills, without which the productive forces of a nation would never become prosperous.[14]

   Pfeiffer copies (no reference!) the first part of the sentence ("Verstand eines Volkes aufklären": "brighten the intelligence of a people," p. 499), leaving out the most interesting part of the sentence.

   Pfeiffer himself is not quoted very often; he is not even dealt with in Small (1909), who examines ten important cameralists, of whom he treats the works by Sonnenfels and Justi more extensively than those of the others.

   Sometimes, the titles of books are quoted, but the authors are not mentioned. Poor references seem to characterize the cameralists; Justi is no exception, nor is Pfeiffer. It is a pity that he shares also with Justi a verbose style. But copying other authors is a general phenomenon of that time. Pfeiffer does not even mention Adam Smith whose *Wealth* he knew.

   To my knowledge there is no reference to Adam Smith in other cameralists as well, but, as Schumpeter mentioned, although *The Wealth of Nations* was soon translated (1776–1778), it took time to become effective (Schumpeter

[14] See von Pfeiffer (1783, p. 54): "Die Wissenschaften, indem sie den Verstand eines ganzen Volkes aufklären, bringen demselben dasjenige Genie, und diejenigen Fähigkeiten und Geschicklichkeiten bei, ohne welche der Nahrungsstand einer Nation niemals blühend werden kann."

1954, p. 501).[15] Even then, was a reference useful since most cameralists, and Justi in particular, were already free traders. Smith, just as the cameralists, admitted exceptions to the general free trade principle. That Smith does not mention what he learned from the cameralists who preceded him is not surprisingly; he is also not famous for his acknowledgements. Moreover, Schumpeter notes that the *Wealth* "does not contain a single analytical idea, principle, or method that was entirely new in 1776" (p. 184) and "cannot rank with Newton's *Principia* or Darwin's *Origin* as an intellectual achievement" (Schumpeter, p. 185). After all, nearly all the concepts used in *The Wealth of Nations* could be found in the cameralist literature.

2. Many economists, even Schumpeter (1954) call Cameralism the German form of mercantilism.[16] Nevertheless, there are important differences: Germany attached much more importance to population policy. It is understandable after the catastrophe of the Thirty-Years War (1618–1648), when German population declined from about 20 million to approximately 8 million. On the other hand, what is the sense of limiting imports in an area where everything is missing? Moreover, the Treaties of Münster and Osnabrück cut up Germany politically in small pieces, ipso facto destroying the advantages of political unity.

   Typical is the cameralists' greater care for the welfare of the whole population. All of them stress this main objective of good governments. Pfeiffer, for example, writes

   > Welfare (for all) is without doubt the main objective of all republics. Consequently, the first and supreme law. Nevertheless it cannot justify any unjust action nor can it be invoked in problems between free states.[17]

   Seckendorff believes already 120 years earlier, like many others, that welfare for all was more important than the welfare of the prince.

   Hence, it would be understandable and advisable to make a distinction between the cameralists and the (other) mercantilists. In 1909, Swann wrote an extensive and coherent book on the cameralists.

   Anyway, speaking of Hörnigk as an "Austrian mercantilist" is a *Schönheitsfehler* (Ellsworth 1950, p. 46); an example of surprising ignorance of both mercantilists and cameralists. Kenen writes:

   > … Classical economists defined national prosperity in terms quite different from those used by the mercantilists. They were concerned with the welfare of the crown's subjects, not that of the crown itself (Kenen 1985, p. 7).

---

[15]Cf. e.g., Böhle (1940): " … Quesnay and Smith whose works were also quoted some times, but exerted no noticeable influence" (… Quesnay and Smith, deren Werke auch einige Male zitiert wurden, aber keinen erkennbaren Einfluss ausübten, p. 133).

[16]Gonnard (1943, p. 163) calls the German expression of mercantilism "the most despotic and the hardest" ("sa forme la plus despotique et la plus dure"). An explanation of such foolish errors may be that the knowledge of languages of the French is generally very limited.

[17]Die gemeinschaftliche Glückseligkeit ist ohne Zweifel der Hauptendzweck aller Republiken, folglich auch ihr erstes und oberstes Gesetz; jedoch macht dieses höchstes Gesetz keine an sich ungerechte Tat gerecht, noch weniger ist es in den Angelegenheiten der freien Staaten gegen einnder anzuwenden (von Pfeiffer 1783, vol. 1, p. 33).

But as I just stressed, the cameralists cared precisely and especially about the welfare of the "crown's subjects"!

3. The prescriptions of the mercantilists cover three centuries. Hence, the many versions of these prescriptions. The cameralists of the eighteenth century have more modern views and are more free trade minded than their earlier predecessors and attach, for example, more importance on competition. Pfeiffer writes:

> As the competition advantage animates activity and this in its turn strengthens trade everything must be done to improve competitiveness. Competitive advantage arises when a nation in a trade fair or a commercial center can sell good products quicker and cheaper than other nations.[18]

The later or "mature" cameralists recognized, for example, that trade can be mutually beneficial and that not all nations can have a positive balance of trade in the long run.

They also take into account, without necessarily mentioning it, the important publications published in the eighteenth century. This is the case, for example, with Mandeville's *Fable of the bees*. We encounter his "private interest" in a text of Justi on the coherence in the production process (as usual, without mentioning a source).

> It is a doubtless, but perhaps not sufficiently recognized truth, that the own interest is the tie that keeps together the whole society; and a society can only be free and nobody have power over the others, as long as the own interest manifests itself in order to bring about the necessary coherence in the production process[19] (von Justi, vol. I, p. 555).

When Justi writes that the government must try to "prevent the people from being inspired by wrong and imaginary interests," and to consider "their true interests"[20] (von Justi, vol. 1, p. 559) one wonders whether the government is sure to be always the keeper of the "true interests."

As I said elsewhere[21] (M.v.M. on Justi), "schools" or "systems" often coexist. They do not succeed each other at a given moment. Classify the cameralists among the mercantilists, although they are much more liberal than the "real" ones, is not adequate. Some of them, just as Justi and Pfeiffer, are rather precursors of

---

[18]Da der Vorzug in der Konkurrenz die Handlung belebt, und alles, was selbigen befördert, die Kommerzien verstärkt, so muss dazu alles beigetragen werden. Dieser Vorzug wird erhalten wenn eine Nation auf Messen, oder grossen Handelsplätzen, gleich gute Dinge geschwinder und wohlfeiler als eine andere Nation verkaufen kann (von Pfeiffer 1783, p. 473).

[19]Es ist eine ungezweifelte, aber vielleicht noch nicht genugsam erkannte Wahrheit, dass das eigne Interesse das Band ist, welches die ganze Gesellschaft zusammen hält; und eine Gesellschaft darf nur frei sein, und keiner in derselben eine Macht über dem andern haben; so wird eben dieses eigne Interesse eine solche Richtung nehmen, und einen solchen Zusammenhang in dem gesamten Nahrungstande hervorbringen, als zu dem blühenden Zustande desselben erfordert wird.

[20]... sie sich bemühet, die Menschen von einem irrigen und eingebildeten Interessse zurück zu halten, und sie auf ihr wahres Interesse zu leiten.

[21]See van Meerhaeghe (2009).

the liberal school. It is a hardy simplification to bring together writers from three succeeding centuries into one group of "mercantilists."

4. Adam Smith passed heavy criticism on mercantilism (Smith 1776, Chap. VIII).

> … who have been the contrivers of this whole mercantile system?; not the consumers, … whose interest has been entirely neglected, but the producers, whose interest has been so carefully attended to; … the interest .. of some other set of producers, has been sacrificed to it (Smith 1776, p. 514).

Schumpeter calls it an "unintelligent criticism" (Schumpeter 1954, p. 361). The historical school (Roscher, Schmoller, Cunningham, Ashley) contended that mercantilism and cameralism were rational in their defense of national autarchy and state power. These ends are even now regarded as reasonable.

Finally, in respect of trade policy, they were the most liberal on the continent. Even then, their "vision of economic policy might look like laissez faire with the nonsense left out" (Schumpeter on von Justi: 1954, p. 172).

> But Smith's attack was successful: the large majority of the economists of the 19th century 'looked upon mercantilists with disapproval and even contempt' (Schumpeter 1954, p. 336), most of them moved by ideological motives. A good example is Viner who believes that mercantilist 'errors' are due to ignorance of 'modern monetary trade theory' (Viner 1937, p. 110). Of course, this 'modern' theory is the 'classical' theory, based on and famous for its many unrealistic assumptions (van Meerhaeghe 1986, Chap. 8). Even Schumpeter regrets the systematic one-sidedness of Viner (Schumpeter 1954, p. 336).

This nineteenth-century haughtiness compares with the presumption of present-day American free traders vis-à-vis European "interventionists." The extreme free trade theory is still raging in the United States and in the globalization dominated by America.[22] To the liberal mind the "interpretation of the German school of historical economists … was certainly no less distasteful …" (Wilson 1959, in Coleman 1969, p. 118).

Keynes provides a famous defense of mercantilism (Keynes 1936, Chap. 23) and criticizes Heckscher (1955) whose work on mercantilism is seen "through the eyes of the classical tradition of liberal economics" (Coleman 1969, p. 9) and is "curiously unrealistic" (Coleman 1957 in Coleman 1969, p. 117). Keynes complains that he was brought up "to believe that it (mercantilism) was little better than nonsense" (Keynes 1936, p. 335) and stresses that the "weight of my criticism is directed against the inadequacy of the *theoretical* foundations of the *laissez-faire* doctrine upon which I was brought up …" (Keynes, ibid., p. 339).

5. As the representatives of the Historical school, and especially Friedrich List, and American economists of the nineteenth century frequently stressed, A. Smith often applied a double standard when free trade and England's interests were

[22] The inadequate sudden implementation of the free-trade principles led to more poverty in the former Soviet republics. There is less unemployment in White Russia because the demonized president was more cautious in following western advice.

concerned. He simply forgot his country's history. Smith admired, for example, the protectionist Navigation Acts (Smith 1776, p. 487). No wonder that these nineteenth century authors spoke of "Do as the English did, not as they said" and that they could repeat today to the less-developed countries "Do as the Americans did, not like they tell you to do."

6. In many countries, mercantilism and cameralism in a different measure fell short of what the doctrine called for. You expect, for example, the leaders in the countries concerned to tax less imports of raw materials needed for the production of industrial goods these countries have to import. But the governments simply cannot miss the revenue! *Nihil novi sub soli!* The equilibrium of the state budget has always – and the situation did not change in the present times – been one of the most difficult objectives to attain.
7. All cameralists and Pfeiffer in particular favored industrialization characterized by increasing returns: they considered it as the main development factor since it stimulates technical change, increases wealth, and ipso facto the potential for tax collection. Widespread wealth seemed to accumulate in the cities, not in the countryside. Moreover, the development of industry is in the interest of agriculture: it transforms agricultural products into industrial products.

   Baron von Leibniz, the great philosopher who wrote also on many other sciences and even on economics with the same authority and therefore rightly called "the Aristotle of the modern era," insisted also on the increasing returns of industry.[23] This was also the case for Roscher.[24]
8. While the Germans regard the state "as primarily a unit, and only secondarily as an aggregate," for the Americans the state is "primarily an aggregate, and only secondarily a unit" (Small 1909, p. 586). In other words, German political theory is primarily collectivist; American political theory is essentially individualistic. What Swann wrote in 1909, still applies today:

   > To understand modern Germany … it is necessary to take account not only of present activities in Germany, but of those formative purposes and tentative institutions which the cameralists represent (Small 1909, p. 596).

9. A consideration of Schumpeter (it's all in Schumpeter!) which has not received the attention it deserves, probably because it praises – horresco referens – the abominable mercantilism, is appropriate to end this paper.

   > If Smith and his followers had refined and developed the "mercantilist" propositions instead of throwing them away, a much truer and much richer theory of international economic relations could have been developed by 1848 – one that could not have been compromised by one set of people and treated with contempt by another (Schumpeter 1954, p. 376).

---

[23] See Reinert and Daastol (2004).

[24] Cf. Streissler (1994). Published as: E. Streissler, Increasing returns to scale and the prospects of small-scale enterprises, in *Wilhelm Roscher and the "Historical Method." Journal of Economic Studies. vol. 22* (pp. 16–25), *nrs. 3/4/5.*

References

Böhle C (1940) Die Idee der Wirtschaftsverfassung im deutschen Merkantilismus. Gustav Fischer, Jena

Chaloupek G (2005) Seckendorff as an economist in comparison with contemporary writers. Eur J Law Econ, pp. 235–247

Coleman D (1957) Eli Heckscher and the idea of mercantilism. In: Coleman D (ed) (1969)

Coleman D (1969) Editor's introduction. In: Coleman D (ed) Revisions in mercantilism. Methuen, London

Der Brockhaus in fünf Bänden FA (2000) Brockhaus, Leipzig-Mannheim, neunte, neu bearbeitete Auflage

de La Fontaine J (1975) The fables. English by Wright E (trans) and illustrated throughout by Gustave Doré, Jupiter, London

Ellsworth P (1950) The international economy. Its structure and operation. Macmillan, New York

Gonnard R (1943) Histoire des doctrines économiques. Lib. Gén. de droit et de Jurisprudence, Paris

Heckscher E (1955) Mercantilism, 2nd edn (trans: Shapiro M, ed: Söderland E). Allen and Unwin, London

Kenen P (1985) The international economy. Prentice Hall, Engle Woods

Keynes JL (1936) The general theory of employment, interest and money. Macmillan, London

Reinert E, Daastol A (2004) The other canon: the history of renaissance economics. In: Reinert E (ed) Globalisation, economic development and inequality. An alternative perspective. Edward Elgar, Cheltenham

Schumpeter J (1954) History of economic analysis. New York, Oxford University Press

Small A (1909) The cameralists. The pioneers of German social polity. University of Chicago Press, Chicago

Smith A (1776) An inquiry into the nature and causes of the wealth of nations. Warwick House, London (1960)

Sombart W (1929) Die drei Nationalökonomien. Duncker und Humblot, München

Streissler E (1994) Wilhelm Roscher als führender Wirtschaftstheoriker. In: Wilhelm Roscher (1817–1894). A century reappraisal. Sixth annual Heilbronn symposium in economics and the social sciences, Heilbronn, 1994

van Meerhaeghe M (1986) Economic theory. A critic's companion, 2nd edn. Martinus Nijhoff, Dordrecht

van Meerhaeghe M (2009) The international aspects of Justi's work. In: Backhaus J (ed) The beginnings of political economy. Johann Heinrich Gottlob von Justi, vol 7, European heritage in economics and the social sciences. Springer, New York

Viner J (1937) Studies in the theory of international trade. New York, Harper

von Justi J (1761), Die Grundfeste zu der Macht und Glückseligkeit der Staaten oder ausfürliche Vorstellung der gesamten Polizeiwissenschaft. G. L. Wolterdorfs Wittwe, Königsberg

von Pfeiffer J (1783) Grundsätze der Universal-Kameral-Wissenschaft. Oder deren vier wichtigsten Säulen, nämlich der Staats-Regierungskunst, der Polizeiwissenschaft, der allgemeinen Staatsökonomie, und der Finanzwissenschaft. In 2 Teilen, Neudruck der Ausgabe Frankfurt am Main. Scientia, Aalen (1970)

Wilson C (1959) The other face of mercantilism. In: Coleman (ed) (1969)

Chapter 10
Pfeiffer and the Foundation of the Science of Forestry

Jürgen G. Backhaus

Introduction

Werner Sombart built his three-volume magnum opus on modern capitalism architecturally like a dramatic opera in three acts. After a general introduction into (comparative) economics as a social science, to be taken as a prelude, the first act is devoted to proto-capitalism, first in phases and then in systematic elements. Act two is devoted to early capitalism and before the intermission (between 1916 and 1927) there is the dramatic final scene, chapter 71 entitled *The Threatening End of Capitalism*.

Act three then on high capitalism followed in 1927, with the concluding scene entitled *The Future of Capitalism*, is often quoted all over the political spectrum.

This short essay comes in three parts in addition to the introduction. Part one reports the reasons for the threatening end of modern capitalism and largely follows Sombart in doing this. The reason is identified as the fact that the capitalist economy and society depended on just one fuel and, in addition, this fuel also was the main raw material that was used by the economy. Hence, this was a single source economy with an ever expanding demand on this single source, wood. As wood necessarily takes time in order to grow and mature, the supply of wood was soon outdone by the demand, deforestation occurred and ultimately rationing was imposed on the most fuel-intensive industries, such as the glass and china industries.

Even in highest places, a need for a new concept of sustainable capitalism was acutely felt. In commenting upon a new industrial development, the landgrave William of Hesse said that this project would make the present generation rich while rendering the coming generation poor.

J.G. Backhaus (✉)
Krupp Chair in Public Finance and Fiscal Sociology, University of Erfurt,
Nordhäuser Str. 63, 99089 Erfurt, Germany
e-mail: juergen.backhaus@uni-erfurt.de

J.G. Backhaus (ed.), *Physiocracy, Antiphysiocracy and Pfeiffer*, The European Heritage in Economics and the Social Sciences 10, DOI 10.1007/978-1-4419-7497-6_10,

After generations of rationing raw materials and regulating fuel-consuming industries, finally Johann Friedrich von Pfeiffer (1718–1887) hit upon the fuel solution: Diversification of the resource base into fuels other than wood and intensification of wood production through the application of scientific methods coupled with a more judicious use of the available wood supply would set economic development onto a new course. The solution was provided essentially in three parts. In 1780, Pfeiffer already published his entire *Anti-Physiocrat*, where he identified physiocracy as the mental block, even stifling off intellectual and economic development. The year 1781 already followed his *Economics of Forestry*, which provided the outline of the basic solution in three parts. In the next year of 1782, Pfeiffer put this system into the more general context of an outline of the science of the economy of the state, and these two books are the subject of part two and part three, respectively.

I

Woods have forever provided pasture for the animals, in particular the pigs, hunting grounds for all kinds of game and, of course, the major product of wood for combustion and also the raw material for construction and most of the crafts.

The single reliance on wood as the material of construction of choice led to recurrent explosions of the demand for timber for construction, whenever a city had become a victim of the flames. The urgency of demand for construction material required extensive cutting, a demand which was simply undeniable and could not be tempered by even the most ruthless of rulers, would he not lose an entire city.[1]

A traditional Thuringian regional (not political) name is "Holzland," land of the wood (not woodlands).[2] The list of the products made of wood is indeed impressive, from the cradle to the coffin. Tools and machines were of wood, furniture, of course, buckets, barrels, bowls, fountains, pipes, printing presses, treadmills, even the first steam engines, spinning wheels, weaving tools, the shafts of guns, all means of transport, but in particular ships. The British navy in the nineteenth century comprised some 10,000 ships. For one medium-sized battle ship, some 4,000 grown oaks were required.

[1] The tale of count Reinhard almost proves the point. The count in gambling had put his entire county on the table and lost. He asked for a postponement of the settlement of the debt until the next harvest, a request which was granted. In his despair, the count is said to have chased out all the farmers off his county and planted a single forest. In this way, he retained his county. While the count is painted as a desperate gambler, we shall return to the tale at the end of this essay. The farmers who told the tale to different tale-gathering professors of German literature, such as the Grimms or Bechstein, had a rather different perspective from the count. To them, losing their farms must have been as traumatic as losing the county must have been to the count. Yet, the tale cannot be taken at face value as an impartial account of economic history.

[2] It is now the name of a mega county comprising the former principality of Schwarzburg-Rudolstadt and the former duchy of Saxony-Gotha-Saalfeld.

Wood was required for combustion, of course. This was not just for heating houses, but in particular for industrial combustion. The Luneburg heath is not an original but a so-called cultural landscape, as it comprised originally woodlands. All the wood has been used up in boiling the salt water and thereby gaining the important salt, before the advent of refrigerators the main medium of preservation of food. We have some spotty numbers of the extensive use of wood and timber for particular areas and purposes. During the eighteenth century and the Harz region we understand that for mining 20,000 stems were used in the mines, for making coals 300,000 cords,[3] for combustion 800,000 cords, for construction 9,000 stems, etc., impressive indeed.

The change of the landscape as a consequence of deforestation was extensive. It is said that formerly you could ride your horse through Spain in the shade. The Balkans and Greece with their now rough terrain were originally forested. The powerful shipping industries of Venice not only took their rowing slaves from the Balkan, they essentially took the timber supplies all the way from the Croatic and Greek and ultimately Lebanese coast. The cypress tree, the preferred tree for shipbuilding in Venice, still is to be seen in the flag of the Lebanon. The scarcity of wood and timber was so extensive that Sombart quotes the "Holznot" from original sources, leading to "Hungersnot" i.e., famine.[4]

II

The winning idea, Pfeiffer's "Science of Forestry," appeared in Mannheim in 1871 and was described as being useful for not only directing civil servants in forestry and the cameral administration, but also for the owners of private estates. The author does neither give his academic affiliation, nor his titles; he rather describes himself not by his name, but by the fact that he is the author of a standard text of economic and cameral sciences (used in Mainz, then the leading cameral school).

The 360 page book, about a standard size at the time, comes in nine chapters, each richly subdivided. The first chapter is a central definition of the science of forestry and what it all comprises. The basic distinction between leaved trees and needled trees which still defines the industry is made by him. As well, chapter 2 dealing with all the relevant types of leaved trees and chapter 3 with all the relevant domestic types of needled trees. In chapter 4, he sets up the principle of a science of sustainable forestry. He explicitly uses the term sustainable (pfleglich), and sets it against efficient. In chapter 5 he goes through all the economic uses of forests and woodlands. Chapter 6 then goes into details of sustainable forestry. Chapter 7, however, takes stock of previous centuries and details the most economic use of the different types of wood. Chapter 8 looks for alternatives to the most extensive use

[3] A cord is roughly a cubic meter.

[4] See Sombart (1916/1917/1927, 1969).

of wood, as a fuel, and extensively discusses the use of subterranean combustibles, notably taking coal from the mines instead of making coal from wood. We should really appreciate that this book appeared in 1781, when there was only extensive coal mining, where the coal came to the surface, but no systematic coal mining had yet sprung up which would later define entire areas in Germany, such as Silesia and the Ruhr region.

Finally, chapter 9 is a most interesting didactic exercise. He defines a principality of A, makes suggestions for forestry policy, sets up objections by the cameralist administration, and counters those objections with his own suggestions for improvement.[5]

III

The "Blueprint of the Science of State" (Grundriss der Staatswirtschaft) prepared for the instruction and warning of future Staatswirte (state economists) is a somewhat smaller book, comprising 284 pages divided into 28 chapters plus a conclusion.[6] The first chapter deals with basic principles of public budgets and their conduct, chapter 2 deals with enhancing revenue, chapter 3 deals with education as being essential for the proper conduct of the state in the interest of the happiness of the commonwealth, chapter 4 deals with agriculture, chapter 5 with mining, chapter 6 with industry and manufacturing, chapter 7 with commerce, public support of commerce is dealt with in chapter 8, and different approaches to the fostering of agriculture and commerce, regulation for development are dealt with in chapters 9 and 10, with more basic considerations in chapter 11. Chapter 12 poses the basic question of the limits to growth. In particular, he makes the point that luxury has no place in conducting economic policy for sustainable development. In the next three chapters, he turns to the duties of the subjects, not only vis-à-vis the state but also vis-à-vis themselves, immediate duties and mediate duties are distinguished. Here, we see early formulations of the subsidiarity principle. Chapters 16–22 discuss different instances of government failure. The term is explicitly used: "Fehlerhafte Beschaffenheit der Staatswirtschaft" with respect to basic principles, the population,

[5] Despite its importance, the book is rare. It has not been reprinted. A couple of years ago, the library of the University of Erfurt at Gotha acquired the book in 2001. As a pre-1850 title, it can only be read there.

[6] By the way, he also proposed a four semester BA curriculum for a future "Staatswirt," i.e., state economist – the term "Wirt" includes not only the manager but also the entrepreneur. In this curriculum the following topics were to be taught:

First semester: encyclopedia, state government science, military economics
Second semester: all agricultural sciences excluding mining
Third semester: urban commerce, technology, factories, manufacture and mercantilism, science of trade
Fourth semester: sciences of police, state, commerce and finance

It should be emphasized that the curriculum also includes technology aspects.

education, agriculture, mining, manufacturing, and finally commerce. Chapter 23 discusses what today probably is the most prevalent form of government failure, government failure through negligence. Chapters 24 and the following refer to different forms of regulation, 24 with respect to luxury consumption, 25 with respect to regulation in general, 26 deals with self-regulation, and this is further discussed in terms of the previous distinction of immediate and mediate duties of the subject.

In all, this is a tour de force which particularly impresses by its prescient use of modern concepts and terminology. The translation of the chapter titles was by no means forced.

Conclusion

As we have seen, Pfeiffer's ideas with respect to facing the threatening end of modern capitalism was to broaden the resource base and to develop principles of economic policy for sustainable economic policy and development in such a way, that the sciences of state, cameral sciences, and the science of forestry could be taught. In his case, the science of forestry also entails as a special case mining of coal. Iron ore mining and the steel industry was not yet in the cards. Teaching requires schools and academies, and, above all, teaching material and teachers. He provided the teaching material and he also provided the ideas. But his efforts at introducing his reforms were met with incredulity and envy in his local minds, but they were avidly taken up elsewhere. Academies of forestry sprang up all over Europe including St. Petersburg, shortly followed by mining academies. By the end of the Napoleonic invasion and the reconstruction of Germany in the form of the German confederation, the country was literally covered by academies of forestry and academies of mining, where the multiplicity of institutions reflected the multiplicity of states in Germany. The author of the Anti-Physiocrat had brought about a scientific revolution which in term laid the foundations for a professionalized discipline of forestry and yet another professionalized discipline of mining.

References

Sombart W (1916/1917/1927) Der moderne Kapitalismus. Historisch-systematische Darstellung des gesamteuropäischen Wirtschaftslebens von seinen Anfängen bis zur Gegenwart, Bd 2: Das europäische Wirtschaftsleben im Zeitalter des Frühkapitalismus, 2. Band, München. Duncker & Humblot, München

Sombart W (1969) Der moderne Kapitalismus: Historisch-systematische Darstellung des gesamteuropäischen Wirtschaftslebens von seinen Anfängen bis zur Gegenwart. Duncker & Humblot, Berlin

von Pfeiffer JF (1780) Der Antiphysiocrat oder umständliche Untersuchung des sogenannten physiocratischen Systems, vermöge welchem eine allgemeine Freiheit und einzige Auflage auf den reinen Ertrag der Grundstücke die Glückseligkeit aller Staaten ausmachen soll. Frankfurt am Main, Esslinger

von Pfeiffer JF (1781) Grundriss der Forstwissenschaft, zum Gebrauche dirigirender Forst- und Kameralbedienten. Mannheim, C. F. Schwann

Chapter 11
Establishing Sustainability Theory Within Classical Forest Science: The Role of Cameralism and Classical Political Economy

Peter Deegen and Cornelia Seegers

Problem Definition and Objective

Ever since the United Nations' World Commission on Environment and Development, chaired by Gro Brundtland, had issued its report "Our Common Future" in 1997 (Brundtland 1997), a world-wide public responded to the notion of "sustainable development." At the report's core stand political objectives that should serve as guiding principles for the behavior of nations. Sustainable development can thus be described as a normative concept (see Pearce et al. 1990).

Norms are based on how humans interpret their natural and social environment. These interpretations are determined through theories, core beliefs, and ideologies. It shapes the prism through which we perceive reality, thus constraining the actions we consider appropriate to undertake (see North 2005, and especially Kant 1781/1997:160).

"Sustainable development" is not an unfettered concept either. Indeed, the mind-sets of the past are living on in today's ideas, drawing our attention and our patterns of action into one direction or another. And since we can trace back the roots of "sustainable development" to developments in resource economics and, even more precisely, to forest resource economics (Endres 2004:114), this article seeks to shed some light on the theoretical background for sustainability in classical forest science.

Sustainable timber production is most likely to represent a very ancient economic management principle, as has been shown by dendroarcheological research about human living in the Modern Stone Age up to 4000 BC in South-West Germany (Lake of Constance/Upper Swabia) and about Etruscan iron mining since 700 BC (Schlichterle and Wahlster 1986 and Keller 1970, as in Köpf 1995/1996). Despite these early

P. Deegen (✉)
Professur Forstpolitik und Forstliche Ressourcenökonomie,
Institut für Forstökonomie und Forsteinrichtung, PF 1117, 01705 Tharandt, Germany
e-mail: deegen@forst.tu-dresden.de

J.G. Backhaus (ed.), *Physiocracy, Antiphysiocracy and Pfeiffer*, The European Heritage in Economics and the Social Sciences 10, DOI 10.1007/978-1-4419-7497-6_11,

practices a cognitive framework only emerged during more recent times (Schuster 2001). We often refer to von Carlowitz' script on *Sylvicultura oeconomica* (1713/2000) as the one giving birth to "sustainability" (see Grober 1999 or Endres 2004). Yet, principles of sustainability have been known and, to some extent, applied within forestry long before that (Schuster 2001, see also Pfeiffer 1972:161). Rather detailed comments were already provided in the so-called *Hausväterliteratur*, guidelines for good family business management. Again, a systemic, scientific foundation for sustainability together with a definition of its principles was only elaborated much later. Schuster (2001) sees their emergence at the time of classical forest science's and forestry's consolidation, in the middle of the nineteenth century. The book published by Hundeshagen (1826) is regarded as one, if not the seminal document.

Considering forestry's enormous economic importance during that era on the one hand, and communication patterns over a given period of time on the other (see Luhmann 1987:191), it seems to be clear that the principles of sustainability adopted by Classical Forest Science are unlikely to be the result of an isolated development. Our efforts should thus be directed at depicting the process of diffusion between forest science and the two competing economic doctrines of the period, Cameralism and Classical Political Economy, which was likely to shape the scientific principles of sustainability in forestry. As a matter of evidence, we are not about to identify clear causal relationships on a continuous time axis. Our objective is much more to work out a combinational logic of filtration and to reveal the scientific methodology underlying classical forestry's sustainability principles.

Principles of Sustainability in Forestry

Starting at the closing years of the Middle Age, two principles have come to build sustainable forestry's fundamental core: not to chop down more wood than will be grown and to reforest forest land bore of timber (Schuster 2001). Implementing these fundamentals required an estimation of the forest's potential yield and a (technical) planning of their spatial realization. In practice, forest areas were most often divided into equal blocks, equal in terms of surface areas or in terms of growing stock. *Short-term overexploitation within a given period of time was evened out by allowing for a certain annual variability, with different scholars in classical forest science assigning different levels of importance to the use of flexibility in planning designs. While Hartig (*1795*) did not think much of it, Heinrich Cotta, founder of the Tharandt Forest Academy, writes as follows: "This is why we need to recur to special measures through which at any time we may undertake modifications, concerning the management as well as the budget, without having to annihilate the management plan as a whole or to waste estimations"*[1] *(Cotta* 1820*:3).*

[1] "Es müssen daher besondere Maßregeln ergriffen werden, durch welche zu jeder Zeit die nötigen Abänderungen, sowohl in Betreff der Einrichtung als des Etats zu machen sind, ohne den Bewirtschaftungsplan im Ganzen zu vernichten oder die Schätzung unbrauchbar zu machen."

The technical discipline facilitating the process organization and also the organizational structure at once was called "forest management planning" (*Forsteinrichtung*). It evolved to become the possibly most important instrument for determining and implementing sustainable timber use in forestry (Schuster 2001:757). Taking into account how closely the development of sustainability's theoretical principles was tied to engineering design and implementation through forest management techniques during the nineteenth century, we may conclude that organizing sustainability in forestry occurred through "forest management planning." We still see these findings illustrated in a recent textbook's subtitle: "forest management panning – sustainable management and regulation of forest resources" (Kurth 1994).

The central purpose of forest management can be summed up as yield determination, sustainable forestry planning and revision and control of forest evolution. Using modern language, we might say that forest management planning tries to provide for sustainable forest development by overcoming uncertainties of the future through strategic planning.

Cameralism

It is well documented that the theoretic principles of sustainability, developing with the evolution of forest science, can also be found in the Cameralists' writings, which were often titled "manual" or "guidelines" for forest science. Among others, we want to name Moser, who published the two-volume textbook *Principles of Forest Economics* (*Grundsätze der Forstökonomie*) in 1757 (quoted in Hasel and Schwartz 2002:323 ff), and von Pfeiffer (1781), whose oeuvre *Outlining Forest Science* (*Grundriss der Forstwissenschaft*) was mentioned by Backhaus during a public lecture delivered in Tharandt in 2005.

Considering von Moser (1757), von Pfeiffer (1781) and also di Paprica (1789), we further propose that forest science as part of cameralistic teaching had been fully developed and adopted as general knowledge by the Cameralists long before the evolution of the forestial classics. di Paprica (1789:26) gives evidence of just how close forest and cameral sciences were entwined: "Von Carlowitz, Beckmann, von Zanthier, von Justi, Cramer, Gleditsch, Reinhard, Käpler, Stahl, Oettelt, Succow, von Pfeiffer, Maurer, von Burgsdorf, von Moser and many others are the true Saints of Foresters and Cameralists." Note that the list comprises not only of straightforward foresters such as Beckmann and Oettelt, but also of Cameralists.

Cameralistic knowledge not only comprised general subject-matters of forest science, but also the idea of "utility in perpetuity," a contemporary paraphrase for sustainability. As an example, di Paprica (1789:27) writes: "It is a firm principle of Cameralism to exploit the forests at the highest possible utility in perpetuity" and "the actual and most noble objective of the forest sciences is the utilization of the woods at maximum benefit in perpetuity" (p. 15). Indeed, there even existed clear-cut conceptions about how to implement this principle. They are reflected in the table of contents of cameralistic forest books and their respective chapter orderings (see again von Moser 1757, von Pfeiffer 1781 and di Paprica 1789). Three major points are stressed throughout the literature:

1. *Reforestation of forest land after harvesting*: While focussing on the crop, authors also present some very detailed essays concerning the choice of tree species depending on site acceptance and the final use of timber. Those chapters treating the subject of afforestation mainly tell us about the contemporary state of art in biology and ecology, whereas in the context of reforestation, wood pasture is mentioned as a major constraint.
2. *Dividing the forests into cutting areas*: The relevant pieces of work concentrate on the presentation of geometrical and mapping techniques. Apparently it had become common belief that only clear-cutting by blocks provided an overview for controlled withdrawal of wood. As di Paprica (1789:336) writes, "finally it is much wiser to cut down a forest in deliberate sections than to thin it out more and more, (…) while this is an impossible thing to do when felling a tree once here once there."[2] The preference for sectional clear-cutting can also be explained through the thus generated quality of the wood (di Paprica 1789:256, von Pfeiffer 1781:137 ff).
3. *Determining the forestry budget*: The forestry budget defines the overall cutting rate and depends on the amount of wood needed to stabilize the current budget and the amount of wood that could actually be exploited sustainability. In this sense, we quote again di Paprica (1789:277) "Determining a forestry budget requires a deep insight into forest science, broad knowledge about manufacturies and factories,… the aggregated real and potential population of the country, the number of craftsmen, …a proper estimation of the annual consumption of lumber … and firewood, and confident calculations about the annual amount of all timber that can be felled in the nobles' and other forestries throughout the country."[3] Since the board for determining the forestry budget would need competencies concerning whole economy, di Paprica (1789:278) proposes a commission assembling men of different expertise: "One enlightens the other, and in this way a wholesome plan for future forestry is created, and the future forestry budget determined."[4]

[2] "endlich ist es doch klüger, einen Wald auf das Geratewohl schlagweise abzutreiben, als ihn mehr und mehr auszulichten, …da hingegen es unter die unmöglichen Dinge gehört, so bald man einen Baum hier, den anderen dort abhaut."

[3] "Die Festsetzung eines Forstetats erfordert tiefe Einsichten in die Forstwissenschaft, ausgebreitete Kenntnisse von den Manufakturen, Fabriken,…der ganzen wirklichen und zukünftig möglichen Bevölkerung des Landes, der Zahl der Handwerker…einen richtigen Überschlag des jährlichen Verbrauchs and Bau- und Brennholz und zuversichtliche Berechnungen alles Holzes, welches aus den herrschaftlichen und übrigen Waldungen im ganzen Land jährlich geschlagen werden kann."

[4] "Einer erleuchtet den anderen, und auf diese Weise entwirft man einen vollkommenen Plan zur künftigen Forstwirtschaft, und setzt den künftigen Forstetat fest."

Today, these points form an integral part of sustainability conditions within the discipline of forest management planning (see Kurth 1994:45 ff). Alas, by no means do we want to evoke the impression that the above-mentioned authors "invented" the conditions, when at least two of them ("reforestation" and "division in cutting areas") can be traced back to the Late Middle Ages (see Sporhan and von Stromer 1969; Bertsch 1951). Rather, we want to demonstrate that Cameralists knew about sustainability conditions in forest science and put them right to practice.

And while the quotations above confirm our view that Cameralists had a complete understanding of forest science and sustainability, we consider it fruitless to engage into discussions about their share in actually developing these ideas. Yet, we sometimes find this sort of statement concerning intellectual ownership in forest science literature. Heinemann (1990:494), for example, judges Moser's essays about sustainability (von Moser 1757) as a systematization of existing individual knowledge rather than newly elaborated ideas, whereas Schuster (2001:756 ff) names non-cameralists like von Langen, Beckmann, and Oettelt as precursors of forest management planning.

Considering again the operating mode of communication as characterized by Luhmann (1987), we can neither assume that cameralists and foresters developed isolated theories of sustainability in parallel, nor that cameralists simply took over sustainability knowledge from foresters. Neither is it helpful to search for authorship or the first quoted thought thread, especially if we keep in mind that the first cameralists emerged around the time of 1500 (Wagner 2001:1), whereas the above quoted statements derive from late cameralists' works, when writing special forest books became common practice. And there is yet another reason for putting into question the validity of the "simple absorption" hypothesis: through their position as custodians and advisors within noble household's management units marked by traditions from an often very ancient past and the ultimate objective of preserving eternal reign, cameralists were well familiar with the concept of perpetuity management, not only in the forestry sector. In fact, we can interpret the parallels in literature as indicating a close exchange between the two groups, if ever there was a sharp division at all. Probably, we should also direct our research efforts much more towards the question of how strongly sustainability ideas are linked to the notion of eternal reign in perpetuity.

Attempting to implement sustainability by means of planning methods seems to be logical then if we depart from this sort of cognitive diffusion between cameralists and foresters. As a matter of fact, cameralists viewed the state essentially as a planning object (Blankart 2006:24). However, their state model resembled less our contemporary nation state but a company with many different enterprises, such as forestry, hunting, mining and manufactories for glass and brewery, and in which taxes as a source of income played a subordinate role (see Wagner 2001). In consequence, we can much better describe a cameralist's function as a person who actively managed and counseled a large family business, rather than a policy expert with mere advisory functions. Under this view planning was more an instrument to overcome uncertainties in a company and not so much an instrument to regulate a state.

The situation started to change at the beginning of the nineteenth century. While nobilities' private forests became public state forests (see for example Hasel 1985:65), Classic Forest Science emerged and brought along the notion of sustainability as a central, self-evident, and precisely defined scientific category (Schuster 2001:757) In a second turn, planning methods became integrated as an indispensable element for regulating sustainability within Classic Forest Science and were subsequently organized in the form of forest management planning (*Forsteinrichtung*) (Hasel 1985:217) even though, and this we wish to state explicitly, the noble family businesses had developed into nations states.

At the same time, cameralistic business-oriented budget management (see di Paprica 1789:277) turned into engineering cutting-rate management. Technical thinking is also expressed in the newly established linguistic terms for forest management, such as *Flächenfächwerk* (method of blocks by area), *Altersklassenverfahren* (method of blocks by age-classes) or *Vorrats- und Zuwachsverfahren* (method of blocks by growing stock and increment).

Given the material at hand, we cannot prove why Classic Forest Science, albeit consolidating preclassical approaches of sustainability planning into a cohesive concept of yield regulation and cutting-rate determination, only concentrated on the forest-based budget and was no longer linked to budgets based on economic factors. Basing our considerations on the Theory of Institutional Change (see North 1990, 2005) and Principal-Agent-Theory (see Pratt and Zeckhauser 1985) we propose the following presumptions:

First, it is easy to imagine that transaction costs for budget determination procedures as described by di Paprica were prohibitively high, favoring subsequent delegation to individual specialists. Since realizing the first two conditions of sustainability demanded engineering expertise, it is quite possible that specialists for forestry, who were used to think in technical terms, transferred this approach to business management and planning, and thus to budget management. Secondly, a general movement away from estimations of the whole economy and towards strictly technical things had taken on momentum. Quite comprehensibly though, given economic estimations' insecure nature experienced during the rise and fall of the Napoleon Empire (see von Kügelgen 1870/2006 for a very lively description). These two possible factors, "delegating decision-power to engineering specialists" and "concentrating on technical parameters in public policy," both influenced the prevailing notion of forestry and forest management planning, and both in the same direction.

We can even add a third factor: the above-mentioned transition from nobilities' private forest ownership to state forests at the beginning of the nineteenth century (Hasel 1985:65) marked a transition towards greater independence for the former family business "forestry department." The hereto related problem of controlling forest administration civil servants' faithful handling of forests as a public asset became quite significant. Even before the transition period, di Paprica (1789:29) had written: "where to take from the capital loan, the well-furnished household, fields and meadows and their daughters' finest dowry in such short time and given such small salary, such large families, good living and splendid clothes? Either these people have found the philosophers' stone or their riches orginate from their forest lands."[5]

The control problem started to intensify as the principal prince was missing. The solution occurred through indoctrinating a particular, in-house forestry culture that we have come to term "forest ethics," by means of newly established forestry academies and forest administration clerkships. Yet, this internal and early "environmental thinking" cannot be regarded as an environmentalist or even ecological movement; it simply provided a basis for protecting forest capital assets against foresters' arbitrary access, serving as an instrument to reduce agency-costs in a situation prone to moral hazard. This in-house forest culture, as we know from Kaufman (1960/2005) and Franck and Pudack (2006), turned out to be a very successful controlling instrument, surely constituting a quite distinctive form of public administration's organizational culture, as described by Wilson (1989/2000:90 ff).

The idea of sustainability occupies a central role within the general "forest ethics" framework. Schanz (1996) demonstrates that modern days' foresters consider it a central symbol of their profession's ideational culture, as it comprises aspects of social responsibility, long-term thinking, and conservation. Sustainability can thus be regarded as a sort of "Oath of Hippocrates" for foresters.

We have thus seen "sustainability" being submitted to a double coding: while its denotation refers to planning techniques for implementing conditions of sustainability, it also carries the connotation of representing a central symbol of forestry's internal culture. It is further assumed that the denotative coding occurred during the preclassical period, while the connotative coding only emerged during the consolidation of classical forestry. The connotation possibly also contributed to a doctrine-like institutionalization of planning methods as a way for regulating sustainability. Otherwise we could not explain the opinion issued by Kremser (1990:274), stating that stand division and yield estimation represent a crucial step for sustainable forest use planning if based not on the demand, but on the state of the forest.

We are now able to reconstruct the history of sustainability in forest science as related to Cameralism in the following picture:

(a) Starting with the closing years of the Middle Age, the ideas of sustainability for forest management began to take shape.
(b) Due to the prevailing communication pattern between cameralists and foresters, implementation of conditions for sustainability occurred more and more through planning instruments, and quite effectively so, given the institutional framework of noble families' "large-scale enterprises."
(c) High transactions costs in determining forest budgets based on indicators of the whole economy, specific problems concerning engineering controlled timber

[5] "Woher in so kurzer Zeit bey höchstschmaler Besoldung, bei der zahlreichen Familie, bei dem Wohlleben und der Kleiderpracht die ausgeliehenen Kapitalien, die wohleingerichtete Ökonomie, die Äcker und wiesen und die reiche Ausstattung der Töchter? Entweder haben diese Menschen den Stein der Weisen gefunden, oder der Reichtum kommt aus ihren Wäldern her."

withdrawal, and a particularly high insecurity about economic estimations during Napoleonic times resulted in classical forest science focusing on engineering parameters for regulating sustainability.

(d) The creation of national state forests at the beginning of the nineteenth century and the hereto related greater discretion of the forest administration increased the monitoring problem of forest civil servants. The problem was met by reducing the moral hazard through establishing an in-house forestry culture that further developed the notion of sustainability into a central symbol of foresters' professional ethics. Sustainability's coding had thus become twofold, with the connotative use possibly contributing to the doctrine-like institutionalization of planning methods as a means for regulating sustainability.

4 Classical Political Economy

Cameralists, or at least the late Cameralists, had already observed the possibility for forests to establish without any planning of "proper annual cutting blocks" (di Paprica 1789:256). "This is why our most splendid woods stem from the Thirty Years' War, when all of a sudden nature sowed the abandoned barren fields."[6] But only Classical Political Economists recognized the phenomenon as an example for price allocation.

In his writing on the "Wealth of Nations"; Smith (1826:186) highlights the impact of price allocation on sustainable forest management: "In its rude beginnings the greater part of every country is covered with wood, which is then a mere incumbrance of no value to the landlord, who would gladly give it to anybody for the cutting. As agriculture advances, the woods are partly cleared by the progress of tillage, and partly go to decay in consequence of the increased number of cattle. (…) The scarcity of wood then raises its price. It affords a good rent and the landlord sometimes finds that he can scarce employ his best lands more advantageously than in growing barren timber, of which the greatness of profit often compensates the lateness of the returns. This seems in the present times to be nearly the state of things in several parts in Great Britain, where the profit of planting is found to be equal to that of either corn or pasture."

The role of price as an institution for sustainability is emphasized most clearly in von Thünen's work (1826/1990). By constructing a national economy based on prices that attains total equilibrium ("The Isolated State"), he not only demonstrates how prices can affect the economy in his isolated world, he also concludes that price allocation would eventually generate timber-producing forestry ("ring of forestry") as a competitive form of land use. Not so surprisingly again, he sums up his findings in the third and purely forestry part of the "Isolated State,": "Our inquiry further

[6]"Daher haben wir unsere schönsten Waldungen von dem dreißigjährigen Kriege her, wo die verlassenen Felder auf einmal von der Natur besät wurden."

shows that any worries concerning the ever increasing prices of lumber wood due to the gradual decay of the virgin forests are completely unreasoned. Quite the contrary, as knowledge about rational forestry will spread ...,the price...for...pine wood will not be able to maintain itself and will have to drop"[7] (von Thünen 1875:118, englisch translation von Thünen 2009). Bearing in mind that Samuelson's (1983:1482) appreciation for von Thünen is less explained by the latter's location theory than by the theory of general equilibrium, we would like to add that von Thünen may just as well count as one of the founding fathers of sustainability theory.

Yet, theoretic approaches based on Classical Political Economy could never encroach upon Classical Forest Science's sustainability theory (see for example Hartig 1795; Cotta 1820; Hundeshagen 1826). Apparently, the feeling of mistrust against sustainable forestry based on prices was large enough for Cotta to write down the following words in his lecture script on public forestry: "Shining through these enquiries and observations is that it is best for the state to own as many forests as necessary to exclude the absolute, for the state really dangerous, scarcity of wood, thus rendering even obsolete any restrictions on private forests. A country that lacks sufficient amount of state forests to serve the above-mentioned purpose must buy or barter as many woods as necessary"[8] (Cotta ?, quoted in Köpf 1991). Of course, statements like these puzzled von Thünen. At the end of the "Isolated State's" third part, the one concerning forestry, he listed as top priority for further research "assessing Mister Cotta's view on private forest owners, who are supposed to always have an interest in devastating their forests" (von Thünen 1875:124).

Some foresters and forest science scholars did recognize the informational role of prizes and used financial rotation cycles for calculating forestry budgets and cutting rates (see König 1813; Faustmann 1849; Pressler 1860). However, their specific impact on long-term land use allocation, or more precisely on product factor allocation, was noticed most casually, if ever. And even though Pressler (1860/1995:78) explains his perennial increment by saying that "if there was a high probability that a similar price increase was to be expected over the next ten years, then it would be obvious that a forester who is not only forestially or technically inclined but also susceptible to market speculations would merit a significant additional contribution to the perennial value increment of his timber; but, however, only for those trees which could or would be cut during that period of rising prices," he puts himself into perspective by adding "in regard to a stand that is to be managed

[7]"Unsere Untersuchung zeigt ferner, dass die Besorgnis, als müsse das Bauholz mit dem allmählichen Verschwinden der Urwälder immer höher im Preise steigen, ganz unbegründet sind. Es wird im Gegenteil, wenn die Kenntnis der rationellen Forstwirtschaft sich verbreitet hat, ...der Preis... für...Kiefernholz sich nicht behaupten können, sondern sinken müssen."

[8]"Aus diesen Untersuchungen und Betrachtungen erhellet, dass es am besten sein muss, wenn der Staat im Besitz so vieler Waldungen ist, als zur Entfernung des absoluten und dem Staate wirklich gefährlichen Holzmangels erforderlich ist, wodurch dann von selbst alle Beschränkungen der Privatwälder unnötig werden. Das Land, dem es an hinlänglichen Staatswaldungen für den obigen Zweck mangelt, muss durch Kauf oder Tausch so viele Waldungen zu erlangen suchen, als für jenen Zweck nötig sind."

sustainably and to be arranged uniformly, this conceivable third increment, as pointed out in our first article (taken from finance theory) cannot exert a principal and systematic influence."

We can thus surely hold the hypothesis that prices' impact on land use and forestry, least of all their role as an institution for sustainability, was not understood during the times of Cameralism or classical forest science. Only Raup's famous essay "The view from John Sanderson's farm: A perspective for the use of land," published in 1966, should eventually offer a forest science illustration of the long-term effects of prices and market competition to forestry.

Integration of Irritation?

At first glance it seems as if Judeich, strongly influenced by Pressler, had blended cameralistic planning and price-based market competition into a reviewed concept of sustainability when writing his oeuvre *Die Forsteinrichtung* (*On Forest Management*) in 1871/1880.

Similar to forest science classics and cameralists he divided the forest in cutting blocks. The number of blocks is determined by the rotation period, as the forest's overall surface is divided by the rotation period. Unlike Cameralists and other Classical scholars, Judeich did not use budget estimation based on details of the whole economy, nor did he calculate a purely forest related yield. Instead, he employed a financial index adopted from his colleague Pressler (as in Pressler 1860) with indicator comprising forest characteristics, such as growing stock and wood increment, as well as factor and product market prices. That makes the indicator resemble very much to the optimal cutting rule formulated as Faustmann–Pressler–Ohlin-theorem in modern forestry economics (see Johannson and Löfgren 1985:80). It is also used in investment theory for analyzing *backup costs* and economic life cycles (see Hirshleifer 1970). Through this approach, Judeich returns to Cameralists' c considerations of the whole economy without having to conduct wholesome economic analyses as described by di Paprica (1789:277 ff). Rather, by reducing economic data to prices he comes close to modern economic techniques.

Can we accept the almost self-suggesting interpretation that by calculating the optimal rotation period as dependent on cutting blocks and price information, Judeich (1871/1880) had combined Cameralists' planning thoughts with market-economic competition information expressed in prices? Another interpretation seems to be possible: Judeich did not recognize the role of prices in overcoming uncertainties of the future, as described by Hayek (1968/2002:17): "It is useful to recall at this point that all economic decisions are made necessary by unanticipated changes, and that the justification for using the price mechanism is solely that it shows individuals that what they have previously done, or can do now, has become more or less important, for reasons with which they have nothing to do. The adaptation of the total order of human action to changing circumstances is based on the fact that the compensation of the various services changes without taking into accounts the merits or defects of those involved." Rather, Judeich only recurred to prices as a planning parameter, without anticipating that by doing so he was crowding out their very function.

In some sense, the dichotomy between the role of prices in market competition and the use of prices in managerial planning calculations is documented, at the latest, in Judeich (1871/1880). Maybe it can also be explained as a result of the above-mentioned transition from Cameralism, as a planning method in noble family businesses, to planning national forest governance.

Results and Some Conclusions

Sustainability as a concept in classical forest science is based on a process of diffusion between forestry and Cameralism that has covered several centuries. But even though scholars of classical forest science apparently also entered into discussion with those teaching classical political economy, economic theories that were based on individual liberalism did not stamp their mark on forest science's principles of sustainability. It is possible though that their period of exchange was too short to generate anything like diffusion.

It is quite true that postclassical Judeich (1871/1880), who has been influenced by Pressler (1860) and other early forest economics (see Helles and Linddal 1997, especially Table 1), tried to combine cameralistic planning with liberal market competition. In doing so, however, he crowded out prices' original function as instrument to discover possibilities for aligning to unforeseen changes (see Hayek 1968/2002). In fact, he employed prices as a reduced and surely cost-effective informational asset concerning the situation of the economy, a method that has become common practice in business economic investment calculations.

There is one thing we want to point out: the present essay does not seek to make a judgement about the respective advantages and failures of "market" and "planning" as institutions for overcoming uncertainties. Rather, the initial question concerns another level of abstraction (Vanberg 1982/1995).

As Cameralism influenced the sustainability term adopted by classical forest science, it also transmitted its underlying methodology: by transferring cameralistic management and counseling of large family business on the national state level, the state was defined as an independent profit-maximizing business unit in the sense of Edgeworth'ian's welfare economics tradition, and stood quite in contrary to the approach by Wicksell (see Backhaus and Wagner 2004). Thus, individualism as the most basic mosaic of social action is only pursued when merged with elitist patterns. We might term this little rigorous interpretation of individualism as "elitist individualism."

We can also understand the Elitist patterns much more thoroughly by focusing on planning as the most important instrument for overcoming uncertainties of economic change. The planning approach seemed justified, though, as it was simply applied to a situation of business management where the large number of

German small states operating as single business units external corrected to external market competition (see Luhmann 1987; Deegen 2004:S. 17). "Failures" in sustainability planning were corrected, at the extreme by threatening small states' existence. The external corrective got lost with the transition of nobel forest into state forests, and the subsequent integration into a tax-financed public budget. Sustainability planning became the only institution for overcoming uncertainties of (economic) change (Deegen 2004), inducing a sort of elitist thinking.

Through it, connotative use – the technique of sustainability planning became part of a forestry in-house culture – whose traces as an informal institution may still be found in our present days. It is important to understand, that a technique became a main-part of a culture.

Further research could focus on investigating whether sustainability as a planning based on "elitist individualism" also materialized as primary institution within the much larger concept of "sustainable development" or whether other sustainability cultures were also transmitted. Such a theoretically-based research approach on forestry history is likely to contribute significantly to our understanding of institution-building and institutional stickiness in general and the establishment of sustainability in particular, thus reaching out beyond the subject-matters close borders. However, the clearness to methodological approach is the source of success.

Acknowledgment We are grateful to Erhard Schuster and Harald Thomasius for very helpful comments and discussions.

References

Backhaus JG (2005) Die Begründung der forstwirtschaftlichen Theorie aus dem Kameralismus. Speech delivered at Tharandt, TU Dresden on 19.10.2005

Backhaus JG, Wagner RE (2004) Society, state and public finance: setting the analytical stage. In: Backhaus JG, Wagner RE (eds.) Handbook of public finance. Kluwer, Boston

Bertsch K (1951) Die Geschichte des deutschen Waldes. Verlag M und H Schaper GmBH, Hannover

Blankart CB (2006) Öffentliche Finanzen in der Demokratie. V.F. Vahlen, München

Brundtland G (ed.) (1987) Our common future: The World Commission on Environment and Development. Oxford University Press, Oxford

Cotta H (1820) Anweisung zur Forst-Einrichtung und Abschätzung. Teil 1. Anoldische Buchhandlung, Dresden

Cotta H (?) Lecture script "Staatsforstwirtschaftslehre" (Public forest economics). Public and University Library of the Free State of Saxony, Tharandt branch

Deegen P (2004) "Ansätze einer ökonomischen Theorie der forstlichen Nachhaltigkeit." Perspektiven forstökonomischer Forschung. Schriften zur Forstökonomie, vol 25. J.D. Sauerländer, Frankfurt a.M

di Paprica C (1789) Gedanken über verschiedene Gegenstände der Forst-Cameralwissenschaft nebst eines Forst-Catechismus für Jünglinge, die sich dem Forstwesen zu widmen gedenken. Grattenauer V. Nürnberg

Endres A (2004) Natürliche Ressourcen und nachhaltige Entwicklung. In: Döhring R, Rühs M (eds.) Ökonomische Rationalität und praktische Vernunft. Königshausen & Neumann, Würzburg

Faustmann M (1849) Berechnung des wertes, welchen Waldboden, sowie noch nicht haubare Holzbestände für die Waldwirtschaft besitzen. Allgemeine Forst – und Jagdzeitung

(Dezember):441–455. Translated into Contemporary English by Linnard W (1968) and reprinted (1995) Calculation of the value which forest land and immature stands possess for forestry. J Forest Econ 1(1):7–44
Franck E, Pudack T (2006) Die Einheit von Hoheit und Betrieb – Anmerkungen aus ökonomischer Perspektive. Forst und Holz 7:258–263
Grober U (1999) Der Erfinder der Nachhaltigkeit. Die Zeit:98
Hartig GL (1795) Anweisung zur Taxation und Beschreibung der Forste, oder zur Bestimmung des Holzertrags der Wälder. Heyer, Gießen
Hasel K (1985) Forstgeschichte. Ein Grundriss für Studium und Praxis. Hamburg, Berlin
Hasel K, Schwartz E (2002) Forstgeschichte. Ein Grundriss für Studium und Praxis. Verlag Dr. Kessel, Remagen
Hayek FA (1968) Der Wettbewerb als Entdeckungsverfahren. Kieler Lecture Series No. 56. Translated into English by Snow M (2002) Competition as a discovery procedure. Q J Austrian Econ 5(3):9–23
Heinemann G (1990) Wilhelm Gottfried von Moser. In: Hartig Foundation G-L (ed) Biographien bedeutender hessischer Forstleute. J.D. Saulerländer, Frankfurt a.M
Helles F, Linddal M (1997) Early Danish contributions to forest economics. J Forest Econ 3(1):87–103
Hirshleifer J (1970) Investment, interest and capital. Prentice-Hall, Englewood Cliffs
Hundeshagen JC (1826) Die Forstabschätzung auf neuen wissenschaftlichen Grundlagen, nebst einer Charakteristik und Vergleichung aller bisher bestandenen Forsttaxations-Methoden. Lauppsche Buchhandlung, Tübingen
Johannson P-O, Löfgren K-G (1985) The economics of forestry and natural resources. Blackwell, Oxford
Judeich F (1871/1880) Die Forsteinrichtung. Schönfeld's Verlagsbuchhandlung, Dresden
Kant I (1781/1997) Kritik der reinen Vernunft. Suhrkamp, Frankfurt a.M
Kaufman H (1960/2005) The forest ranger. A study in administrative behaviour. Resources for the Future, Washington DC
Keller W (1970) Denn sie entzündeten das Licht. Geschichte der Etrusker – die Lösung eines Rätsels. Droemer Knaur, München
König G (1813) Anleitung zur Holztaxation. Becker, Gotha
Köpf EU (1991) Tharandter Lehren – Zum forstpolitischen Beitrag Heinrich Cottas. Tharandter Forstarchiv 62:94–95
Köpf EU (1995/1996) Nachhaltigkeit: Prinzip der Waldwirtschaft – Hoffnung der Menschheit? Scheidewege- Jahresschrift für skeptisches Denken. Special edition:307–317
Kremser W (1990) Niedersächsische Forstgeschichte. Rotenburger Schriften (Sonderband 32), Rotenburg (Wümme)
Kurth H (1994) Forsteinrichtung. Nachhaltige Regelung des Waldes. Deutscher Landwirtschaftsverlag, Berlin
Luhmann N (1987) Soziale Systeme. Suhkamp, Frankfurt a.M
North DC (1990) Institutions, institutional change, and economic performance. Cambridge University Press, Cambridge
North DC (2005) Understanding the process of economic change. Princeton University Press, Princeton
Pearce DW, Barbier EB, Markandya A (1990) Sustainable development: economies and environment in the Third World. Elgar Earthscan, London
Pfeiffer G (1972) Wasser und Wald als Faktoren der städtischen Entwicklung in Franken. Jahrbuch für fränkische Landesforschung 32:151–170
Pratt JW, Zeckhauser RJ (1985) Principals and agents: the structure of business. Harvard Business School Press, Boston
Pressler MR (1860) Zur Verständigung über den Reinertragswaldbau und dessen Betriebsideal. Allg. Forst- und Jagdzeitung (Mai):173–191. Translated into Contemporary English by Löwenstein W, Wirkner J (1995) For the comprehension of net revenue silviculture and the management objectives derived theory thereof. J Forest Econ 1(1):45–87

Raup HM (1966) The view from John Sanderson's farm: a perspective for the use of the land. Forest Hist 10:2–11

Samuelson PA (1983) Thünen at two hundred. J Econ Lit 21:1468–1488

Schanz H (1996) Forstliche Nachhaltigkeit – Sozialwissenschaftliche Analyse der Begriffsinhalte und –funktionen, vol 4. Schriften aus dem Institut für Forstökonomie, Freiburg Im Breisgau

Schlichterle H, Wahlster B (1986) Archäologie in Seen und Mooren. Den Pfahlbauten auf der Spur. Theiss Verlag Stuttgart

Schuster E (2001) Einige Bemerkungen zur Geschichte der forstlichen Nachhaltigkeit. Forst und Holz, Nr. 23/24, S. 754–757. Schaper. Alfeld

Smith A (1776/1826) The wealth of nations, vol 1. Arlington House, New Rochelle

Sporhan L, von Stromer W (1969) Die Nadelholzsaat in den Nürnberger Reichswäldern zwischen 1469–1600. In: Zs. F. Agrargesch. U. Agrarsoz. 17, S. 79 ff

Vanberg V (1982/1995) Markt und Organisation. Die Einheit der Gesellschaftswissenschaften, Bd. 31. J.C.B. Mohr (Paul Siebeck) Tübingen

von Carlowitz HC (1713/2000) Sylvicultura oeconomica. Anweisung zur wilden Baum-Zucht. Reprint der Ausg. Leipzig Braun 1713, bearb. von Klaus Irmer und Angela Kießling. Freiberg: TU Bergakad. Freiberg: Akad. Buchh

von Kügelgen W (1870/2006) Jugenderinnerungen eines alten Mannes. Hellerau, Dresden

von Moser WG (1757) Grundsaetze der Forst-Oeconomie. Bronner, Frankfurt

von Pfeiffer JF (1781) Grundriss der Forstwissenschaft. Zum Gebrauch dirigierender Forst- und Kameralbedienten, auch Privatguthsbesitzern. Verlag Schwan, Mannheim

von Thünen JH (1826/1990) Der isolierte Staat in Beziehung auf Landwirtschaft und Nationalökonomie. Scientia V., Aalen

von Thünen JH (1875) Der isolierte Staat in Beziehung auf Landwirtschaft und Nationalökonomie. Dritter Teil: Grundsätze zur Bestimmung der Bodenrente, der vorteilhaftetsten Umtriebszeit und des Werts der Holzbestände von verschiedenem Alter für Kieferwaldungen. V. von Wiegandt, Hempel & Parey. Berlin

von Thünen (2009) The isolated state in relation to agriculture and political economy Part III: principles for the determination of rent, the most advantageous rotation period and the value of stands of darying age in pinewoods. Edited by Ulrich van Suntum Palgrave Macmillan Hamsphire

Wagner RE (2001) The cameralists: fertile sources for a new science of public finance. In: Backhaus J (Hrsg) Founders of modern economics: Masstricht lectures in political economy. Edward Elgar (forthcoming), Cheltenham (Version Hompage R. E. Wagner)

Wilson JQ (1989/2000) Bureaucracy. What government agencies do and why they do it. Basic Books, New York

Index

J.G. Backhaus (ed.), *Physiocracy, Antiphysiocracy and Pfeiffer*, The European Heritage in Economics and the Social Sciences 10, DOI 10.1007/978-1-4419-7497-6,

Q

CPSIA information can be obtained at www.ICGtesting.com
234655LV00001B/14/P

9 781441 974969